D0934604

SOLDIERS DON'T GO MAD

SOLDIERS DON'T GO MAD

A Story of Brotherhood, Poetry, and
Mental Illness During the First World War

CHARLES GLASS

Penguin Press
New York
2023

PENGUIN PRESS
An imprint of Penguin Random House LLC
penguinrandomhouse.com

Image credits appear on page 315

LIBRARY OF CONGRESS CATALOGING-IN-PUBLICATION DATA

Names: Glass, Charles, 1951– author.
Title: Soldiers don't go mad : a story of brotherhood, poetry, and mental illness
during the First World War / Charles Glass.
Other titles: Story of brotherhood, poetry, and mental illness
during the First World War
Description: New York : Penguin Press, 2023. |
Includes bibliographical references and index.
Identifiers: LCCN 2023007303 (print) | LCCN 2023007304 (ebook) |
ISBN 9781984877956 (hardcover) | ISBN 9781984877963 (ebook)
Subjects: LCSH: World War, 1914–1918—Psychological aspects. | Sassoon,
Siegfried, 1886–1967. | Sassoon, Siegfried, 1886–1967—Mental Health. |
Owen, Wilfred, 1893–1918. | Owen, Wilfred, 1893–1918—Mental Health. |
Post-traumatic stress disorder. | World War, 1914–1918—Literature and the
war. | War neuroses—Patients—Great Britain—Biography. | World War,
1914–1918—Medical care—Great Britain. | Craiglockhart War Hospital
(Edinburgh, Scotland)—History. | World War, 1914–1918—Veterans—
Mental health—Great Britain. | Soldiers—Great Britain—Biography.
Classification: LCC D524.5 .G53 2023 (print) |
LCC D524.5 (ebook) | DDC 616.85/212—dc23/eng/20230228
LC record available at https://lccn.loc.gov/2023007303
LC ebook record available at https://lccn.loc.gov/2023007304

Printed in the United States of America
1st Printing

Designed by Amanda Dewey

In grateful memory of Rob Morrell,
Alessandro de Renzis, and P. J. O'Rourke

And it's been proved that soldiers don't go mad
Unless they lose control of ugly thoughts
That drive them out to jabber among the trees.

—Siegfried Sassoon,
"Repression of War Experience," 1917

CONTENTS

INTRODUCTION

All the armies in the Great War had a word for it: the Germans called it *"Kriegsneurose"*; the French *"la confusion mentale de la guerre"*; the British "neurasthenia" and, when Dr. Charles Samuel Myers introduced the soldiers' slang into medical discourse in 1915, "shell shock." Twenty-five years later, it was "battle fatigue." By the end of the twentieth century, it became post-traumatic stress disorder (PTSD).

In December 1914, a mere five months into "the war to end war," Britain's armed forces lost 10 percent of all frontline officers and 4 percent of enlisted men, the "other ranks," to "nervous and mental shock." An editorial that month in the British medical journal *The Lancet* lamented "the frequency with which hysteria, traumatic and otherwise, is showing itself." A year later, the same publication noted that "nearly one-third of all admissions into medical wards [were] for neurasthenia"—21,747 officers and 490,673 enlisted personnel. Dr. Frederick Walker Mott, director of London's Central Pathological Laboratory, told the Medical Society of London in early 1916, "The employment of high explosives combined with trench warfare has produced a new epoch in military medical science."

This development need not have surprised Britain's military physicians. Major E. T. F. Birrell of the Royal Army Medical Corps (RAMC) had observed nervous breakdowns in surprising numbers while supervising a Red Cross medical mission to the Balkan Wars between Turks and Bulgarians in 1912 and 1913. The new heavy weapons that Germany's Krupp and other European industrialists sold to both sides inflicted carnage that doctors had not witnessed before. Modern science was creating modern war. Explosive rifle cartridges penetrated flesh more deeply than balls from single-shot muskets. High-explosive artillery shells released not only the shrapnel shards of old, but ear-shattering thunder, blinding light, and a concussion so fierce that it sucked the air away. The shells demolished the strongest ramparts, leaving no refuge. Rapid-fire machine guns mowed down hundreds of men in an instant. Hospital wards received, in addition to those who had lost arms or eyes, disabled soldiers without marks on their flesh. They suffered unexplained blindness, mutism, paralysis, shaking, and nightmares. A surgeon from Belgium's Saint Jean Hospital, Dr. Octave Laurent, documented the Balkan wounds in his book *La Guerre en Bulgarie et en Turquie.* Laurent removed metal shards from broken bodies, but surgeons could not cure paralysis, trembling, nightmares, blindness, stammering, and catatonia.

Laurent posited physical causes for the symptoms. This accorded with medical and military doctrine of the day that fighting men did not become hysterical. Practitioners in the new field of psychiatry shared the view of Sigmund Freud in Vienna that hysteria, a word derived from the Greek for "uterus," was a female condition. Laurent referred to the soldiers' malady as *la commotion cérébrospinale*, a variant of what American Civil War doctors had called "windage," undetectable molecular disruption of the spinal cord from the vibration of speeding bullets and shells. Concussion had caused some, but not all, of the neuroses. Laurent's and the RAMC doctors' denial of the emotional causes of physical disabilities would influence the military response to mental illness when Europe's Great War began in the summer of 1914.

Industrial-era weaponry deployed on a mass scale from August 1914 to November 1918 exacted a greater toll in dead and wounded than in any previous war. For the first time in history, millions of men faced high-velocity bullets, artillery with previously unimaginable explosive power, modern mortar shells, aerial bombardment, poison gas, and flamethrowers designed to burn them alive. British casualties soared on August 26, 1914—a bare three weeks into the war—when German artillery ravaged the British Expeditionary Force (BEF) at Le Cateau in northeast France. In October, the Battle of Ypres produced so many cases of mental shock that the War Office dispatched a leading neurologist, Dr. William Aldren Turner of London's National Hospital for the Paralysed and Epileptic, to France to discover the causes. Examining otherwise healthy men afflicted by deafness, deaf-mutism, blindness, stammering, palsies, spasms, paraplegia, acute insomnia, and melancholia, he concluded, "In many instances he [the soldier] may persevere with his work until a severe psychical shock—such as seeing one of his friends killed beside him, severe shelling, an upsetting experience, or bad news from home—unsteadies him, and precipitates a definite attack of neurasthenia, requiring rest and treatment at home." As the war progressed, doctors recorded an escalating proportion of mental breakdowns alongside the usual statistics of killed, wounded, and missing. The percentage increased as the war froze along a static cordon of opposing trenches from the English Channel south more than four hundred miles to the border of neutral Switzerland. Along this deadly frontier, troops of both sides endured the relentless hammering of devastating artillery in a dark underground world from which the only escape was injury or death.

Debate among military physicians and between doctors and senior officers raged over how to deal with the unblooded wounded. Dr. Myers criticized the military for regarding shell-shocked soldiers as "either insane and destined for the madhouse or responsible and should be shot." The question persisted throughout the war: should men who broke down on the field of battle be disciplined or receive medical attention? By war's end, firing squads had executed some, practitioners had administered punishing electric shocks to others, and psychiatrists offered Freudian psychoanalysis to a lucky few. But even then, the treatments' purpose was to thrust shattered boys and men back into the violent conditions that had caused their breakdowns, troubling physicians who had to weigh duty to patients against military necessity.

The problem of soldiers' mental health became a crisis in the summer of 1916, when British general Sir Douglas Haig launched an all-out assault to break the German line in northern France's Somme Valley. Preparatory, uncamouflaged massing of forces and supplies, together with a weeklong artillery barrage to reduce enemy defenses, alerted the Germans to the impending onslaught. At 7:27 on the morning of July 1, British artillery subsided and an eerie silence prevailed. Two minutes later, a mountain of earth rocketed into the sky from a spot behind the German lines called the Hawthorn Redoubt, where British sappers detonated a 40,000-pound underground charge. That was the signal for thousands of men laden with 66-pound backpacks to climb over the parapets of the British trenches and march into No Man's Land. German defenders, who had sheltered deep under the surface during the barrage, emerged to fire machine guns, artillery, and mortars at their attackers. Twenty-one-year-old Captain Wilfred Nevill, known fondly as Billie to the men of his East Surrey Regiment, kicked a soccer ball onto the battlefield and charged forward. As he dribbled the ball into the barbed wire, German gunners cut him down. A fellow officer, Lieutenant Robert Eley Soames, followed with another ball, urging the men to kick it into goal. Few of them made it.

Novelist and official war propagandist John Buchan, whose swashbuckling imperial heroes like Richard Hannay had inspired many youngsters to volunteer, described the carnage in his 1917 book, *The*

Battle of the Somme: "The British moved forward in line after line, dressed as if on parade; not a man wavered or broke rank; but minute by minute the ordered lines melted away under the deluge of high explosive, shrapnel, rifle, and machine-gun fire." The Germans pitied the boys falling before their bullets, calling them *Kannonenfutter*, cannon fodder.

It was not combat so much as slaughter. Between dawn and dusk, nearly twenty thousand British soldiers died, while another forty thousand suffered wounds or went missing in action—the highest one-day loss in British military history before or since. The men and boys who straggled back to their trenches had witnessed unprecedented horror. Close friends, in some cases their own brothers, had been cut to pieces before their eyes. It was more than many could bear. Thousands turned up in Casualty Clearing Stations (CCS) without visible wounds but unable to speak, hear, walk, or stand still. Many were incoherent. Some, fearing terrifying nightmares, dared not sleep. They came from all ranks, a high proportion of them junior officers. Haig pressed the Somme offensive for four bloody months of mounting casualties without breaking through.

Dr. Arthur Hurst, a physician in Britain's RAMC, filmed many of the broken men. His *War Neuroses* and *The Battle of Seale Hayne* depicted men and boys trembling, blinded, paralyzed, babbling, hiding under beds, and frozen in what Americans in Vietnam fifty years later would label "the thousand-yard stare." Hurst's motifs resembled those of the epoch's silent horror movies, stricken creatures struggling with deformities, spectral figures casting sinister shadows against white backgrounds, eyes bulging and transfixed, paralyzed limbs, shaking bodies, all so terrifying that the images were not shown to the public. Although the British Army High Command was reluctant to acknowledge that war wounds could be mental as well as physical, it could not avoid addressing a phenomenon that was depriving the fighting forces of the men needed to prosecute the war.

Many of the broken men recorded their experiences in diaries, letters, illustrations, and poems. Two young officers treated for shell shock, Siegfried Sassoon and Wilfred Owen, rank among the finest poets of the war. Yet much of their verse would not have been written but for their psychotherapy. Chance brought the two poets together, and chance assigned each to a psychiatrist suited to his particular needs. These analysts acted as midwives to their works by interpreting their nightmares, clarifying their thoughts, and encouraging them in their creations. Owen, who in another context might have been left to languish in trauma, benefited from intensive therapy under Dr. Arthur Brock. Brock's interest in science, sociology, folklore, Greek mythology, and nature studies accorded with Owen's. It was Brock who expanded Owen's horizons and gave him the self-confidence to tackle sundry outside tasks and restore his mental balance. Sassoon, in contrast, enjoyed intellectual engagement with his psychiatrist, Dr. William Halse Rivers, who did not trouble him with the outside activities that Brock imposed on Owen. Had Rivers treated Owen and Brock been responsible for Sassoon, this would have been a different story. Had both young officers been sent to different hospitals, they would not have met, and the poems they wrote would have been vastly different from the masterpieces the world knows.

Following the disaster of the Somme, the War Office opened new hospitals expressly to deal with shell shock and treat what had become an epidemic. The best was a place in Scotland called Craiglockhart.

. . . in this battle of Marathon . . . Epizêlus, the son of Cuphagoras . . . was in the thick of the fray, and behaving himself as a brave man should, when suddenly he was stricken with blindness, without blow of sword or dart; and this blindness continued thenceforth during the whole of his after life. The following is the account which he himself, as I have heard, gave of the matter: he said that a gigantic warrior, with a huge beard, which shaded all his shield, stood over against him; but the ghostly semblance passed him by, and slew the man at his side. Such, as I understand, was the tale which Epizêlus told.

—*The History of Herodotus*, book 6, chapter 117, translated by George Rawlinson, 1910

CHAPTER ONE

The Hydro

Historians surmise that Craiglockhart took its name from the Scots Gaelic *Creag Loch Ard*—"crag or hill [on] the high lake," although the hill boasts neither lake nor great height. There is a pond, but men dug it long after the outcrop received its name. Its twin peaks, known as Easter and Wester Craiglockhart hills, lay claim to the lowest altitude—a bare two hundred feet above the sea—among seven hills that, like Rome's, defined the topography of Scotland's capital city. A stone castle protruded from the crag until the thirteenth century, but it played no significant role in the country's turbulent history of dynastic and religious wars. It was already rubble when the Act of Union sealed Scotland's connection to England in 1707. By the nineteenth century, a southwestern suburb of Edinburgh, Slateford, had absorbed the crag while retaining it as a rural sanctuary.

The crag's woods and meadows afforded a pastoral retreat from the somber stone mansions, filthy tenements, and notoriously disputatious politics of the city. Craiglockhart boasted unpolluted air, pure underground water, and panoramic views, not only of Edinburgh's spires a mere three miles northeast, but of the Firth of Forth estuary and the twenty-mile ridge of green wilderness known as the Pentland Hills.

These natural advantages of curative waters, smokeless skies, invigo-
rating vistas, and proximity to the capital's wealth attracted a company
of canny Scots merchants to erect a health spa of gargantuan propor-
tions on thirteen fertile acres.

Expense was the least consideration for investors who engaged two
of Scotland's most prestigious architects, John Dick Peddie and Charles
George Hood Kinnear, in 1877 to design the extravagant Craiglockhart Hydropathic Institution. This was the era of sumptuous health
retreats for beneficiaries of Britain's growing imperial bounty to "take
the waters." More than twenty such establishments sprang up in late
nineteenth-century Scotland beside the lochs and up the glens, promising respite from counting houses, mills, and coal-infused air. Peddie
and Kinnear adopted a design similar to another luxurious spa they
were building forty miles northwest of Craiglockhart, near the town
of Dunblane. Both hydros would be massive fortresses of fine-cut ash-
lar sandstone playfully mixing Italian Renaissance motifs with the
stolid mass of a Scots baronial manor.

In 1878, workers demolished an old farmhouse, laid foundations,
and erected scaffolds on a grassy hillock facing west from Wester
Craiglockhart Hill. Over the following months, the villa's imposing
280-foot-wide façade took shape, soaring from deep basements up three
stories of bay windows and a classical balustrade to a pitched gray slate
roof. Peddie and Kinnear mimicked fashionable styles from Doric col-
umns on second-floor windows to a Japanese pagoda capping the five-
story central tower's Italian belvedere. Wings at either end stretched
behind and housed four floors of long corridors and multiple bedrooms. Turret-like gables and chimneys at irregular intervals lent the
otherwise brooding structure a fairy-tale aura. A 50-by-20-foot swimming pool with Turkish bath in the basement offered, in the promot-
ers' words, "all the varieties of hot and cold plunge, vapour, spray,
needle, douche and electric baths."

Outdoors, gardeners cleared pathways through a forest of beech and Scotch pine. The landscape provided acres of lawns for an archery range, bowling greens, tennis courts, and croquet grounds. Harried Scottish burghers could exercise without straining themselves.

The mock classical exterior belied interior conveniences as modern as any in Victorian Britain, including indoor plumbing for water closets, showers, and baths. The Tobin system of interior ventilation, metal tubes within wall cavities to recirculate the air, filtered smoke from the many fireplaces in bedrooms and common rooms alike. Guests could tumble out of bed, step down a marble staircase, and skip along the 140-foot hallway to the dining room for a full breakfast of porridge, eggs, bacon, sausage, black pudding, toast, and tea. From there, they could wander into the billiard room, reading room, or Recreation Hall. Those in need would find the office of the medical superintendent, Dr. Thomas Duddingston Wilson, on the ground floor.

The Craiglockhart Hydropathic's elegant portals opened to Edinburgh's "worried wealthy" in 1880. Carriages and hansom cabs deposited patrons from Edinburgh at the foot of the stone walkway leading up a grass verge to the villa. Guests, while valuing the Hydro's amenities, proved too few to cover the costs of construction, maintenance, staff, and taxes. The owners sold it in 1891 to a fellow Scotsman, fifty-year-old architect James Bell. Bell already managed Peddie and Kinnear's Dunblane Hydro, which he left to live and work at Craiglockhart as principal shareholder and managing director. He renamed it the Edinburgh Hydropathic.

Accompanying Bell to Craiglockhart was Dunblane's head gardener, forty-one-year-old Henry Carmichael. The rugged and conscientious Carmichael brought his wife, Catherine, and their eleven children to live in one of the "Hydro Cottages" on the Craiglockhart property. Two of the older boys assisted their father with the lawns, shrubs, flowers, and woods. Catherine bore two more children, Archibald, known as Archie, and Elizabeth, at Craiglockhart. In tribute to Henry's employer, Elizabeth's middle name was Bell. Soon after the girl's birth, Catherine contracted typhoid. No doubt weakened from bearing and rearing thirteen children, she died on August 1, 1894. Henry cared for the children with the help of his oldest daughter, Janet, until 1897, when he married again. His second wife, Mary Comrie, gave the family one more son, John, and another daughter, Euphemia.

Like the Carmichael family, Craiglockhart's gardens flourished. Henry and his older sons seeded and mowed grass fields for the Hydro to host the Scottish Croquet Championship in July 1897. The precision with which the Carmichaels nurtured the grounds led to the championships' taking place there for seventeen more years. Bell took part in the competitions, and he proudly presented the prizes at the conclusion of each tournament.

Bell's astute management transformed the Hydro's fortunes. Its reputation spread, attracting rich patrons in want of rejuvenating therapies. The kitchen provided hearty Scottish fare, the Carmichaels maintained the grounds, maids kept the bedrooms in good order, and athletic staff guided overweight plutocrats in exercises and games to mitigate the effects of years of indulgence. Craiglockhart's popularity pointed toward good fortune as the new century approached.

Craiglockhart, along with the rest of Britain, mourned the death in 1901 of Queen Victoria, who had popularized holidays in Scotland with her acquisition of Balmoral Castle and her many summers there. The transition from Victorian to Edwardian eras with the accession of King Edward VII continued the Hydro's prosperity, as gentlemen and ladies from England as well as Scotland sought its cures. On Edward's death in 1910, his son George V inherited a kingdom whose subjects envisioned a long reign of peace.

Events in the summer of 1914 dispelled their illusions: the assassination by a Serbian nationalist of the Austrian grand duke at Sarajevo in June, Austria-Hungary's ultimatum to Serbia, the mobilization of continental armies from France to Russia, and, on August 4, Imperial

Germany's invasion of Belgium. Britain declared war on Germany the same day, a decision few in Scotland or England questioned. The secretary of state for war, Lord Kitchener, appealed for volunteers to join his expanding New Army. Young men, among them the Edinburgh Hydropathic's patrons and workers, converged on military enlistment centers throughout the empire. In Scotland, volunteers were so numerous in early August that Edinburgh's recruiting bureau stayed open all night. Two of Henry Carmichael's sons, Archie and Alexander, enlisted in the Royal Scots Regiment in September. One grandson, John Henry Carmichael, also joined the colors in 1914 to serve in the Royal Field Artillery. Soon afterward, Henry's youngest son, John, who had been born at Craiglockhart, became a signaler in the 8th Battalion of the Regiment of Scottish Rifles, popularly called the Cameronians. With three sons, a grandson, and two of his nephews in the armed forces, Henry Carmichael relied on his other boys to help with the backbreaking work of keeping the grounds up to prewar standards. By this time, Carmichael was sixty-four.

The Carmichael boys, like all the other volunteers in the first wave of recruitment, were unprepared for warfare in the modern era. Raised on tales of imperial battles against Indian rebels and Zulu warriors, they harbored the patriotic delusion that battles would be decisive, few would die, and victory would be swift. Lieutenant Bernard Law Montgomery, who would live to command British armies in the Second World War, was not alone when he wrote, "At least the thing will be over in three weeks." The poet Rupert Brooke welcomed the release from peacetime ennui:

> Now, God be thanked Who has matched us with His hour
> And caught our youth, and wakened us from sleeping.

Cavalry officers carried lances and their infantry counterparts brought swords across the English Channel to face the Germans. They were

soon disabused of romantic ideas about gallant battles and a rapid conclusion. By Christmas, when many imagined they would have beaten
the "Hun," a million would be dead. More were wounded in body and
mind. Horses, swords, and lances proved useless against German fire-
power. Men were returning to Britain with tales of explosives whose
force sucked the air out of their lungs and ripped open their eardrums.
A man could die of internal injuries without a projectile touching him.
A new kind of war was leaving men with new types of injury. It was
enough to drive anyone crazy.

DESPITE THE WAR, James Bell hosted the Scottish Croquet Championships at Craiglockhart as usual in September 1914. Spectators from
Edinburgh and farther afield converged on Henry Carmichael's im-
maculately trimmed lawns, while Bell competed against croquet masters from Scotland, England, Ireland, and Wales. Bell awarded the
trophy to a twenty-four-year-old Englishman, Gaston Wace. Patriotic
disapproval of such frivolity in wartime, however, forced Bell to cancel
future competitions for the duration.

The Carmichael boys posted letters from their training camps
and the front lines to the family at Craiglockhart. Private Archibald
Carmichael, twenty-four years of age and a hearty five foot ten and
154 pounds, wrote to assure them of his good health before he embarked from Liverpool on May 25, 1915, aboard His Majesty's Transport (HMT) *Empress of Britain*. The ship reached Alexandria, Egypt,
on June 1. Eight days later, Archie's 4th Battalion of Royal Scots sailed
from Alexandria to reinforce their beleaguered comrades on the
beaches of Germany's ally, Ottoman Turkey. Britain had launched an
amphibious invasion on April 25 at Gallipoli, where British, Austra-
lian, New Zealand, and French troops suffered nine thousand casualties in the first week.

No further letters arrived from Archie, but his platoon commander, Lieutenant R. Mackie, wrote to his twenty-seven-year-old sister, Elizabeth, from Turkey. Mackie's family owned the shop where Elizabeth worked, J. W. Mackie & Sons confectioners, on Edinburgh's elegant Princes Street. "I grieve very much to have to send you such sad tidings of your brother Archie," the letter began. Mackie explained that a shell burst had struck her brother in the head, wounding him too severely for doctors to save him. Archie, he wrote, was "a quiet steady young soldier whom we all liked and now miss." Mackie hoped the family would take consolation knowing that Archie had not suffered. Henry Carmichael continued to tend the gardens, knowing that other sons, nephews, and a grandson faced the same dangers Archie had.

Scotland, unlike England's south coast that reverberated to artillery blasts from the French side of the English Channel, was aloof from the war until Sunday night, April 2, 1916. At 7:00 p.m., Edinburgh police announced that two German Navy zeppelins, the giant dirigibles invented by Count Ferdinand von Zeppelin in 1900, were cruising over the North Sea toward the city. Similar airships had already bombed industrial centers and naval bases in England, but this was their first foray so far north. Although Edinburgh lacked air defenses, the fire brigade, Red Cross, and security services mobilized to deal with casualties and fires.

The first zeppelin appeared just before midnight, bombing the docks at Edinburgh's Port of Leith and setting Innes & Grieve's Scotch whisky warehouse on fire. Following the course of the river known as the Water of Leith, it bombarded neighborhoods on both banks. The high explosives and incendiaries devastated two hotels, several houses, and many business premises. One bomb narrowly missed the highest landmark in the city center, Edinburgh Castle.

Soldiers stationed in the castle manned its famed One O'Clock Gun, a 32-pound ceremonial cannon that had fired daily since 1861 for ships' captains to set their clocks. Blank charges, however, did not deter the airships. The second zeppelin trailed the first over the city, releasing most of its explosives on empty fields.

The raid, visible from Craiglockhart, lasted thirty-five minutes. Seventeen German incendiaries and seven high-explosive shells had taken thirteen lives and left twenty-four wounded. Among the dead were a one-year-old baby and a soldier, Private Thomas Donohue of the Royal Scots, on leave from the trenches in France.

The war, which Edinburgh's citizens knew secondhand from newspapers and their sons' letters, had come to Scotland. Its mental victims were not far behind.

CHAPTER TWO

The War Hospital

A t the outbreak of the late European War," wrote British Army psychiatrist Dr. C. Stanford Read, "there was little foresight shown or preparations made for a large influx of mental cases." Dr. Read ran the army's only mental asylum, the Royal Victoria Hospital's D Block in Netley, Hampshire. Founded in 1870, D Block was better suited to locking up the incurably insane than to returning men to normal life. It had only 121 beds for enlisted men and 3 for officers, insufficient for the thousands of mental cases the Great War was turning out every month. The government needed more beds, more hospitals, more psychiatrists, more nurses. It opened psychiatric institutions, starting in November 1914 with a special hospital for officers beside London's Kensington Palace, and Moss Side Red Cross Military Hospital at Maghull near Liverpool. Maghull filled to capacity within two months, forcing the War Office to requisition additional hospitals throughout the British Isles—"hospitals," not "asylums," wrote Dr. Read, "to obviate, if possible, the stigma that might be felt to attach to the name." In 1915 alone, nervous collapse claimed 21,474 officers.

As the Somme bled Britain's armed forces throughout the summer of 1916, the War Office turned to James Bell's Edinburgh Hydro-pathic. Its swimming pool, Turkish bath, common rooms, and twelve rural acres offered essentials for traumatized officers to begin their recovery. The government requisitioned the Hydro, and Bell moved to another property he owned nearby. The Hydro required little renova-tion. The massive villa had beds for 174 patients with two or three to a room. Its administrative offices easily converted to psychiatric con-sulting rooms. It was as if Peddie and Kinnear had designed Craiglock-hart for victims of shell shock.

Craiglockhart War Hospital opened in October 1916 for "officers only." Segregating officers from men was common practice in all European armies. No one questioned the separation of officers from "other ranks" in any realm, be it dining, accommodation, or, in this case, mental health treatment. Military necessity provided an additional motive for concentrating medical resources on officers. They were des-perately needed at the front, where they were dying and breaking down out of all proportion to their numbers.

Craiglockhart's O. C., officer commanding, was fifty-year-old phys-ician Major William H. Bryce of Scotland's Lowland Field Ambu-lance. Although a career officer in the RAMC since his 1903 enlistment in Glasgow, Bryce recoiled at military formality. It was his belief, he wrote, that "there should be little to indicate hospital régime beyond the few regulations necessary to ensure order." His priority was the welfare of patients rather than arbitrary rules of etiquette and dress. Parade ground drill had no place in his mental hospital. It did not bother him if patients wore bathrobes and bedroom slippers all day. His own uniform often lacked a cap and the officer's traditional cross-shoulder Sam Browne belt. Subordinates were not required to salute him; and, as one astonished observer at the hospital noted, he "spoke to his Staff as *equals!*" While such affronts to military propriety irri-tated his superiors, Bryce's objective was not to break men, but to make them whole.

Bryce in the autumn of 1916 benefited from the presence of two remarkable psychiatrists, who excelled as much at psychology as in fields far removed from medicine. It seemed they understood Trinidadian intellectual C. L. R. James's famous question long before he wrote "What do they know of cricket who only cricket know?" The principal medical officers were a Scotsman, Dr. Arthur John Brock, and an Englishman, Dr. William Halse Rivers. Both had qualified as neurologists and psychiatrists. Brock's other interests, on which he wrote and lectured, were sociology, rural Scotland, classical Greece, and the relationship of mental health to the environment. Rivers had sailed as an anthropologist to South Sea islands, Egypt, and India; made scientific studies of eyesight and nerve regeneration; and written books on color perception, primitive tribes, kinship, and heredity. Brock's and Rivers's extracurricular interests diverged, but the two shared a humanistic, holistic approach to mental illness at odds with the era's military orthodoxies. Most senior officers, including many Medical Corps physicians, regarded shell shock as nothing other than malingering or cowardice that demanded not treatment, but punishment. Brock and Rivers, encouraged by Major Bryce, sought to demonstrate that sympathetic therapy worked better than harsh discipline.

PHOTOGRAPHS TAKEN AT Craiglockhart show a clean-shaved, lean, tall, and ascetic Arthur Brock in his starched captain's uniform, usually at his desk. Aged thirty-eight in 1916, he had a high-pitched voice, abundant energy, and what one patient called "a long peaked nose that should have had a drip at the point." He adorned his consulting room in Craiglockhart's villa with objects akin to his intellectual pursuits: a pen-and-ink drawing of a wrestling match between two stripped and entwined ancient Greek wrestlers and, on shelves below, volumes of Greek myths, ancient medical classics, and Scots Gaelic folklore alongside texts by his mentor, Scottish sociologist Patrick Geddes.

Brock was born just outside Edinburgh on September 9, 1878, the son of a gentleman farmer and a poet, Florence Walker. On completion of his degree in classics at Edinburgh University, he planned to become an artist. When his father vetoed that career, he enrolled in medicine at Edinburgh in 1896. A meeting with Patrick Geddes, an autodidact Renaissance man regarded in Scotland as the father of town planning, had a profound influence on the young medical student. Twenty-four years his senior, Geddes introduced Brock to the philosophies of Auguste Comte and Henri Bergson, kindled his interest in sociology, and taught him the importance to mental health of environment and community. The admiration between the two men was mutual, Geddes writing that Brock was "pragmatic in mind, activist in temper, not content with any specialised view or treatment."

Brock spent months in Europe's preeminent centers of psychological discovery, Vienna and Berlin, both before and after graduation in 1901, to expand what he called his "mental horizon." A succession of Scottish hospitals employed the young physician, notably Woodburn Sanatorium for Consumptives in 1910 and 1911. His study of tuberculosis patients gave him insights into depression that would serve him at Craiglockhart. He noted that at Woodburn "even a patient with only mild tuberculosis soon goes to pieces morally if he has nothing to do." In line with Geddes, he believed that lengthy rest was more curse than cure. Patients needed to walk outdoors, to study the world around them, and, most important, to work. Idleness was lethal.

In 1915, Brock married Swedish physiotherapist Siri Marianne von Nolting and enlisted in the army. His first posts were aboard hospital ships to India and off the coast of France, where he ministered to casualties straight from the front lines. His next assignment was as medical officer at the Aldershot Garrison, "the home of the British Army," in Hampshire. While there in 1916, he completed his translation of *On the Natural Faculties* by second-century C.E. Greek physician Galen.

Brock believed Galen, along with Hippocrates a father of medical science, had much to teach modern doctors about natural healing and close observation of disease.

The army transferred Captain Brock to Craiglockhart in time for its inauguration. The shell-shock hospital seemed to him "a microcosm of the modern world, showing the salient features of our society (and especially its weaknesses) intensified, and on a narrower stage." With his wrestlers' sketch suspended like a banner over garish floral-print wallpaper, his eclectic library stacked on shelves, and notebooks open on his desk beside a wicker wastepaper basket, Brock prepared to test his and Geddes's theories on men shattered in the most merciless test of endurance that history had yet contrived for young warriors.

BROCK'S COLLEAGUE AT Craiglockhart was one of the most accomplished scholars of his generation. Dr. William Halse Rivers was a polymath with notable achievements in neurology, clinical psychiatry, medical research, anthropology, and linguistics. Yet the impression he gave on first meeting was of shyness and diffidence. He stammered when he spoke and tired so easily that he was often unable to work more than four hours a day. The four hours nonetheless were more productive than the full days of younger, healthier men. Born near Chatham in Kent on March 12, 1864, Rivers was fourteen years older than Brock. Unlike his clean-shaved colleague, Rivers sported a swirling moustache and wore wire-rim glasses. Where Brock took inspiration from classical medicine and Geddes's sociology, Rivers applied lessons learned from peoples whom most Europeans regarded as backward. His empathy for South Sea islanders and other colonized peoples diminished his faith in, as he said, the "Great White God." "I have been able to detect no essential difference [in intellectual concentration] between Melanesian or Toda and those with whom I have been accustomed to mix in the life of our own society," he wrote, displaying a mind free of prejudice and receptive to fresh ideas. One such idea was Freudianism, which Rivers had studied, as had Brock, in Germany.

The Riverses were a naval family. Two ancestors, a father and son both named William, fought at Trafalgar aboard Admiral Horatio Nelson's flagship, HMS *Victory*, in 1805. The younger Rivers, then a seventeen-year-old midshipman, was wounded in the mouth and lost a leg during the battle; but he went on fighting and allegedly killed the Frenchman who fatally wounded Nelson. Family legend had it that Nelson's last words were "Take care of young Rivers." The midshipman's son, who would become William's grandfather, was the last Rivers to serve in the Royal Navy. His son, William's father, Henry, became an Anglican clergyman. Henry and his wife, Elizabeth Hunt, had four children, William, Charles, Ethel, and Katharine, between 1864 and 1871. Although Henry was also a speech therapist, he failed to address William's stuttering.

The speech impediment was not the boy's only handicap. At the age of five, he walked up the stairs of the family house and entered a room. What happened there must have been traumatic. From that day, he had no visual memory. Loss of the ability to see images in the mind, *aphantasia*, from the Greek for "absence of imagination," was so rare that it would not receive a name in medical literature for many years. Only in dreams could Rivers conjure images of people, places, and objects. Not even in dreams, however, could he recall what occurred in that upstairs room.

William and his brother, Charles, attended boys' day schools together, first in Brighton and later in Tonbridge, Kent. William's intention on leaving Tonbridge School was to follow his grandfather and father to Cambridge University, but illness kept him out of his final year and prevented his sitting for the scholarship examination. A friend and colleague, Grafton Elliot Smith, recalled that he "always had to fight against ill health: heart and blood vessels." Rivers studied instead at the University of London's teaching hospital, Saint Bartholomew's, becoming, in 1886 at the age of twenty-two, its youngest ever Bachelor of Medicine and member of the Royal College of Surgeons.

Rivers's poor health prevented him from pursuing a career, like his illustrious forebears, in the Royal Navy. In 1887, however, he signed on as ship's doctor for voyages to Japan and North America. His love of the sea saw him taking vacation cruises to Norway, Portugal, Madeira, the Canary Islands, and the United States. While sailing home from the West Indies, he enjoyed lengthy conversations with Irish wit and playwright George Bernard Shaw. Saint Bartholomew's awarded him a doctorate in medicine in 1888, after which he served a two-year residency at the Chichester Infirmary. Next came research in neurology and psychology back at Saint Bartholomew's. Curiosity about the brain and nervous system led him to the National Hospital for the Relief and Cure of the Paralysed and Epileptic in London's Queen's Square. Rivers was drawn to Germany, as Brock would be, to learn more about psychology. Spending 1892 in Jena and Heidelberg, he mastered German, studied philosophy as well as psychology, and attended concerts and art exhibitions. It was not long before he was publishing academic papers in German. With the German experience heightening his interest in the mind, he noted in his diary, "I should go in for insanity when I return to England." So he did, practicing at London's Bethlem Royal Hospital, founded in 1247 as England's first mental asylum and known in the vernacular as "Bedlam."

Achievements mounted, from a lectureship at University College London, to another at Saint John's College, Cambridge. Saint John's gave him a place to live in its cloistered grounds beside the River Cam. His students felt free to call on him in his rooms at any time. One recalled that "he had an extraordinary way of making us feel that we were taking part in a discussion on a plane of equality with him." He became founding director of England's first two psychology laboratories in London and Cambridge. Lured in 1898 by his medical students Charles Samuel Myers, who would later coin the term "shell shock," and William McDougall, Rivers ventured on a rigorous expedition to the Torres Strait between Australia and Papua New Guinea to study the islands' inhabitants. Going out as a doctor, he returned a dedicated anthropologist. It was a discipline his maternal uncle, James Hunt, founder and first president of the Anthropological Society of London, had pioneered. Rivers's methodology for ethnographic research and classification became standard practice. He traveled to Upper Egypt in 1900, to the Toda people in the Nilgiri Hills of southeast India in 1901 and 1902, and, five years later, to the Solomon Islands in Melanesia to study customs, kinship, and color perception. His books on the Todas in 1906 and the Melanesians in 1914 became instant classics in the emerging discipline of anthropology.

While practicing and teaching psychology in London and Cambridge, Rivers continued his work in anthropology. In the summer of 1914, he was in Australia attending an anthropological conference of the British Association for the Advancement of Science, when Britain and Germany went to war. British and German scientists alike sailed home, but Rivers went to the New Hebrides to do field research. He returned to England in the spring of 1915 and immediately volunteered for frontline service in the RAMC. The army, considering the fifty-year-old physician's health too fragile, turned him down.

Dr. Grafton Elliot Smith recruited him in July as a civilian psychiatrist at Moss Side Military Hospital, then becoming the preeminent treatment center for the war's mentally wounded. Among its clinicians were the two former students who had accompanied Rivers to the Torres Strait, Charles Samuel Myers and William McDougall. The patients were not officers, but "other ranks." Rivers found that healing them was hindered by their distrust of authority, inhibitions about their private lives, and suspicions that doctors wanted to trick them into saying something that would return them to the front. Their intellectual and educational level, compared with that of his Cambridge students, further distanced Rivers from them. The conscientious psychologist persevered, working himself to exhaustion while keeping up with academic research.

In October 1916, the War Office sent him as a commissioned RAMC captain to Craiglockhart. The "officers only" establishment allowed Rivers to discuss with educated young men their dreams, the causes of their collapse, and the restoration of their mental health. The challenge had awaited him all his professional life, and he embraced it. "Rumour has it," wrote a Craiglockhart inmate, "that when a fresh convoy arrived, Capt. Rivers walked round them & took his pick. Strange to say, nearly all the interesting patients floated his way."

THE RED CROSS SUPPLIED most of the hospital's nursing and ancillary staff from its Voluntary Aid Detachments (VADs), mainly young women of all classes seeking to help the fighting men. Craiglockhart's seven staff nursing sisters, eighteen VAD junior nurses—among them Scottish ingenues Florence Mellor, Mary McGregor, and Grace Barnet—and the housekeepers worked under the supervision of Matron Margaret MacBean. Miss MacBean, a formidable Scotswoman born in 1864, the year of Rivers's birth, had entered the nursing profession at the age of twenty-three. With twenty-four years in general hospitals behind her, she became matron in 1911 of the Govan District Asylum at Hawkhead near Glasgow. A letter of reference from its medical superintendent, Dr. James H. MacDonald, stated, "She is not only a highly trained and experienced nurse but a most efficient Matron, who commands the respect and esteem of the Staff and patients alike and, indeed, all with whom she comes in contact." Some colleagues referred to her as "the fiery matron." Her responsibilities encompassed nursing staff, kitchen, laundry, and housekeeping. It was a coup for Craiglockhart to engage a nursing director who, despite not having served in the military, claimed five years' experience in mental health. The War Hospital was seeking excellence in all aspects of the care of traumatized soldiers.

Henry Carmichael persevered as head gardener, assisted by the sons who had not gone to war. Summer gave way to the chilly Scottish autumn. Purple foxgloves and pale hedge bindweeds were wilting, beech and ash leaves changing color and falling to earth. While the Carmichaels burned leaves and dead branches in glowing bonfires, Rivers's and Brock's first patients staggered into Craiglockhart.

CRAIGLOCKHART'S INITIAL INTAKE of eight officers arrived on October 27, 1916, in a state of shock, eyes glazed and barely able to take in their surroundings. The oldest was thirty-four-year-old John Sandison. Edward Curwen and Gilbert Davidson were thirty-two, John Douglas twenty-seven, and John Oliver twenty-six. The youngest, George Lightfoot, Charles Greaves, and Ernest Clayton, were twenty-two. All were second lieutenants, all "neurasthenic."

Second Lieutenant Sandison came to Craiglockhart straight from the Somme's Transloy Ridges, where twelve days earlier German artillery buried him alive and left him unconscious for thirty-six hours. The men who dug him out found a trench shovel stuck into his abdomen and shrapnel embedded in his left ankle. Sandison, a company commander in the 10th Battalion of the Seaforth Highlanders Regiment, had no memory of the explosion that nearly killed him. His legs were immobilized and wracked with pain.

Sandison's long military record gave the lie to a common belief that only fresh recruits, unaccustomed to military discipline, broke down at the front. The six-foot-three-inch Scotsman had joined the Royal Scots Regiment in 1898 at age sixteen and retired in 1912 as a quartermaster sergeant. That should have ended his military career, but the war drew him back, first as a sergeant in the Royal Scots and, from spring 1916, as a commissioned officer in the Seaforth Highlanders. He had endured the Somme slaughter for three and a half months before coming to Craiglockhart. Soon after he checked in, he met the psychiatrist who would treat him, Dr. Arthur Brock.

Brock's therapy revolved around the ever-present portrait of the mythological wrestling match between Hercules and Antaeus framed on his wall. It was no haphazard decoration in an otherwise dreary medical office. Brock, the classicist and translator of ancient Greek texts, explained to Sandison and his other patients that the picture was a metaphor for their predicament. The giant Antaeus, a fearsome king in Libya, was the son of the sea god, Poseidon, and Gaia, goddess of the earth. His prodigious strength emanated from the ground, his mother earth, the way Samson's did from his hair. When the hero Hercules arrived in Libya, Antaeus challenged him to a wrestling match. Hercules threw Antaeus to the ground again and again. Each time Antaeus hit the earth, his muscles grew. Realizing the source of his opponent's power, Hercules lifted Antaeus into the air and broke his back. Brock felt that each officer at Craiglockhart "recognises that, in a way, he is himself an Antaeus who has been taken from mother earth and well nigh crushed to death by the war giant or military machine."

The key for Brock was to ground his charges in everyday reality through vigorous physical and mental activity. He encouraged patients like Sandison to rise early, "take a cold bath or swim before breakfast," then to go outdoors and survey the land. Some officers locked themselves in the lavatories to avoid the doctor's wake-up calls, until Brock had the bolts removed. One patient "boasted that if he lay flat under his bed, so that the untidy bedclothes hid him, as if he were an early riser, he escaped." While Craiglockhart offered cricket, golf, badminton, water polo, tennis, and two full-size billiard tables, Brock recommended more productive pastimes like carpentry, photography, debating, music, and writing. Cure depended on reintegration into a community through productive labor. His mantra, derived from Geddes, was "Place-Folk-Work," with productive labor connecting the patient to his environment and to the community. Brock took the name of his method, "ergotherapy," from the Greek for "work," *ergo*, and for "healing," *therapeia*. It was the cure for "ergophobia," fear of work.

Brock rejected American Dr. Silas Weir Mitchell's popular prescription for neurasthenics in Philadelphia: rest, massage, isolation, and a milk diet. War hospitals utilizing the Weir Mitchell therapy produced mixed results that left some patients in long-term lassitude. The worst course for any patient, in Brock's view, was to confine him to bed. Moreover, he believed, hospitals that advised traumatized soldiers not to think about the war were hindering their recovery. His psychoanalysis required soldiers to confront and thus render ineffective memories of their disabling experiences. Finally, he insisted his patients become self-reliant: "If the essential thing for the patient to do is to help himself, the essential thing for the doctor to do—indeed, the only thing he can profitably do—is to help him to help himself." Brock had encountered neurasthenic symptoms in civilians before the war. "Shell-shock," he observed, "was but the pre-war 'nervous breakdown' with added terrors and frightfulness."

The "added terrors" included asphyxiation by chemical weapons of the kind Second Lieutenant George Walpole Lightfoot survived on September 2, 1916, on the Somme at Delville Wood. All the Royal Welch Fusilier (RWF) officers and men beside him died in the gas attack, but stretcher-bearers found Walpole unconscious and carried him to the nearest CCS. Three days later, doctors declared him a shell-shock case. A ship ferried him with other wounded to Southampton on September 16, a date, like that of his gassing, that he could not remember when asked. A Medical Board of RAMC physicians at the 4th London General Hospital noted: "He looks pale & ill. He has a cough and there is a little soreness in the sternum . . . He is startled by noises and is troubled by terrifying dreams. He is very weak and is unable to stand any fatigue." The board ordered him to report to Craiglockhart on its opening day.

Thirty-two-year-old Edward Curwen fell to poison gas in April 1916 near Loos in front of the Germans' fortified Hohenzollern Redoubt, where he was serving with the British 12th Division's Trench Mortar Battery. An art teacher in Scottish secondary schools before the war, the blue-eyed subaltern, junior officer, received treatment at a base hospital in France. When his lungs recovered, his superiors sent him back to the front. There he suffered a nervous collapse. He wrote, "I was compelled to go to hospital on October 3rd after being about 10 weeks on the Somme." The Medical Board that examined him in France sent him to England on October 20 and, six days later, to Craiglockhart.

The same Medical Board examined Canadian John Douglas of the Seaforth Highlanders' 7th Battalion and commented that "he had been 13 months at the front. He feels very shaky & incapable of any sustained bodily or mental effort." At Eaucourt l'Abbaye, a shell that exploded a few feet from him killed two of his friends and trapped him under a ton of debris. When comrades dug him out, his hands trembled, his head ached, and nightmares blighted his sleep. The once healthy, five-foot-six-inch Toronto native had enthusiastically answered the call of King and Country in September 1914 at the age of twenty-four. By the time he reached Craiglockhart, his hair was gray.

Another casualty from Eaucourt l'Abbaye, Percy Pickering, came to Craiglockhart on its second day. The twenty-year-old second lieutenant of the Royal Welch Fusiliers' 18th Battalion stood five feet seven inches and weighed 136 pounds. He had enlisted in December 1914 and received his commission the following September. On the front lines, heavy artillery blew him off his feet and left him bleeding. He refused to leave his men. Physicians, noticing that he "was unable to control much twitching" and suffered headaches, insomnia, and depression, pulled him out of the line. A Medical Board in France examined him on October 9, concluded that his injuries were "Severe. Not permanent," and recommended treatment in Britain. Care of the dazed youngster fell to Dr. Brock.

Two days after Pickering arrived, Second Lieutenant Alexander Scott Freeman of the Queen's Own Cameron Highlanders limped through Craiglockhart's portals. Genuine physical ailments had afflicted him since November 8, 1915, when a high-explosive shell wounded him at the hotly contested Hill 60 near Ypres in Belgium. When an appendectomy failed to relieve his stomach pains, doctors put him on a diet. That worked so badly they had to pump his stomach. While recuperating, he contracted pneumonia and gastritis. The twenty-three-year-old soldier, who had enlisted in the first month of the war, was a mental and physical wreck by the time a Medical Board examined him on October 27, 1916, and wrote that "his admission to Craiglockhart War Hospital is strongly recommended."

The first eight officers and those who joined them in the following weeks lounged in the common rooms, read newspapers, smoked, traded gossip, and enjoyed a variety of sports as if they were rich clients of the old Hydro. Craiglockhart seemed more officers' club than mental asylum. Major Bryce wrote, "The officers' hospital should be run socially on the lines of a country house, or, more correctly speaking, on the lines on which a country club might be organized." Doctors encouraged the men to write to their families and in some cases to invite their wives or parents to visit. Craiglockhart's surface normality reassured its patients that they had no cause for shame and their minds could heal like broken legs. Normality reigned by day. At night, though, chilling screams echoed along bare corridors to the terror of young VAD nurses.

While the nightmares distressed their victims, Dr. William Halse Rivers saw them as openings to his patients' psyches. He urged them to discuss their dreams in detail. Although he had studied Freud before the war, he did not begin reading the Austrian's *The Interpretation of Dreams* until beginning work at Craiglockhart. Rivers shared Freud's view that dreams were "wish fulfillment," but nightmares of unimaginable wartime horror led him also to see "dreams as prominent symptoms of nervous disorder." Nightmares of those who repressed their memories were the most frightening and persistent. "It has been found over and over again," he wrote, "that when this process of repression is given up, the dreams no longer occur, or, if they continue, lose their terrifying character."

Officers in Rivers's consulting room did not lie on a couch. That "usual analytic procedure," Rivers felt, produced a "morbid transference" of trauma from patient to doctor that achieved nothing for either of them. Rivers's patients sat in chairs for face-to-face conversations that made "the analysis a matter in which the patient and I are partners." He called it "talking therapy," which he had developed with enlisted men at Maghull but felt he could employ more effectively with the better-educated and less-inhibited officers at Craiglockhart. One of the men he treated, Lieutenant William Evans, recalled that Rivers "had a quick, dry sense of humour that would always seem far ahead of our own. By the time we thought of an answer, he'd be ready with the next line. If you were lucky you got to spot the mischief hidden in his eyes. I used to enjoy those verbal sparring matches and, I think, so did he." Rivers offered cups of tea, while he drank milk. He let the men narrate their dreams so that "the main lines of analysis were already clear as soon as the dream had been related." A straight line, he believed, led from dream to cause.

Rivers followed Major Bryce's lead in eschewing military etiquette. One patient observed that "he had to be forcibly reminded that he must not go his rounds unless fully equipped for all emergencies in full panoply of uniform including cane." Rather than salute VAD cooks, Rivers bowed courteously, "another grave breach." Some of those he treated, like his students at Cambridge, remembered the way Rivers pushed his eyeglasses up his forehead and clasped his hands around one knee when an idea excited him. One Craiglockhart patient observed, "When walking he moved very fast, talking hard, and often seeming forgetful that he was being carried along by his own legs."

Rivers shared Brock's rejection of advice from other hospitals that patients "banish all thoughts of war from their minds" in favor of "beautiful scenery and other pleasant aspects of experience." The men needed a balance between confronting their terrors and being overwhelmed by them, an equilibrium some never achieved. Rivers the scientist was finding his way through trial and error, admitting that he approached his first cases with "diffidence."

Patients visited their psychiatrists a few times a week. Rivers left his free to do as they liked the rest of the time, while Brock imposed a regimen of rigorous work and study. When the Scottish rain wasn't pouring, the young men played soccer. Most had the privilege of going into Edinburgh to visit museums, eat in tea shops, and stroll along the magnificent Georgian thoroughfare that was Princes Street. Yet even simple outings risked danger. At one o'clock each afternoon, Craiglockhart officers in uniform with hospital blue armbands heard the blast of Edinburgh Castle's cannon, the traditional but outdated signal for ships' captains to set their clocks. Some of the veterans shook with fear or froze where they stood, as the harmless explosion hurled them back to "the hell where youth and laughter go."

At Craiglockhart, the men learned skills like growing vegetables and developing photographs. From the original eight patients, the hospital's population soon grew to more than one hundred. Three-doctor Medical Boards convened regularly, usually with Major Bryce presiding, to determine each man's future: remain at Craiglockhart, return to the war, take up light duties in Britain, or receive a medical discharge. For every patient who left, others were waiting to take his place. In the second half of 1916, the number of Britain's shell-shock victims, compared with the previous six months, more than quadrupled, to 16,138. Craiglockhart's doctors were dealing with an epidemic.

CHAPTER THREE

Interpreting Dreams

Major Bryce and Captain Brock convened Craiglockhart's first Medical Board on November 30, 1916. Among those examined was Second Lieutenant Percy Pickering, the twenty-year-old Royal Welch Fusilier who had come to the hospital on its second day. Under Brock's care, he was making "rapid progress towards recovery and now shows no signs of nervous disability." The memory of heavy shelling that buried him alive at Eaucourt l'Abbaye no longer tormented him. The board elected to grant him six weeks' rest at his family home in Lancashire. On his return to Craiglockhart in mid-January 1917, he was hardly the same man. His hands trembled. Intolerable insomnia and terrifying nightmares dogged his every night. The recurrence of symptoms that Brock seemed to remove demonstrated that therapeutic progress was reversible. The board met on January 18 and voted to keep him for another month. In February, Pickering appeared again before the board's psychiatrists, who concluded they could do nothing more for the young soldier and transferred him to the Prees Heath Military Hospital in Shropshire. Craiglockhart had experienced its first failure.

By the first of March, Craiglockhart had taken in 125 officers, from whom the medical staff learned more about the nature of shell shock. Rivers distrusted the term "shock," which implied a single cause, and preferred "anxiety neurosis" to "neurasthenia," an "absolutely worthless word." He was coming to the view that the causes of breakdown were many and accumulated over time. Rivers called it "erosion," the steady loss of the fabric of life under the constant stress of fear, deprivation, and confinement in trenches from which soldiers could not escape. They feared not only the artillery fire above, but volcano-like eruptions from explosives planted by German tunnelers below. Breakdown, he believed, was a normal reaction to abnormal circumstances. Anxiety neurosis was inevitable in sensitive men forced to choose between duty and life, between "fight and flight." The irresolvable conflict resolved itself in mental collapse with its concomitant symptoms. Rivers's task was to make his patients understand and cope with fear as natural under life-threatening circumstances. Brock adopted a universal view: shell shock was no different from nervous breakdowns suffered by men and women trapped in industrial societies that severed them from nature and their communities: "Are not these horrors of war the last and culminating terms in a series that begins in the inferno of our industrialized cities?" For Brock, all that the victims of industrial servitude in peace and war had to do, as E. M. Forster wrote in another context, was to connect, "Only connect! . . . Live in fragments no longer."

MARK "MAX" PLOWMAN, one of the officers who found himself at Craiglockhart in March 1917, was born in Tottenham, then an industrializing suburb north of London, on September 1, 1883. The family were Plymouth Brethren, a small Protestant sect formed in 1825 that dispensed with clergy and clung to a belief in Christ's Second Coming and strict interpretation of Holy Writ. Plowman's father owned a brickworks, where Max went to work after quitting school at age sixteen. Four years later, he abandoned the Plymouth Brethren while embracing a noninstitutional Christianity modeled on that of William Blake, the Romantic poet and artist he most admired. "It is impossible," wrote Plowman, "truly to love anybody without loving God." Ten years in his father's factory engendered a strong identification with the working class. Aspiring to become a writer, he apprenticed in a bookshop in 1909, became a journalist, and wrote poetry. He and Dorothy Lloyd Sulman married on May 1, 1914. When the war began three months later, his reaction was ambivalent: he wanted to punish Germany for invading neutral Belgium, but his Christianity condemned war as nothing more than organized murder.

Plowman's compromise between fighting the aggressor and resisting the evil of war was to enlist in the RAMC. Instead of killing and wounding German boys, he would tend the wounds of his countrymen. He wrote to his brother on December 18, 1914, "Repairing's bloody enough work, I suppose but I seem to fancy it before progging hog's flesh with a bayonet." The RAMC inducted him as a private on Christmas Eve, his enlistment papers recording him as "a reviewer for the *Daily News*" with "No religion." He drilled with the 4th Field Ambulance as a "waggon orderly" alongside composer Ralph Vaughan Williams. His equivocal role as a noncombatant uniformed soldier troubled him, and by August 1915 he was considering an officer's commission in "a decent regiment." "Who am I," he wrote, "that I should say to another man—You do my killing?" Having enjoyed the benefits of British nationality, he recognized a duty "to reap its disadvantages & the fruits of its mistakes & if I decline to do so then patriotism is less than nothing." Added to that was his belief that Britain had "to teach Germany that war is not beneficial."

Officer instruction with the Yorkshire Regiment began in spring 1916 at a camp near Stafford in the West Midlands. To prove himself to the younger recruits, thirty-two-year-old Plowman ran a five-and-a-half-mile cross-country race in thirty-four minutes, coming tenth in a field of thirty. The next day, though, age caught up with him during bayonet practice when he pulled a muscle. The regiment posted him to its 10th Battalion in France on July 13. The battalion had yet to recover from the loss of twenty-two officers and over seven hundred men two weeks earlier on the Battle of the Somme's first day. Survivors' accounts of that massacre informed Plowman's first impression of the conflict: "The idea of a war to end war died that day, when the flower of Kitchener's Army was destroyed."

He confessed in letters home his terror of incoming artillery: "Shell fire is a terrible thing, much more terrible than I had ever troubled to imagine . . . To sit in an inferno of noise & light & wait to be blown to nothing with small earthquakes all round is a disgusting experience. Its *stupidity* strikes everybody up there." His first weeks along the Pommiers Redoubt pitted him against sweltering summer heat, hard chalk soil, merciless artillery, and frustration at not being able to fight back. When a shell killed most of the men in one of the battalion's trenches, a lone soldier crawled out, glared wide-eyed at him, and exclaimed, "Why, this isn't war at all. It's bloody murder!" It was not the war the press was reporting. Plowman wrote: "The newspapers on the war are nauseating, much more than they were in England. Whether the general censorship is to blame or not I don't know but it's all unreal—the horror & terror & misery are all 'written down' or covered with sham heroics by cheap journalism." The war's "stupidity" and "absurdity," mentioned often in his letters, did not lessen his willingness to fight.

Shrapnel and bullets were not the only causes of injury, as he discovered when an unwounded young soldier named Brown passed out. Plowman loosened Brown's tunic and tried to revive him. He sent for an RAMC doctor in the dugout mess. The irate doctor came outside and shouted at the stricken youth, "You damned young scrimshanker, get up! What the devil do you fancy you're playing at. Leave him there if he doesn't get up and don't call me again." Brown's comrades lifted him up, calling the physician "brute" and "swine." The sergeant explained, "He had the fever in Gallipoli, and he gets these attacks." Brown would collapse again two months later, but a new medical officer sent him to a hospital.

In early August, shells battered the 10th Battalion's frontline trenchworks for sixty hours nonstop. Plowman's platoon struggled to restore parapets crumbling under the barrage. After the shelling, he was drinking tea from a tin cup in a cramped dugout when something struck his neck. He imagined another officer had slapped him: "No one looks guilty, and putting my hand up I find my neck bleeding, and there at my feet was an inch of shrapnel I had not seen before." He finished his tea and walked to a dressing station for an anti-tetanus injection. The wound was too light to take him out of the line or affect his resolve. He wrote to a friend, "I'm awfully glad I did get out here."

The war's caprice was becoming obvious, as he wrote from a support trench on September 16: "And you know, my dear mother, there's nothing but good luck between one & very sudden death out here." There was also the pointless deployment of tear gas. It made eyes water and food inedible without changing anything on the battlefield. "This futile waste," he wrote, "seems an epitome of the childishness of modern war. The kind of mind that now devises inventions for war would be kept in an imbecile home in any civilised society; such a mind is as far beneath reprobation as contempt."

Nothing he witnessed caused him to oppose or condemn the war. Instead, he questioned "the causes that brought about the war. And those I believe to be chiefly commercial avarice & international antagonism based on ignorance." He felt guilty as a beneficiary of the system in which he and others thoughtlessly compelled "less fortunate neighbours to live lives so devoid of beauty & reflection that they have never had the opportunity of seeing any other vision of the earth but grab and grasp." He wrote to his novelist and pacifist friend Hugh de Selincourt, "Cally," on October 18, "Wouldn't I love to believe that the war was just a huge beast let loose upon us by a few crafty self-seeking devils of hell! . . . Wouldn't I like to be able to say sincerely—To hell with Belgium what have I to do with mouldy agreements signed before I was born. I really don't know, Cally. I *really* don't know."

October saw Plowman undergoing advanced infantry training at a base behind the lines. Soon after settling in, he wrote that "the whole battalion marched out to a quarry not far from here and, in the natural amphitheatre, heard a lecture by a Scottish officer on 'The Spirit of the Bayonet.'" The officer was Major Ronald Campbell, a pugnacious Highland Scot whose bayonet-fighting lessons made a marked impression on the many soldiers who attended them. Campbell was famous for urging his listeners, "Kill them! Kill them! There's only one good Boche, and that's a dead one!" Veteran war correspondent Philip Gibbs heard him entreat the trainees, "You may meet a German who says, 'Mercy! I have ten children.' . . . Kill him! He might have ten more."

Campbell's bellicose performance troubled Plowman less than it did others: "From a purely military standpoint it was excellent. Why, indeed, should we spare a fat German just because he throws up his hands and shouts 'Kamarad,' when, as the lecturer says, if we let him live, he may become the father of ten more Huns? Killing is the job for infantrymen, and if we don't like killing, why did we join the infantry? The bayonet is the logical conclusion of all fighting; there you get to the real thing; and a proper lust for blood is what you need to use a bayonet." The lesson nevertheless gave him "a weak stomach."

Back on active duty with the battalion, Plowman marched to Frohen-le-Grand, a desolate hamlet on the Picardy plain. Depressed by tenebrous sleet, he mused that he had become too old for war. To flee such a nonlife made sense. He sympathized with any man who deserted, despite the risk of a firing squad, whose action was "at least of his own volition." Plowman could not run away himself: "The Germans are still in France. While that is so, who can talk of peace?" He added, "I shall go on, even gladly. But it is hell."

One of the officers in Plowman's company, Lieutenant Rowley, received a letter from prominent citizens in the north of England pleading for a woman who had lost two of her three sons in recent fighting. They were petitioning the prime minister to release the third son, Private Stream, for less hazardous duty. Lacking authority to pull Stream out of the trenches, Rowley showed the letter to the battalion colonel. The colonel promised to act on it as soon as possible. A week later, the company sergeant reported that a shell had blasted his trench and killed one man. The man was Private Stream. Plowman wrote,

> Only one casualty in the company all the while we've been here, and this, this boy blown to pieces so that there is literally nothing left to bury! What will it mean to the lad's mother? We feel a weight of gloom as if fate and the Devil himself were one.

Taking advantage of a full moon, Plowman's commanding officer ordered him "to go across No Man's Land, and cut the throat of the nearest German lad on sentry, and bring back the tabs of his tunic for identification." The mission epitomized the war's senselessness: "It involved a simple act of complete self-violation. Once over that stile and there is nothing more to be said." His memoirs did not say whether he carried out the task.

In November, two four-day tours in the front line crippled a dozen of his fellow officers and "I don't know how many of the men" with scabrous trench feet. He wrote to his friend Janet Upcott, an *Economist* journalist, "The place was a nightmare of mud & deep shell-holes full of water, & we were very unlucky for it rained for 6 days out of our 8 [at the front]." The 10th Yorkshires suffered more killed and wounded that month than at any time since he joined the battalion.

Plowman's next assignment was Transport, delivering rations by night, usually in heavy rain and under fire, to frontline soldiers. He clawed his way through "liquid mud" in communication trenches, leading mules packed with food, water, and rum. Nearing the command post, he stumbled. "Look out, sir!" a soldier warned. "That's a dead man."

Plowman's platoon brought the supplies forward, "devilish hard work," and stopped abruptly when one soldier dropped down beside a ration bag. "Sorry, sir, I'm whacked," the man said. Plowman ordered him back to work. He answered that he was weak from lack of food, which Plowman knew to be true. "Moreover," he reflected, "the man is forty and not very strong. Yet the frontline troops had to be fed." The exchange continued:

> "Look here," I say, "if you don't get up, it's my duty to shoot you for disobeying an order."
> He does not stir, but after waiting a moment replies in the voice of one turning over to sleep:
> "Then, sir, I'm afraid you'll have to shoot."
> I'm second best at this encounter.

Rain drenched the 10th Yorkshires for another week. On the first day of clear sky, Plowman observed a deserted village about fifteen hundred yards away and wondered why soldiers from the opposing armies did not gather there for a drink. "What base, pathetic slaves we are to endure such idiocy! No doubt it's good to fight when indignation and hatred boil up as they did in 1914. But these passions have long since spent themselves. Why are we fighting still?"

Although conditions grew more desperate in December, he remained steadfast: "I still hope to 'do my bit in the Great War,' and am fully conscious it won't have been done till certain yards of French territory have been gained wherein I am concerned." By January 1917, his frontline platoon lacked hot food, rum, socks, and waterproof boots. An outraged Second Lieutenant Plowman wrote a letter that London's *Morning Post* printed on January 16: "We have all welcomed out in France your excellent leader on soldiers' leave pay . . . Can you also use your influence to see that the men holding the line on the Western Front get more fuel, more rum, more leave and more waders?" Supplies piling up in abundance behind the lines were not reaching the front. Most of his men had received only one day's leave in two years, which he judged both "unfair & inadequate." Perhaps out of caution, he signed the letter, "A Subaltern."

January's snow froze the ground near Lesboeufs, where two 10th Battalion companies manned positions—"really a rough line of converted shell-holes"—at the edge of No Man's Land. A fresh operation to push the Germans back began at noon on January 13, when British artillery rained fire on the opposing trenches. In response, German guns battered the 10th Battalion. Plowman and three other men scrambled out of a corrugated iron shelter seconds ahead of an incoming shell. Amid the mayhem, Plowman shouted at the men to disperse: "That's it! Get some distance between you. Look there, Burt, you've water-boots on. You can go through the water down to . . ."

Those were his last words. Several hours later, as the sun was setting, his eyes opened. Prostrate on a plank at the bottom of a trench, he saw a lance corporal looking down at him. The young man said, "We thought you was dead."

His head burned "like a furnace," and his ears were bleeding. He asked about fellow soldiers who, he should have remembered, had died long before. The men carried him to the doctors, who diagnosed shell shock and sent him home. On March 1, a Medical Board in England noted, "He still gets headaches after exertion . . . His memory is poor and his family doctor states that his mental processes are wholly slower than before." By the time he reached Craiglockhart on March 9, his memory was no better. Sleep, when it came at all, was marred by terrifying dreams. His head throbbed in pain. Yet he did not exhibit other neurasthenic symptoms like trembling, stammering, or paralysis.

Dr. Rivers took his case. Plowman's gaunt frame spoke of appetite loss, although he remained a stately figure with a craggy, clean-shaved face, long, straight nose, and dark, wavy hair parted neatly on the left. The eyes, set deep below bristly eyebrows, stared out as if struggling to focus. His uniform carried two wound stripes, both for shrapnel injuries. Because his concussion in the field was the result of a shell burst, Rivers diagnosed the cause of his illness as "commotional" rather than "emotional." Nonetheless, Plowman needed therapy to get at the root of his nightmares.

Rivers treated him for a week and then, for reasons missing from Plowman's war record, transferred him to Craiglockhart's Bowhill Auxiliary Hospital. Bowhill House was a regal country palace that the Duke of Buccleuch had made available on January 17 to Craiglockhart's overflow. A second auxiliary opened for yet more patients at Major Walter and Lady Clementine Waring's Lennel House on February 3. Bowhill, situated forty miles from Slateford on the Scottish Borders amid grassland and forest, was both more tranquil and luxurious than Craiglockhart. Rivers regularly saw patients there. Plowman, between consultations with Rivers, reflected not only on his condition but on the war that had landed him in a mental asylum.

RIVERS READ FREUD'S *Interpretation of Dreams* twice at Craiglockhart. He finished the last chapter, "Psychology of Dream Activities," for the second time on Monday, March 19, with misgivings. Freud's view of dreams as hallucinatory "wish fulfilment" jarred with what shell-shock victims were telling him. Their dreams, in addition to fulfilling wishes as Freud asserted, performed multiple functions: "the expression of different affective states such as fear, anxiety, shame, grief, etc." They also exposed repressed memories and resolved mental conflicts. His own dreams, which he analyzed methodically, appeared to confirm his conclusion.

Rivers woke early on March 20, "feeling very tired and unfit for work" and read a report in London's *Times* that seventy-three-year-old Alexandre Ribot had become premier of the new French government. Perusing the list of ministers, Rivers observed that the previous prime minister, socialist Aristide Briand, was missing. The absence of the formidable statesman who had led France as both prime minister and foreign minister since October 1915 hinted that French commitment to the war was wavering. Rivers sensed that the Triple Entente allies, Britain, France, and Russia, suffered from "a lack of co-ordination" in the war against Germany. The Russians had overthrown the czar five days earlier, raising the possibility that the new regime would make a separate peace with Germany. But that same day, March 20, President Woodrow Wilson's cabinet voted for the United States to declare war on Germany. If Congress approved, Britain would gain an ally to replace the one it stood to lose. Russia might desert any day, but America needed a year to mobilize an army. Rivers wondered what the changes portended.

Another publication Rivers read on March 20 was *The Cambridge Magazine*, a pacifist journal to which he had contributed a scientific article before the war. *The Cambridge Magazine*, founded in 1912 by recent Cambridge graduate Charles Kay Ogden, was Britain's largest-selling university weekly. Part of its appeal to readers was "Notes from the Foreign Press," translations of articles from a selection of two hundred overseas newspapers. These included German and Austrian journals not available elsewhere. French pundits were writing "that the economic crippling of Germany was incompatible with the extraction of any indemnity from her in case of a successful conclusion of the war." The idea prompted Rivers to question, though not renounce, his support for the war. He had long accepted, albeit with decreasing certainty, that the German aggressor had to be defeated. Yet a Germany in ashes would destabilize the postwar order. Moreover, disabled soldiers at Craiglockhart, whose recollections of trench warfare contradicted the official narrative, were giving him other qualms.

At the end of Rivers's workday on March 20, a colleague, probably Dr. Brock, asked him "to deal with a case of a very difficult kind, involving a disciplinary aspect." Rivers did not record the name of the patient or what the problem was, but he confessed to employing a "somewhat violent procedure, where milder measures might have been sufficient if I had shown more patience and forbearance." He went to his room to read and prepare for bed, while reproaching himself for his behavior.

He dreamed about a letter from "a Cambridge friend," whose signature was not legible but whose identity was clear. The letter admonished him for his political views. Rivers assumed that meant his pro-war sentiments. As he lay between sleep and waking, he imagined looking again at the names of France's new ministers in the newspaper. A question came to him: did the change of government mean France would no longer fight to the finish?

Upon waking, Rivers, whose earlier dreams revealed "anxieties connected with my hospital work," immediately wrote down all he could remember of the dream. This began self-analysis of the kind Freud had practiced on his own dreams. What was the dream telling him? What lurked in his unconscious? What could he learn from his dreams to understand his patients'? He considered what might have prompted what he called "The Reproachful Letter Dream," probing his memory of the previous day's events for clues. *The Cambridge Magazine*'s translation of the French commentary on Germany came to mind, but the more important element appeared to be self-criticism over his mishandling of the disciplinary case. Considering the problem all that day, he felt that the meaning of the dream must lie in the dream itself, the reading of the letter, and not in the "half-waking, half-sleeping thoughts" that immediately followed.

Rivers's relentless analysis of his own dreams gave him insights into the nightmares of the men for whose mental well-being he was responsible. To know his patients, he had to know himself.

〰〰〰〰〰〰

RIVERS WOULD LATER COME to analyze the dreams of an English officer who had been buried by a shell explosion in France. When the officer regained consciousness, he experienced severe headaches, vomiting, and bed-wetting. Yet he stayed at the front for two more months. Then, one night, he went out to search for a missing officer, who was also a friend, in No Man's Land. All he found was his friend's headless, limbless torso. That was when the dreams began. Rivers recorded, "Sometimes the officer appeared as on the battlefield; again as leprous. The officer would come nearer and nearer in the dream, until the patient woke pouring with sweat and in utmost terror." Sleep became impossible, and the man spent his days dreading nightfall. Doctors at his first hospital advised him not to think about it. His condition deteriorated, and he came to Craiglockhart.

After hearing the patient's dreams, Rivers tried to soften their effect by telling him that the near-total destruction of his friend's body meant that death had been instantaneous. There would have been no terror and no pain. It was worth thinking about, Rivers said. A few nights passed without nightmares until the man dreamed again that he was back in No Man's Land. He knelt beside his friend's mangled corpse as if in prayer. More dreams, each less fearsome than the last, followed. In one, he achieved a kind of benediction when he unbuckled his friend's Sam Browne belt to send it to the family. In another, he and his friend talked about what happened. The fear had gone.

Rivers took on another patient, who was able to sleep only with a light on. Even with the light, he lay awake for hours until dreams dragged him back into the warren of trenches, tunnels, and filthy dugouts. He was reliving the terror that had caused his breakdown. During the day, he fought to forget what happened in France. Again at night, the memories preyed on him. He described the nightmares to Rivers, who advised him, as he had other patients, to dredge up his memories and "transform them into tolerable, if not pleasant, companions." The man made the effort, and during a subsequent consultation he told Rivers about the war as he had lived it. That night, for the first time in five months, he slept in peace. Over the following week, sleep again became difficult, but not stressful. As the talking therapy progressed, his health, mental and physical, improved. "He was," noted his Case Study, "at last able to return to duty."

Another patient was having nightmares so severe that Rivers worried he could not help him. This English officer had been hurled by a shell blast into the rotting corpse of a German soldier, immersing his face in dead flesh. He choked on the man's insides, the smell and taste knocking him unconscious. Although he recovered sufficiently to return to duty, the lingering sensations made him vomit. His condition became so bad that the army sent him to a succession of hospitals before Craiglockhart. Rivers attempted his usual method of suggesting positive aspects of unsettling incidents. However, as a subsequent report on the case stated, "Rivers' psychotherapeutic plan of finding a redeeming feature in the experience, upon which the patient might concentrate, failed because there was no redeeming feature." The hospital allowed him a short leave in peaceful countryside, where his nightmares dissipated. On his return to Craiglockhart, Rivers gave up hope of a cure. The man left the army to find what peace he could somewhere in the country. It was unlikely he would recover.

One patient suffering unexplained war nightmares baffled Rivers. No amount of probing uncovered their cause, and Rivers concluded that either a "submerged experience" or perhaps "no experience" explained his headaches and depression. When the dreams and the depression worsened, Rivers felt powerless. The man's anxiety was so pronounced that a Medical Board released him from the army.

An older officer treated by Rivers explained that a shell concussion had destabilized him. His treatment at other institutions involved "baths, electricity and massage, whereupon he rapidly became worse."

When one Medical Board asked him about his time at the front, he broke down and wept. By the time Craiglockhart admitted him, he was emaciated, "with an expression of anxiety and dread, paresis [weakness] of legs, sleeplessness and war dreams." Rivers counseled him to discuss the war, read about it, and think about what happened to him. The patient made a vague attempt. The only relief from his symptoms, he told Rivers, had come during periods of leave from the previous hospitals "in the heart of the country, away from relatives, with aspirin and bromides." He slept better there, diminishing the headaches. The Craiglockhart Medical Board had little choice but to let him resign his commission and seek what solace he could on his own. However much he studied his patients' dreams, Rivers did not always find in them the key to a cure.

NOCTURNAL DREAMS CARRIED Craiglockhart's inmates back to the trenches, the rats, the dismembered comrades, and the punishing bombardments. During the day, they organized themselves into teams, societies, and clubs. They were, after all, British officers and gentlemen. It was unacceptable to lie still and wallow in self-pity. As early as February 23, 1917, despite the frost of a Scottish winter, they played tennis on a grass court that the Carmichaels had cleared. James Bell, now living on an adjoining property, donated a plot to the new Gardening and Poultry Keeping Association. Lieutenants Lees and Ritchie oversaw the construction of a henhouse in Bell's garden. Hens soon laid nearly one hundred eggs for the hospital's kitchen, but an experiment in incubating chicken embryos was less successful. "Some unsuspecting person," wrote one officer, "knocked the top off the thermometer, with the consequence that the poor wee things were next roasted in their shells and then frozen."

On April 11, Commandant Bryce and Matron MacBean welcomed Craiglockhart's first high-level visitor, Canadian prime minister Sir

Robert Borden. Borden had sailed to the United Kingdom to take part in British prime minister David Lloyd George's newly established Imperial War Cabinet of leaders from Britain and its overseas dominions. Borden, an imposing figure in a three-piece suit with a well-groomed moustache, thanked Second Lieutenant James Douglas and other Canadian officers for their sacrifices, a rare official acknowledgment that the men of Craiglockhart were no less deserving of gratitude than their comrades whose wounds were physical. No senior British politician made a similar gesture, as opinion over shell shock as a genuine, treatable condition remained contentious.

The new Debating Society, modeled on the verbal jousts that some had known at the Oxford and Cambridge Unions, held its first debate on April 12. The motion was whether "insufficient attention has been paid to pure science as compared with applied science," a noncontroversial topic influenced by the society's official "embargo on sectarian and political questions." Captain Archibald argued for the motion, winning fourteen votes to four among the audience of eighteen. The sparse turnout prompted one attendee to comment that "it is perhaps to be regretted that such a highly technical subject was chosen for the opening meeting." To attract more spectators, the Society rescinded its "embargo on sectarian and political questions."

Billiards became a popular pastime, most of all when rain kept everyone indoors. The men held regular billiard tournaments and invited Major Bryce to compete. At one of the first contests, a witness reported, "A little light relief was provided by the Major, who finding himself forced to pot the white, not only was successful, but accomplished the feat of putting down his ball and the red in addition to making the cannon." Despite Bryce's cannon, striking two balls with the cue ball, Lieutenant Lees won the match.

Craiglockhart's musicians staged concerts every Saturday evening on the stage in the villa's vast Recreation Hall, where they competed with the badminton players for rehearsal space. On April 21, Captain

Bates conducted the hospital orchestra, opening the program with tunes from Paul Alfred Rubens's 1914 musical *To-night's the Night.* Craiglockhart's theater critic, a patient using the pen name "Peas Blossom," wrote, "It's a treat to watch Bates conduct, as he puts one in mind of [John Philip] Sousa or Henry Wood!" Women, usually wives or daughters of patients, took part in the concerts. Mrs. McLagan, Mrs. Tann, and Miss Campbell sang ballads and love songs, after which Miss Campbell's father crooned "The Yeomen of England." The lighthearted entertainment reached a peak with Mr. Clark's rendition of "In Other Words" from the London musical *The Bing Boys Are Here.* Bates's orchestra closed with a jocular march dedicated to the commandant, "Major, Board 'em." Then, wrote Peas Blossom, "we all toddled off to bed in a very happy frame of mind."

Peas Blossom's review appeared in the debut edition of the new house journal, *The Hydra.* The black-and-white cover photo of the sixteen-page fortnightly showed the hospital building with an officer in the foreground. He wore a greatcoat, leaned on a walking stick, and might have been a doctor or a patient. The editors appealed to staff and fellow patients to submit articles, short stories, poems, and jokes. The magazine's name had less to do with Craiglockhart's roots as a Hydro than with the Hydra of Greek myth. Dr. Brock had written that if a psychiatrist "confines himself to dealing with symptoms—it will be as with the head of the Hydra." Cut off one of the Hydra's heads, and another grew in its place. The symbolism was not lost on readers.

"*The Hydra* must be made to pay its own way," declared the editorial. The cover price of sixpence along with advertisements from local tradesmen covered the cost of paper and printing at H. & J. Pillans & Wilson in Edinburgh. The editors asked readers to order subsequent issues in advance to avoid wasting paper on unsold copies during the wartime shortage.

The Hydra's pages teemed with the boyish humor to be expected of young men not long out of school. One satire imagined the advice the Stoic emperor Marcus Aurelius might have given the men:

> Always take the short way, and the short way is not that which the taxi-men take from the Street of Princes to the Hospital.
>
> When thou desirest to enter into a public place to quench thy thirst pay attention to two things: the blue band and the blue brassard—for one of these causes must be removed ere thy desire can be accomplished. But perhaps it is better that thy desire not be accomplished.

Blue brassards were emblems of the Royal Military Police, who prevented soldiers from going into pubs. Blue armbands signified their wearers as Craiglockhart patients, whom publicans were not permitted to serve alcohol. Edinburgh, despite its conviviality, could be alienating to men whose condition and armbands distinguished them from "normal" citizens. Some of *The Hydra*'s contributors made this clear. J. W. O'C. Whitehead, editor of *The Hydra*'s first issue, wrote a poem entitled "Waiting":

> Alone in this great drear city,
> 'Mid the throngs that never end,
> An object of scorn or pity,
> And nowhere a friend.

Much of the journal's poetry was lighter, like this affectionate tribute to Major Bryce by an officer signing himself "D. L. T.":

> Who takes me in hand when I'm "binged a bit thick,"
> And doesn't preach, for that makes me sick
> But generally acts like an absolute brick?
> The Major.

For all the hijinks portrayed in *The Hydra*, a suppressed truth haunted its writers and readers: the war had crippled them in mind and body. Many felt guilt for shaming their families and deserting the men they commanded. To get back to those they left in the trenches, they were fighting tough mental battles. Their struggles emerged in the pages of *The Hydra*. The journal was on its way to becoming a vehicle, not only for the men to voice their woes, but for some of the most profound and heartrending poetry of the war.

CHAPTER FOUR

A Complete and Glorious Loaf

D r. Rivers impressed Max Plowman so much that he wrote to a friend one month into his retreat at Bowhill that his psychiatrist was the "one rather interesting man up here." When he asked Rivers about Freud's theory of dreams, the doctor lent him Dr. Bernard Hart's 1914 *The Psychology of Insanity*. Plowman thought it "an interesting little introduction to the study of the human mind & well worth reading." Hart's thesis dwelled less on dreams than on another theme important to Rivers, the "repression" of distressing experiences. Rivers's loan of the book, as between equals, pleased Plowman. So too did Rivers's acquaintance with famed Edinburgh University geneticist Arthur Darbyshire, who had died of cerebral meningitis on military duty in France in December 1915. In one important area, however, Rivers proved a disappointment: "But I gave him up when he said he could no longer read poetry; not, *really*, because I wanted to inflict mine on him, but because now & from henceforth & for evermore I will not trust a mind which has become so divorced from nature that it cannot appreciate poetry."

Plowman had no complaints about Bowhill House, with its vast parkland and paintings by Holbein, Gainsborough, and Reynolds: "The

Ducal Mansion is perhaps preferable to snow on Vimy Ridge & I have no doubt that I have missed a good deal worth missing when I see that all my old company officers are now back or dead." One question troubled him: "Why do they still keep me? . . . I asked that so long ago that I've got tired of asking it, & now I'm beginning to get settled here for the duration." He feared he would not leave until 1947 and then "in a long black box." Concern for his wife and young son's financial security led him to apply for a "wound gratuity," extra pay to which he was entitled, on April 26. His request to the War Office stated that he had been wounded twice and was still "suffering concussion from a shell explosion which rendered me unconscious with subsequent loss of memory, and cut both ears permanently deforming the left one."

His support for the war in his first month of therapy remained as strong as it had been at the front. On April 29, he wrote that "as long as those devils sit rooted in France I'm all for clearing them out by force." He objected to the *way* it was fought: lives wasted in fruitless offensives, the supply chain that left soldiers hungry and cold, the army staff's indifference to the men's fate—"And I speak feelingly having nearly starved to death at Lesboeufs in October–November 1916." Yet he was willing to endure it again to drive the Germans out of France.

AMONG RIVERS'S OTHER patients that spring was Captain William Arnold Middlebrook, who arrived at Craiglockhart on April 10. He had enlisted at age twenty at the war's outset, taking his second lieutenant's commission on October 10, 1914. Rising to the rank of captain in the East Yorkshires' 4th Battalion, Middlebrook had fought throughout the sixty-four-day struggle to capture a hill at Bois des Fourcaux, High Wood to the British, in July and August 1916. By the time German troops retreated from the obliterated copse, the British had suffered so many dead that their commander, Major General Charles Saint Leger Barter, was relieved of command for the "wanton waste of men." On October 29, German artillery battered British troops holding High Wood. One of the high-explosive shells blew Captain Middlebrook high into the air. When he crashed back to earth, he lost consciousness for three days. A succession of military hospitals in France and Britain treated him without success, recording deafness in his left ear, shaking, failing memory, diminished eyesight, and depression.

Middlebrook was twenty-three when he began "talking therapy" with Rivers. Mutual respect grew, as Middlebrook came to admire and depend on the psychiatrist. Their exhausting sessions, however, were not improving his condition. His medical report noted he was "absolutely incoherent in speech & unfit to carry on his duties." Rivers accepted that Craiglockhart could do no more for the young man, and he was released a month later. He returned to his home city, Hull, where civilian Dr. Arthur C. Johnson treated him for the rest of his life.

The Hydra's second issue went on sale at Waverley Station and in Edinburgh's bookshops on May 12. More businesses were placing advertisements to support the hospital. As quid pro quo, *The Hydra* published a map clearly marking each advertiser's address. The editors reminded fellow patients to supply material for the journal's expanding length, accusing noncontributors of being "so convinced of their inability to write that they don't even try." Those who did try made the journal as entertaining as it was informative.

All arriving patients automatically became members of the Officers' Club, which helped them to adjust to life in the new surroundings. The Merchants of Edinburgh Golf Club invited the officers to use its course without charge, and "a number of gentlemen" formed a cricket club. Badminton and early morning swims proved popular. The Gardening and Poultry Keeping Association attracted so many new members, encouraged by Major Bryce and Captain Brock, that they were negotiating to obtain more land. The would-be farmers took advantage of the warmer weather to dig all of Mr. Bell's garden and plant vegetables. The hens were laying, and the association was constructing a chicken run.

In "Edinburgh. A Vindication," one patient wrote a travelogue of the city that Dr. Brock was advising his patients to study as a means of connecting to their environment. Calling the city the "Modern Athens," the writer ended on a mournful note: "We are, meantime, far removed from the horror and devastation of war, but the memories of past tragedies still linger with us." Another writer criticized civilians who shirked their obligations to King and Country, asking whether it was "right that her brave men should fight and her cowards remain at home to do the thinking and to wield the whip over passive soldiers?"

The May 12 issue included four poems, one of them by a new contributor who signed himself "Cockney." "Crucifixion" began with an address to "ye birds that mate in seasons due" and condemned those who served Mammon rather than the love represented on the Cross:

> Make of our heavenly light the fires of hell.
> Oh, set us wholly instinct free,
> That like the birds and beasts we dwell
> In sweet unquestioned liberty.
> Freed from the anguish
> Of those who languish
> In self-confined and self-consumed flames,
> Proffering ought before thy Name of names.

"Cockney" was Max Plowman. Writing poetry and letters provided a mental escape from what he called "a private lunatic asylum." He was collecting his poems for publication later in the year by Oxford publisher Basil Blackwell, to include many he wrote before he had gone to France and those he was producing in Scotland. His latest, "The Dead

Soldiers," showed a disgust for the war that was missing from the correspondence in which he endorsed continuing the struggle against Germany:

> God in every one of you was slain;
> For killing men is always killing God,
> Though Life destroyed shall come to live again
> And loveliness rise from the sodden sod.
> But if of life we do destroy the best,
> God wanders wide, and weeps his unrest.

On April 23, the Debating Society discussed a more engaging topic than the relative merits of pure and applied science: "that the electoral laws of Great Britain require no alteration in their relation to women." Votes for women had become a pressing issue throughout the United Kingdom. Suffragettes were protesting in major cities, and police incarcerated many of them. In January, a British parliamentary committee had recommended extending the franchise to women, but only to those who owned property. In March, Russia's new regime granted the vote to all women. The officers at Craiglockhart rose to the occasion with a robust exchange of opinion. At debate's end, an overwhelming majority voted to grant women the vote. Only four officers opposed. *The Hydra* quipped that "the suggestion that there were only four married men present must be treated as malicious libel by the anti-suffragists."

Captain Bates conducted the Craiglockhart orchestra for enthusiastic audiences of patients and staff at the Saturday concerts on April 28 and May 5. The first commenced with tunes from the previous year's West End musical comedy *Chu Chin Chow*. Mr. Clark played two piano compositions that *Hydra* critic Peas Blossom thought "didn't go off as well as they might have done." Peas preferred the violin solo by Miss Grieve, a former Craiglockhart nurse who returned for the concert. Show tunes and poetry recitals followed. At the end of an

Irish love song by Miss Goldie Scott, Peas wrote, "our guide, philosopher, and friend, Major Bryce, sang a little Scotch ballad called 'Burd
Ailie.'" The major, according to Peas, "did justice by it." Bates led the
orchestra in the "Soldiers' Song" from Charles Gounod's opera *Faust*.
Its refrain, sung in French, may not have been clear to everyone: "Immortal glory of our ancestors / Be loyal to us / Let us die like they did!"
At the concert's conclusion, Peas reported that "we sought out our rum
ration—I beg pardon—our cocoa, and our couches, with the feeling
that once more our weekly concert had been a success." The following
week's performance, in Peas's view, was "one of the best we ever had."
To the familiar mix of musical comedy, violin solos, and ballads, resident thespians added a full scene from *Julius Caesar*. The concerts were
making Saturday evenings the highlight of Craiglockhart's week.

MILITARY PSYCHIATRISTS DISAGREED on the relation between a patient's prewar experiences and his susceptibility to breakdown. Some
held that any exhausted soldier could become shell-shocked, while the
opposing view was that only those who had been emotionally unstable
before the war were vulnerable. Brock leaned toward a connection between their prewar lives and their breakdowns. "Amongst soldiers exposed to the same amount and degree of shell-shock, some developed
shell-shock and some did not," he wrote. "In many cases men stood the
long strain and anxiety of trench-warfare for many months, and only
finally collapsed when their moral resisting power was beaten to
pieces." Other men broke down the moment they heard cannon fire.
He felt that "the small stock of will-power which they had inherited
from their parents, or developed (or been allowed to develop) by education, was practically annihilated by relatively small strain." In 1917,
there was insufficient data to prove or disprove a link.

On May 5, an officer who had suffered from prewar disabilities
registered at the hospital. Twenty-six-year-old Second Lieutenant

W. R. C. Snape was Craiglockhart's 240th patient. Rivers assumed his care. Snape, who appeared anxious and depressed, told Rivers that the train journey to Scotland was enough to rattle his nerves. Noise, whether of airplanes or gramophones, terrified him. Sleep, when it came at all, brought nightmares. Memory and concentration were failing. His head, especially around the right ear, which had been wounded by shrapnel, ached all the time.

His right ear had suffered an abscess, perforating his eardrum, when he was eight. His mother and father died soon afterward, leaving Snape without brothers or sisters. The wounding of an ear that had debilitated him in childhood, coming after a year of strain in the trenches, possibly explained his psychological reaction. Rivers, always learning from his patients, explored the possibility. Whether he could help Lieutenant Snape was another matter.

Snape had studied at the prestigious Malvern College before taking his degree at Queen's College, Cambridge. The outbreak of war found him studying French at the Université de Poitiers, when he dashed back to England as one of the army's first volunteers. The Leicestershire Regiment commissioned him second lieutenant in its 6th Battalion on August 24, 1914, and sent him to France a year later. He secured a creditable field record until he was wounded in July 1916. "At first," his medical record stated, "he made excellent progress but after that he started having headaches which increased in severity." A thunderstorm, flashing and booming like heavy artillery, had sparked the first headache. A succession of Medical Boards in Britain noted improvement followed by relapses into headaches, nightmares, lethargy, and an inability to concentrate. After granting him several periods of home leave, the physicians concluded that his mental state obviated a return to active service.

A Medical Board on January 27, 1917, sent him to a hospital in Leicestershire, where he appeared to recover. Six days after his release to light duty in England, however, his condition deteriorated. Doctors noted that his jaw, arms, and knees jerked uncontrollably and that his self-confidence had collapsed. On April 23, he was transferred to the Moray Lodge officers' hospital in London. There, he suffered "marked nervous instability all the time" and depression "with acute phases in which he breaks down and weeps." One of the Moray Lodge staff, a Dr. Guthrie, "strongly recommends that he should be invalided out." The army, as yet unwilling to give up on the promising officer, sent him to Craiglockhart.

Nine days into therapy with Rivers, he enjoyed his first sleep without nightmares. His headaches, however, persisted, as did his tears when the pain was unbearable. Rivers wrote, "The hearing in the right ear is very defective and there is great weakness of convergence of the eyes and blurring of print when he reads." Snape's hand trembled, and he suffered alternately from constipation and diarrhea. Rivers's treatment was having a partial effect, but not enough to return him to the front lines.

WHILE MAX PLOWMAN MARKED time at Bowhill House, devastating news from France hit him hard. Harold Baker, the young son of his friend W. F. Baker, had been killed. Plowman had urged the boy to take a commission, which would have removed him temporarily from danger during officer training in England. Now it was too late. He wrote on May 7, "I feel it's one of the biggest & most irredeemable tragedies of the war, & one, almost *the* one, I'd have given almost anything to prevent." He sent a letter of condolence to Baker *père*, which he felt was inadequate to the enormity of the older man's grief. "There seemed nothing to say," he admitted. What he did say left him dissatisfied, especially the platitude that "the lad quite definitely died for liberty . . . for an ideal of liberty as cleanly & as clearly as any martyr ever died."

Plowman wandered into the woods above Bowhill a few days later to think and write. Harold Baker's memory haunted him, inspiring a poem of remembrance:

> Amid so many dead—
>   Why should I sing of you?
> Or seek to crown your head
>   With wreath of rue
> Who wear the immortal crown ordained for you?
>
> . . .
>
> You died for Liberty.
>   'Tis she doth weep
> And in her heart your dear remembrance keep.

The poem seemed as feeble in capturing the meaning or meaninglessness of the boy's death as his letter to Harold's father. Plowman's next Medical Board was scheduled for May 22. Craiglockhart's physicians, including Rivers, would then tell him whether he needed more time at Bowhill or was fit to return to battle and, possibly, the fate of Harold Baker.

CRAIGLOCKHART'S ELEVEN MET the students of Merchiston School for a hotly contested, rain-drenched cricket match on May 9. Major Bryce, despite twenty years away from the sport, batted for Craiglockhart. *The Hydra* commented that he had "a sound bat, with a good eye," and was his side's second-highest scorer. Bryce's dexterity did not prevent the schoolboys from defeating the veterans, 120 to 93.

One spectator, Lieutenant James Haygate Butlin, noted in his diary, "Fine morning. Inclined to rain. Went to watch cricket against Merchiston School. Coldish." This was Butlin's fourth day as a patient. His cryptic journal entries provided little insight into either his personality or life at Craiglockhart, but letters he wrote to his closest friend from schooldays, Basil Burnett Hall, did. Butlin had cut short his undergraduate studies at Wadham College, Oxford, in December 1914, when he was eighteen, to enlist in his native county's Dorsetshire Regiment. Burnett Hall stayed at Oxford until graduation and then worked at the Foreign Office. Butlin chided him, "When are you going to join the army? It is the duty of every able-bodied citizen to defend his country."

Butlin sent Burnett Hall his first impression of Craiglockhart on May 5, the day after his arrival: "It is a magnificent hydro standing on palatial grounds fitted with all the comforts that man's ingenuity can contrive." Butlin thought he might write a book rather than exert himself gardening or playing bowls. Time away from the trenches appealed to him: "provided one is in by six o'clock & conforms to a few simple rules life is a complete & glorious loaf." The same letter mentioned that the hospital's other "inhabitants" propagated two theories to explain their presence there: first, they were "lunatics under careful surveyance but none the less dangerous"; and second, they were "victims of venereal disease & confined here as punishment. From the looks of the population I gather that the second theory is most strongly held." He lamented that he had not had a drink for two weeks, and he wanted his tennis racket sent from home, "as I see I shall go mad with nothing to do." His diary refers to playing bridge, strolling through Edinburgh, and seeking female company.

Butlin's next letter to Burnett Hall, on May 11, described his physician: "I have been interviewed by the Doctor: he is a clever man, a bit of a philosopher, an eminent nerve specialist & somewhat of a crank." While the doctor was unnamed, the treatment pointed to Brock rather than Rivers. Butlin told "the Doctor" that he liked playing bridge, but the doctor disapproved, because it "tended to keep you too much in the house." Butlin added that he enjoyed literature, "rather a false step as he then asked me to join the staff of the 'Hydra.'"

The young soldier, while amusing and gregarious, had survived long periods in vermin-infested, muddy trenches and endured some of the war's most savage battles. He held the Star and Victory campaign medal for soldiers who fought in the early stages of the war. In May 1915, his regiment played its part in the futile Battle of Festubert. The botched offensive sacrificed sixteen thousand Indian, Canadian, and British casualties for a few hundred yards of barren terrain. Butlin confessed to Burnett Hall that the fight had drained him so much that he ordered his men to shoot surrendering German soldiers. His excuse was that German snipers were shooting at his company and "my nerves were shattered." Much to his subsequent relief, the men refused.

The army granted him a short leave in Britain, where he wrote of his desperation not to return to France. But he was soon back with his regiment, writing from the front, "My nerves are not what they were, I can tell you." More months in the filth of pestilential trenches gave him an acute ear infection. In March 1916, doctors sent him to England, where he moved from one hospital and military base to another for nearly a year. His letters reflected his war weariness: "I've done 12 months of it and that's enough in the infantry." At the end of the year on home duty, he returned to the Dorsets in France. The regiment was bracing for the Battle of Arras.

On the eve of the Arras offensive, Butlin had a premonition of death and asked Burnett Hall to write to a young Frenchwoman he loved, Juliette Pécard in Rouen, if the worst happened. At first light on April 9, the British attacked. Butlin, as he wrote to his mother a week later, led his men "over the top near . . . one of the most important strong-points in the German line of defence." His company encountered "tremendous artillery & machine gun fire but gained our objective all right." He reassured his mother that no officers in his A Company had fallen, although C Company lost all but one. Everything in his letter pointed to his having recovered his courage: "How one stands it is a marvel to me but still one does & cheerful into the bargain."

His letter of the same day to Burnett Hall could have been from a different man: "I am not very clear on dates & days. The cold was awful & some of the nights spent in the open amidst snow & mud & shell fire are among the worst in my experience." He wrote to his friend three days later from a captured German dugout "about 40 feet below the earth," complaining of relentless rain with nothing but biscuits and bully beef to eat. Only the daily rum ration kept him going. He and his men watched helplessly as one of their comrades ran from a German warplane firing its machine gun at him: "It must have been an awful death though practically instantaneous." The struggle to secure countryside around the city of Arras and along the Vimy Ridge ended on May 7, with more than 158,000 British and empire soldiers dead, wounded, or captured.

Butlin lingered through two more weeks in the trenches, until medical officers examined him and diagnosed shell shock. One week after taking up residence at Craiglockhart, he wrote to Burnett Hall, "Do you know, Basil my lad, that even a 'complete and glorious loaf' palls after a few days." The therapy was more strenuous than he had hoped, another clue that he was in Brock's care: "Can you imagine me, my dear Basil, getting up & taking a swim before breakfast? Doing a little gardening & poultry farming after breakfast? . . . Viewing natural scenery after tea? Reading & writing after dinner & then to bed?" The humor and amorous adventures in Butlin's letters pointed to the improving mental health he enjoyed at Craiglockhart, but the goal of Brock's therapy was to send him back to the very conditions that made him break down.

In mid-May, Max Plowman wrote a short essay, "Thoughts on the Human Body," and another poem, "The Incarnate Word," for *The*

Hydra. The essay and poem were confused, if sincere, homages to the beauty of human forms as "temples of the Holy Ghost." Plowman challenged prevailing notions of the body as shameful and in need of covering: "Those who do not regard the human body as the highest expression of beauty have perverted minds." To Plowman, "desexual-ised" cherubs, satyrs, mermaids, and spirits sprang from "minds inca-pable of the highest sense of beauty." The passage finished with an invitation to readers to "sing the following hymn which has not yet appeared in any ancient or modern book":

The Incarnate Word

If man can speak his mind,
What of his soul?
Whose voice is never heard
Save as he find
Spirit and flesh speak whole
The incarnate word.

. . .

O form so long despised!
So long enslaved!
To ignorance enchained.
By shame disguised!
To thee I have behaved
With cruelty ingrained.

But love shall set thee free . . .

After submitting the baffling essay-poem under his pseudonym "Cockney" to *The Hydra*, Plowman reported on May 22 to a Medical Board of Rivers and two other doctors. The verdict was unanimous: "He is fit for duty." His fitness, however, was only for light duty in Britain for at least three months. The board granted him three weeks' leave, and by the time his essay-poem appeared in *The Hydra* of June 9, he was at home in London with his wife, Dorothy, and their baby son, Tim. His time with them would last until June 14, when he was due to proceed to the West Yorkshire Regiment base at Whitley Bay in Northumberland.

MEDICAL BOARDS DETERMINED whether to keep an officer at Craiglockhart, return him to the front, assign him to light duty in Britain, or discharge him from the service. The life-and-death decisions could save or destroy a man. Send him back too soon, he might break down again. Keeping him too long could leave him unfit for battle. Discharge him into the abyss of a local lunatic asylum, he may never come out. Light duty in Britain was a compromise that gave officers time to reintegrate into military life before returning to battle. Craiglockhart, a repair shop to fix those who could fight again, did not waste limited resources on those the military could no longer use.

Among disappointments was Second Lieutenant W. R. C. Snape. His therapy was not producing results. There were potential keys to explain his war trauma: among them his wounded ear and its damage in childhood; losing his parents at an early age; seeing friends die in battle; and the strain of long service under fire. Craiglockhart was not a research laboratory. Snape's lack of progress and persistent nightmares compelled Rivers to recommend his release after only forty-five days, when the army would discharge him from the service. On the day of Snape's departure, June 20, Craiglockhart admitted its 321st patient, Royal Engineers lieutenant C. E. Tooley. As war on the Western Front intensified, the number of officers waiting for beds at Craiglockhart grew longer every day.

MAX PLOWMAN WAS STILL under clinical observation, appearing before Medical Boards every few weeks, when he reported to the West

Yorkshire Regiment on June 14. His wife and son joined him in an officer's billet overlooking Northumberland's Whitley Bay. When not busy running the mess, Plowman ruminated on the war that had caused his and so many other men's breakdowns. The result was an outpouring of words, in poems and one long essay, that clarified his thoughts. Confronting the war and resurrecting memories accorded with Rivers's methodology of reducing fear by facing it head-on.

Dorothy would remember him in their seaside cottage, "pencil in hand and notebook in front of him, sitting at the table." While he wrote, young Tim handed toys to a visiting officer who was trying to relax on the sofa. Plowman began his essay with a question that Tim's presence may have inspired: "If a child is born has it a right to live?" Plowman's answer was an unconditional "Yes." The "yes" was changing his mind about the war. "The war came," he wrote, "and with it the right to die." Titled "The Right to Live," the essay challenged fundamental beliefs not only about the war but about the economic structure of society. For a serving officer to write it was a risk, and nothing he had written before had taken him as deeply into the causes of the war and its longevity. He was finding his way back to sanity through an unexpected avenue: pacifism.

Weren't he and his fellow patients in Scotland sane compared with politicians who sent them to kill and die? Was it crazy for a man to collapse under the constant terrors of high explosives and poison gas in a filthy subterranean realm shared with feral rats and lice? Would a sane mind subject people to such madness?

Poor men who had slaved for paltry wages flocked to the army as if mesmerized by the Pied Piper: "They were clothed, they were fed, they were housed, they were honoured, and many a one who had spent all his days in fear of penurious life now reclined at ease upon the opulent couch of death." War propaganda declared they were fighting for liberty, and they believed it. Plowman continued:

And for liberty they have suffered the torments of the damned. They have been shot and stabbed to death. They have been blown to pieces. They have been driven mad. They have been burned with liquid fire. They have been poisoned with phosgene. They have been mutilated beyond description. They have slowly drowned in mud. They have endured modern war.

To what end? For what liberty?

The modern soldier lived with death longer than any fighter since the Hundred Years' War. "Moreover," Plowman argued, "he is not a comparatively small portion of the nation, but may be numbered in millions. In ultimate potentiality he *is* the nation . . . And this is the man who 'wants to live!'" Plowman called for nothing less than a revolution to overthrow a system that stood "in fierce opposition to the precepts of Christ and out of harmony with the rudimentary principles of humanity." In common with Brock's view of industrial society as antihuman, Plowman saw inhumanity in the scientific age: "We are no longer masters of science but slaves to it. Science has developed into a tyranny, and so complete has our enslavement become, we are fast losing any power of choice in our way of life." He appealed to men emerging from the trenches, "You faced death. Now you have to face life." The postwar world needed to reject the ideology of competition and avarice that required perpetual war.

At the end of the essay, he repeated its opening sentence about a child's right to live: "I do not presume to answer the question, except with this evasion. Ask the child's mother."

With financial support from bookseller W. F. Baker, whose son Harold's death played a part in turning him against the war, Plowman planned to publish the essay as a pamphlet. The military was unlikely to prosecute him for the simple reason that he did not put his name to it.

The antiwar poems he was writing, however, bore his name. They would appear in a book, *A Lap Full of Seed*, that Basil Blackwell scheduled for publication in September. His conversion from stalwart warrior to pacifist was no longer a secret, but he was willing to take the consequences of refusing to return to the front. Rivers the psychiatrist had helped to restore his mental balance, but he had failed as an army physician to make him fight again.

CHAPTER FIVE

Out of Place

D r. Arthur Brock went to his consulting room on the morning of Wednesday, June 27, 1917, to meet a patient who had arrived the evening before. A bare-bones report from the Welsh Hospital in Netley, Hampshire, did not tell him much. The twenty-four-year-old second lieutenant in the Manchester Regiment "fell down a well at Bouchoir and was momentarily stunned" in March. Hospitalized with concussion for three weeks, he returned to the front. In mid-April, a shell burst blew him skyward and knocked him unconscious. When he woke, he went back to the trenches. On May 1, comrades noticed his shaking and stammering. The Regimental medical officer sent him for observation to Number 41 Stationary Hospital at Gailly on the River Somme. The patient wrote home, "Do not for a moment suppose I have had a 'breakdown'! I am simply avoiding one." The eminent neurologist Captain William Brown oversaw his care at Gailly. Brown's use of Freudian "abreaction," psychocatharsis to elicit and dispel suppressed fears, was restoring 70 percent of his shell-shock patients to active duty after two weeks. Brown made an impact on his charge, who wrote, "The nerve specialist is a kind of wizard who mesmerises when he likes: a famous man." The famous man's efforts, however, failed to alleviate his symptoms. Diagnosing severe neurasthenia, Brown sent him to the American-run Number 1 General Hospital at Étretat on the Normandy coast. Three weeks later, on June 16, he proceeded to Netley's Welsh Hospital and appeared before its Medical Board on June 25. The board observed his "highly strung temperament" and ordered him to Craiglockhart "for special observation and treatment."

That was all Brock had to go on. There was nothing in the man's file about his family, his education, or his interests. Brock would elicit that from the man himself. The shell-shocked subaltern who walked into his office that morning was an unimposing figure, a mere five foot five and looking younger than twenty-four. The only hints of the years that warfare adds to youth were strands of gray in his otherwise dark, well-brushed hair, parted wide in the middle. A wisp of moustache hinted that he had not been shaving long. One acquaintance recalled, "His eyes were, I suppose, what struck one first in his appearance—dark and vivid eyes, flashing now and then a startled look that indicated quickness of apprehension and extreme sensitiveness." His name was Wilfred Owen.

Owen was not a career soldier. Nor had he joined with the first volunteers in Lord Kitchener's massive New Army in 1914. His background was modest for an officer. Born in Owestry, Shropshire, on March 18, 1893, Wilfred Edward Salter Owen was the son of a railway inspector and a mother with social pretensions and evangelical convictions. Thomas Owen, having been a merchant seaman, worked for the railways to support his wife, Susan Shaw, and their four children—Wilfred, Harold, Colin, and Mary. Debts left at the death of Susan's father, who had been mayor of Owestry, put them in reduced circumstances for most of Wilfred's childhood. Susan dominated the household and kept Wilfred close. His brother Harold recalled, "My mother from the beginning was jealous that my father should exert any strong influence over us children and most especially over Wilfred." Tom

Owen withdrew as his wife "created a bond between herself and us children, especially Wilfred," an intimate bond that Harold believed harmed his brother.

Wilfred had few friends, apart from the children of his mother's favorite sister. The cousins were Emma, Leslie, and Vera Gunston, with whom he founded an Astronomical, Geological, and Botanical Society that explored Shropshire's meadows and hills. This led them to the remains of an ancient Roman settlement, Uriconium, where the children became amateur archaeologists. Wilfred wrote a poem about Uriconium as well as other juvenilia inspired by William Wordsworth, John Keats, and Percy Bysshe Shelley. The adolescent polymath also interested himself in botany, geology, astronomy, and, courtesy of his mother, theology.

Owen left the Shrewsbury Technical School in 1911 at age eighteen with the ambition to be the first in his family to study at a university. All he needed was a scholarship to cover the costs, which his family could not afford. He passed the University of London entrance examination, but his grade was insufficient to garner financial support. His mother placed him as assistant to a Protestant clergyman, Reverend Herbert Wigan, at his vicarage in the village of Dunsden, west of London. This was an unhappy experience for the young man, who grew more sympathetic to the poor of the village than to the wealthier congregants courted by Reverend Wigan. Maternal indoctrination had familiarized him with the Bible, which he could quote at length; but his reading of Shelley's radical poetry put him at odds with conventional religion. "Then will oppression's iron influence show," Shelley had written, "The great man's comfort as the poor man's woe." Owen confessed in a letter that would have disturbed his mother, "Escape from this hotbed of religion I now long for more than I could ever have conceived a year ago." He left Dunsden in January 1913 in ill health that hinted at a nervous breakdown. His mother put him to bed for a month. He sat the entrance exam for University College, Reading.

Once again, his pass mark fell short of a scholarship. While his brother Harold joined the merchant marine and sailed to India, Wilfred was unsure what career to pursue. Delaying his decision, he went to Bordeaux in September to improve his French and teach English at the Berlitz School.

When the war began nearly a year later, he was tutoring for a French family in the Pyrenees Mountains near the Spanish border. He confided in a letter to his sister, Mary, that if he had foreseen the coming conflagration, "I should certainly have borrowed six-pence and bundled over into Spain. In August 1914, when the moon was red, I used to go up at night to a hill-top, and look at Spain." A few days into the war, he wrote to his mother that, while most local men had vanished into the French Army, "I continue meanwhile to be immensely happy and famously well." Letters over the following weeks, mostly to his mother but also to his father, brothers, and sister, rarely mentioned the battles raging in Belgium and northeastern France. When the German Imperial Army was overwhelming British and French defenses, Owen wrote to Mary of his delight at meeting "a great French Poet," Laurent Tailhade. Through the older man, Owen discovered the French poetry that would influence his style as much as Keats and Shelley. Tailhade, a dashing aesthete and pacifist who had nonetheless fought seventeen duels, interested him more than any British general. When the bisexual French poet made a pass at him, Owen ignored rather than rebuffed it.

Owen moved that September from the Pyrenees back down to Bordeaux as the French government, fearing the German conquest of Paris, was arriving. The authorities requisitioned the university where he was studying, and the school that employed him as an English teacher closed. He remained detached from the conflict even as British and French forces launched a counterattack along the River Marne to save the capital from the advancing Germans. One of his former students, Dr. Sauvaître, thrust the war in his face by inviting him to an emergency hospital for wounded soldiers. Physicians at the converted school were treating bloodied and dying men despite "no anaesthetics— no time—no money—no staff for that." Owen wrote to his brother Harold on September 23 that he had watched a surgeon amputate a man's leg and sketched other injuries—a bullet hole through a head, a crushed shin, and a shattered knee. The gore failed to horrify him: "I was not much upset by the morning at the hospital."

In early November, following the poet Tailhade's conversion from pacifism to militarism, Owen pondered whether to enlist. "It is a sad sign if I do," he wrote to his mother on November 6, "for it means that I shall consider the continuation of my life of no use to England. And if once my fears are aroused for the perpetuity and supremacy of my mother-tongue in the world—I would not hesitate, as I hesitate now— to enlist." Accepting that a poet's income was unlikely to provide a living, he considered diplomacy and business. But he could not banish the army from his mind. "I suffer a good deal of shame," he wrote to his mother on December 2. "But while those ten thousand lusty louts go on playing football I shall go on playing with my little axiom—that my life is worth more than my death to Englishmen." He remained in Bordeaux to tutor four young brothers whose return to boarding school in England had been delayed by the war.

His preoccupation with the war prompted him to write a sonnet, "1914," that began, "War broke: and now the Winter of the world / With perishing great darkness closes in." It was his first poem about war, and, as with earlier works, he did not publish it. Needing to cover expenses, he accepted a French mercantile firm's commission to represent it at a London trade fair in May 1915. In London, a noticeboard in his hotel displayed "an announcement that any gentleman (fit, etc.) returning to England from abroad will be given a Commission—in the 'Artists' Rifles.'" The Artists' Rifles were a popular London regiment, founded by painters, sculptors, musicians, actors, architects, and writers during the Crimean War—an appropriate choice for a young man with literary aspirations.

On his return to Bordeaux, he wrote to his mother about the Artists' Rifles and insisted, "I now do most intensely want to fight." Still he procrastinated. In August, a full year into the war, his thoughts turned to working in a government office or joining the Italian Cavalry. In September, he took two of the brothers he was tutoring to London. After putting the lads on a train to their Catholic school in Somerset, he moved to Tavistock Square in Bloomsbury, then London's literary quarter. His French boardinghouse, Les Lilas, stood within walking distance of poet and publisher Harold Monro's Poetry Bookshop at 35 Devonshire Street and the 28th London Regiment (Artists' Rifles) headquarters in Duke's Road. He visited the bookshop first. His next stop, on September 20, was Duke's Road for the army physical examination. Doctors declared him healthy. He swore an oath the next day to serve King and Country, writing with excitement to his mother, "This time it is done. I am the British Army!"

Private Owen's initial military training took place in London parks due to the rapidly expanding army's shortage of cantonments. Drilled to exhaustion during the day, he listened to readings at night in the Poetry Bookshop's barnlike back room where William Butler Yeats, among others, lectured. In November, he rented a room "right opposite the Poetry Bookshop," where Harold Monro encouraged his poetic ambitions. Two weeks later, the Artist recruits moved to Romford in east London. Owen achieved "very high marks in Musketry, Reconnaissance, and Drill—full marks for Drill—But in Military Law I came pretty low!" The army transferred him in mid-June to the 5th Battalion, Manchester Regiment, for further training at Mitford Camp near Guildford in Surrey. The 5th Manchesters, a Territorial Regiment similar to an American National Guard unit, lacked the prestige of a regular army detachment.

To his satisfaction, the Manchesters commissioned him in the 2nd Battalion—"a Regular Regiment, so I have come off mighty well." He sailed across the English Channel on December 29, 1916. "There is a fine heroic feeling to being in France," he wrote to his mother on the first of January, "and I am in perfect spirits." From Calais, he moved east to Halloy, a hamlet near Beaumont Hamel, to join the regiment. Its men and officers were then returning from two months of hard fighting along the Somme front. Their faces showed Owen what they had been through: officers had "a harassed look," while the men were "expressionless lumps."

As Owen and another subaltern shivered in a two-man tent, the temperature dropped below zero. Batmen, enlisted men working as officers' servants, brought them food, lit fires, and cleaned their quarters. Owen soon moved with two other officers into an abandoned house where no amount of cleaning removed the mud that penetrated "that Sanctuary my sleeping bag, and that holy of holy my pyjamas."

The noise, if not the danger, of war reached him on January 7: "As I was making my damp bed, I heard the guns for the first time. It was a sound not without a certain sublimity." The guns were British, firing out. Incoming fire would be less sublime. Two days later, drawing closer to the front, he came to Bertrancourt, a ruined village he called "Gehenna." As the new commander of A Company's Number 3 Platoon, he went the next day to inspect a captured German trench his men were to take over. Trench Standing Orders required platoon commanders to "visit the trenches on the day previous to that on which relief takes place. They will gain as much information as possible from the company commanders they are relieving." Owen was reconnoitering the area around the trench, when shells exploded near him. Back in camp, he censored the men's letters and made them smear whale oil on their feet. Oil protected against trench foot, whose open sores and fungus made marching painful and could lead to gangrene and amputation.

On Friday, January 12, Owen led Number 3 Platoon into No Man's Land, the contested and cratered terrain between armies that the British called "England." Owen and twenty-five men of the platoon jumped into the former German trench while sleet churned the ground into a torrent of mud and submerged paths of duckboard planks. They unpacked their equipment and huddled inside a dugout, a reinforced bunker burrowed into the trench bank. The rest of the thirty-six-man platoon took its position in another trench. Outside, high-explosive shells and rapid-fire machine guns ravaged the earth. Rising rainwater left barely four feet of air to breathe. Packed tight and trapped all of Saturday and most of Sunday, they endured fifty hours of relentless bombardment. Owen called it "the agony of my happy life . . . every ten minutes on Sunday afternoon seemed like an hour." His thoughts turned to suicide: "I nearly broke down and let myself drown in the water that was now slowly rising over my knees."

Owen had stationed sentries "half way down the stairs during the more terrific bombardment. In spite of this one lad was blown down and, I am afraid, blinded." The blinding of the young man tormented him. The artillery barrage slowed at sunset, and Owen seized the moment to find the rest of his platoon in the other trench. He moved belly-down across the barren soil of No Man's Land, wading through waterlogged shell holes and ducking to avoid "our own machine guns from behind." Crossing a mere 150 yards took a half hour. When he reached the men, they were alive. Replacements appeared, and Owen returned to base with his equipment and all his men.

The platoon next to his had lost two sentries. One was a young enlisted man Owen had declined to take on as a servant, because the man's bayonet skills made him more valuable as a fighter. His death left Owen with a sense of guilt: "If I had kept him he would have lived, for servants don't do Sentry Duty."

Two brother officers in Owen's battalion had more to regret. The one who relieved him in No Man's Land was court-martialed for abandoning three Lewis light machine guns when he withdrew. The other had been "completely prostrated," presumably shell-shocked.

Owen's zeal for battle was waning, as he wrote to his mother: "I have not been at the front. I have been in front of it . . . I have suffered seventh hell."

He was next billeted with fellow officers in the single habitable room of a ruined farmhouse. The roof leaked melting snow. Shell-pocked walls offered no respite from glacial winds. His bed was a hammock weaved from rabbit wire. The place was "wretched beyond my previous imagination—but safe." Less safe was No Man's Land, through which Owen led his platoon on the night of January 18. A furious blizzard blinded them, and they lost their way. Owen forged ahead for about a half mile to scout the terrain. Suddenly, a shell burst beside him. It spewed, as he wrote to his mother in capital letters, "GAS!" Chemical weapons terrified soldiers more than bullets. There was no shelter from vapors that permeated the air they breathed. "It was only tear-gas from a shell," he wrote, "and I got safely back (to the party) in my helmet with nothing worse than a severe fright. And a few tears, some natural, some unnatural." He described No Man's Land in religious terms for his mother: "It is the eternal place of gnashing of teeth; the Slough of Despond could be contained in one of its crater-holes; the fire of Sodom and Gomorrah could not light a candle to it—to find the way to Babylon the fallen." His feet went numb, one of the men froze to death, and the rest were "half-crazed by the buffeting of the High Explosives."

On February 4, Owen's commanders pulled him away from the front, posting him to the Advanced Horse Transport Depot in Abbeville. Before beginning the course to become a transport officer, Owen was confined to bed for twenty-four hours with a severe cold and cough from the previous week in the snow. Owen, although an able rider, had trouble mounting one particularly temperamental horse: "When at last I swung over, and before I could get the reins properly gathered, he bolted. It was not so much a gallop, as a terrific series of ricochets off the ground, as if we had been fired from a Naval Gun." Between lessons, he wrote, "I am settling down to a little verse once more." He thought about his first month at war. Most shocking was the havoc modern explosives were wreaking on human flesh and the natural world that he, following Keats and Shelley, romanticized: "Hideous landscapes, vile noises, foul language and nothing but foul, even from one's own mouth (for all are devil-ridden), everything unnatural, broken, blasted; the distortion of the dead, whose unburiable bodies sit outside the dug-outs all day, all night, the most execrable sight on earth."

Two weeks at Abbeville provided relief from the trenches, but it was time wasted. He learned when he reported to the 2nd Manchesters on February 27 that the regiment did not need another transport officer. Instead, his popular commanding officer, forty-five-year-old Boer War veteran Lieutenant Colonel Noel Luxmoore, transferred him from A to B Company and put him in charge of a platoon. This delighted Owen, as did the fact that B Company's commander was a poet, Lieutenant (Acting Captain) Sebastian Sorrell.

The older officer shepherded the twenty-three-year-old subaltern through the dangers of battle, nurturing a friendship that Owen told his mother he valued above all others in B Company. On their first night together, Sorrell and Owen went forward to direct trench digging close to the German line. Owen was overseeing the work from a parapet, when a private called out, "Get down, sir!" Owen dived as a German sniper's bullet flashed past. The man who saved his life was a private Owen remembered from basic training in England—"One of those to whom I swore I would never tolerate near me at the Front."

By this time, as Owen wrote to his brother Harold, he had insomnia. Nonetheless, he performed his platoon commander's duties with aplomb, while writing frequent letters home and a few poems. One evening, Sorrell offered him a choice between "writing a Sonnet before 7.30 or going with the next Fatigue Party!!" Owen did not say which he chose, but he wrote to Susan that he was happier with Sorrell and

B Company's "fine sergeants" than he had been in A Company: "I sleep well; I eat well; I am well." On March 8, B Company withdrew from their trench and marched to Beaufort to rest. The village, like all the others on the contested ground of eastern France, had been devastated by shelling. The houses and barns in which they slept were "not half so cosy as dug-outs."

A replacement officer, thirty-one-year-old Second Lieutenant Hubert Gaukroger, joined B Company. Gaukroger, with a wife and two sons, was more mature than Owen and had a longer history of warfare. Fighting against Turkish forces in Mesopotamia from January to March 1916 left him so badly wounded that he was invalided for a year. Owen called the red-haired Manchester native, with affection, "Cock Robin." B Company soon moved toward the front for what Owen called "a soft job" of constructing dugouts in the trench banks. They worked when it suited them, allowing Owen the occasional luxury of sleeping late. He wrote to Susan from the basement billet he shared with Gaukroger and two other officers on March 11, "How I hope it will last. It may spin out 3 weeks."

It didn't last. A week later, he was writing from "a hospital bed (for the first time in life.)" The reason was a concussion. He had been searching for "a man in a dangerous state of exhaustion" on the night of March 13 at Quesnoy-en-Santerre. The ground gave way, he dropped fifteen feet, and his head crashed into a rock, rendering him unconscious. When he woke, he was half blind and unable to find his watch and his revolver. Lighting a candle in what appeared to be an abandoned cellar, he made several attempts to climb out before he reached the surface. He returned to his platoon "with nothing more than a headache, for three days." Then the concussion hit. He "developed a high fever, vomited strenuously and long, and was seized with muscular pains." A forward medical post sent him to the rear on March 16, first to a military hospital at Nesle and a day later to Number 13 Casualty Clearing Station at Gailly. When he wrote to Susan on

March 18 from his bed at Gailly about his "vile headache," he forgot it was his birthday. He was twenty-four.

His next letter from Gailly to Susan, on March 21, expressed hope that, by the time she read it, "I shall be starting back to overtake my battalion, if it is not chasing along too fast." The pain in his head was diminishing, but snow kept him indoors. He and the ward's ten other officers huddled around a woodstove in cotton-padded kimonos, "very pleasant to wear." The hiatus freed him to read Elizabeth Barrett Browning and work on poems of his own. He sent "SONNET—with an Identity Disc" to his youngest brother, sixteen-year-old Colin, on March 24, with the ending,

> For let my gravestone be this body-disc
> Which was my yoke. Inscribe no date, nor deed.
>
> But let my heart-beat kiss it night & day . . .
> Until the name grow vague and wear away.

"I stickle that a sonnet must contain at least 3 clever turns to be good," he apologized. "This has only two." Warmer weather and improving health took him outdoors for long walks and a "joy ride" in a Daimler ambulance to a recently liberated village. A fourteen-year-old French boy told him that retreating Germans had taken all males over the age of fifteen with them, but they had left the villagers five days' bread rations before setting fire to their houses and blocking up the well. In bed the next morning, Owen woke to the rumble of British artillery strafing the German line. In the evening, he assisted the nurses with other patients, one a pilot with a fractured skull and abdominal injuries. "Constitutionally I am better able to do Service in a hospital than in the trenches," he wrote on March 28. "But I suppose we all think that."

The CCS released Owen at the end of March, and he set off on his own to find the regiment. Walking and hitching rides on mud-clogged roads made for slow progress; but, as he wrote to Susan, "Journeying over the new ground has been most frightfully interesting." A family of refugees gave him shelter on the night of April 3. Owen wrote that the mother, father, and five children were from "a good class socially, and of great charm personally" and treated him "as a god":

> In 24 hours I never took so many hugs & kisses in my life, no, not in the first chapter even. They took reliefs at it. It would have astounded the English mind.—While, just the night before I was in blues as deep as the Prussian Blue—not having heard an affectionate spoken word since I left you . . . I am now in the Pink.

As Owen traveled, his 2nd Manchester comrades were moving forward to confront some of their toughest battles. On April 2, they took a denuded copse called Savy Wood, where a German rearguard killed two of their officers and twelve men and wounded seven officers and fifty men. The dead officers were Second Lieutenant Heydon, who had been Owen's friend in A Company, and newly arrived Second Lieutenant Gaukroger, "Cock Robin," of B Company. The fighting along a railroad line through Savy Wood had been so fierce that the British could not retrieve their dead.

Owen was reassigned to A Company, where he missed the comradeship of his poet friend, Acting Captain Sorrell. A Company's commander, Captain H. R. Crichton-Green, sent Owen out with his platoon to reconnoiter No Man's Land on the night of April 4. To pinpoint German positions in driving snow, Owen drew fire on himself. He and the men made it back to their trench unharmed.

The British were preparing an offensive in conjunction with French forces. They would advance from Savy Wood to the outskirts of the medieval town of Saint-Quentin, whose Gothic cathedral spire was visible for miles around. "It is the town on which the hopes of all

England are now turned," wrote Owen on April 4. The Saint-Quentin attack, though, was postponed. The real hope of all England for Field Marshal Douglas Haig was not Saint-Quentin, but nearby Vimy Ridge. Haig called it "an important tactical feature, possession of which I considered necessary." Many, including Winston Churchill, disagreed. America's declaration of war against Germany on April 6 was altering the battlefield equation. Churchill asked in the House of Commons, "Is it not obvious that we ought not to squander the remaining armies of France and Britain in precipitate offensives before the American power begins to be felt on the battlefield?" Churchill and others urged caution until the Americans arrived.

Haig's assault began anyway at 5:30 on the morning of April 9, with four Canadian divisions in the lead. By one o'clock, the Canadians had captured the ridge and taken eight thousand prisoners. Although the British suffered sixteen thousand casualties, Haig wrote, "This is small considering the three successive strong positions, each one deeply wired, which have been taken." Not everyone agreed, as indicated by the name that the troops gave that month: "Bloody April."

Owen, who had been in reserve during the Vimy Ridge battle, led his platoon three days later in a thrust from Savy Wood toward Saint-Quentin. "Twice in one day we went over the top, gaining both our objectives," he wrote. "Our A Company led the Attack, and of course lost a certain number of men." The "certain number" was thirty. A Company then charged over ravaged, cratered ground through razor-sharp barbed wire toward the Germans' Dancour Trench. Owen survived "some extraordinary escapes from shells & bullets" and was relieved he did not have to use his bayonet. He described the encounter in a long letter to his youngest brother, Colin:

> The sensations of going over the top are about as exhilarating as those dreams of falling over a precipice, when you see the rocks at

the bottom surging up to you. I woke up without being squashed. Some didn't. There was an extraordinary exultation in the act of slowly walking forward, showing ourselves openly.

There was no bugle and no drum for which I was very sorry. I kept up a kind of chanting sing-song: Keep the Line straight!

Not so fast on the left!

Steady on the Left!

Not so fast!

Then we were caught in a Tornado of Shells. The various "waves" were all broken up and we carried on like a crowd moving off a cricket-field. When I looked back and saw the ground all crawling and wormy with wounded bodies, I felt no horror at all but only an immense exultation at having got through the Barrage. We were more than an hour moving over the open and by the time we came to the German trench every Bosche [*sic*] had fled. But a party of them had remained lying low in a wood close behind us, and they gave us a very bad time for the next four hours.

The 2nd Battalion commander, Lieutenant Colonel Luxmoore, was so proud of his unit's performance that he issued a communiqué: "The leadership of officers was excellent, and the conduct of the men beyond praise." Owen griped that their reward was another twelve days in the line, although in fact they withdrew after nine. The nine days proved eventful. The Manchesters and other regiments of the 32nd Division pursued German forces pulling back along the River Ancre. The Germans were in the midst of a massive strategic retreat to their new heavily reinforced defensive line, the Siegfriedstellung, which the British dubbed the Hindenburg Line for German field marshal Paul von Hindenburg. While ceding territory to their enemies, the Germans shortened their front line by twenty-five miles and put their forces behind massive fortifications in depth along a salient between Reims and Arras. As they withdrew, they scorched the terrain to deny the British sustenance and cover.

War correspondent Philip Gibbs of *The Daily Chronicle* accompanied the troops and described the hellish landscape:

> It was like wandering through a plague-stricken land abandoned after some fiendish orgy, of men drunk with the spirit of destruction. Every cottage in villages for miles around had been gutted by explosion. Every church in those villages had been blown up. The orchards had been cut down and some of the graves ransacked for their lead.

The Tommies negotiated a morass of collapsed bridges, blighted villages, booby traps, roads blocked by hewed trees, and thick barbed wire, often under fire by expert German snipers. In one advance during a heavy rainstorm, the trench mud was so thick that a weakened Owen risked enemy fire by walking on the ground above. A high fever drenched his forehead in sweat, and his muscles ached. Worse was coming. The platoon settled for the night on the ground beside a railway embankment in Savy Wood, while heavy sleet drenched their coats. Owen was sleeping on the ground, when:

> A big shell lit on the top of the bank, just 2 yards from my head. Before I awoke, I was blown in the air right away from the bank! I passed most of the following days in a railway Cutting, in a hole just big enough to lie in, and covered with corrugated iron. My brother officer of B Coy, 2/Lt Gaukroger lay opposite in a similar hole. But he was covered with earth, and no relief will ever relieve him, nor will his Rest be a 9 days-Rest. I think that the terribly long time we stayed unrelieved was unavoidable; yet it makes us feel bitterly toward those in England who might relieve us, and will not.

He survived the ordeal, but he could not banish Gaukroger's butchered corpse from his mind. Maggots began feasting on corpses within hours, and Gaukroger had been dead for ten days. Such sights sickened even the gravediggers.

A replacement force came on April 21, allowing Owen to withdraw from the front. The 2nd Manchesters marched eight miles to the hamlet of Quivières and, for the officers, a snug billet in a cellar. This was a time of regrouping, as the men drilled each morning, played soccer in the afternoon, and attended lectures in the evening. On April 23, Acting Captain Sorrell of B Company left the regiment. The company commander who shared Owen's poetic aspirations had won the Military Cross (MC) for bravery under fire, but the experience of being blown up and buried twice during combat left Sorrell severely shell-shocked. He was not alone.

Owen began to show troubling symptoms at Quivières: trembling limbs, halting voice, and confused memory. Major James Finlay Dempster, filling in for Lieutenant Colonel Luxmoore as brigade commander, saw Owen on May 1. It was obvious to Dempster that the junior officer needed medical treatment. The next day, Owen was on his way to Gailly. From there, Dr. William Brown dispatched him to Craiglockhart.

CRAIGLOCKHART DID NOT impress Owen. "There is nothing very attractive about the place," he wrote to his mother the night he arrived, "it is a decayed Hydro, far too full of officers, some of whom I know." All he could do was wait for morning "to see the MO [medical officer]." He put his service revolver on a side table before falling asleep. When he woke, the revolver was gone. A nurse had removed it. Firearms were not permitted in an institution where suicide remained a constant temptation.

Dr. Brock, having read Owen's medical report, received him in his consulting room after breakfast. Although Brock's case notes disappeared or were destroyed after his death, a critic with access to them before they were lost quoted the doctor's view of Owen as "a very outstanding figure, both in intellect and character." Owen opened up to

Brock, revisiting the "seventh hell" of his six months in France. His disintegration seemed gradual, its origins less in a single event than in constant tension, exposure to danger, loss of comrades, and injuries that knocked him senseless. The war had been rough on him, but it had on thousands of others. He could not explain why he was there, why he needed to be there.

Brock detected a strong Shropshire accent that contrasted with the officer corps' traditional upper-class clip. Owen's voice, like his body, was shaky. Having observed every speech defect from slight stammers to total mutism over his eight months at Craiglockhart, Brock interpreted Owen's stuttering as the mind's dissociation from its surroundings. Owen had literally been hurled into the air, like Antaeus by Hercules in Brock's wall drawing. To bring Owen back to earth, Brock utilized what he called "steps in a progressive series:—(1) Psychoanalysis . . . (2) Therapeutic conversations . . . (3) Ergotherapy."

Brock's method often meant treating two shell-shock victims together: "If each patient can be induced to constitute himself a doctor to at least one of his fellows who is in worse straits than himself, so much the better. It will 'take him out of himself.'" Brock's choice to accompany Owen in some of his consultations was Second Lieutenant Charles Mayes of the Royal Garrison Artillery, a nineteen-year-old who had been at Craiglockhart since March.

Owen recounted his war experiences to Brock, who believed that dwelling on morbid memories was not on its own a cure. Owen needed work, not as a distraction from his problems, but to engage with his environment and find a place in a community. Grounding himself in this way would restore his mental balance and conquer his symptoms. Owen mentioned an interest in literature, and Brock encouraged him to write poetry, essays, and articles. The psychiatrist disapproved of ars gratia artis. Art needed a purpose outside itself. Owen's first assignment was to come up with something about those symbols of trauma, Antaeus and Hercules, on Brock's wall.

LIEUTENANT JAMES BUTLIN was falling in love. His "latest pure passion" was an ingenue named May Mackay: "She is twenty (just) with blue eyes & fair hair, a lovely complexion & a slight Scottish accent which is very pretty." Confiding this development to school friend Basil Burnett Hall on June 14, he boasted of tennis triumphs and jibed, "I consider your remarks re venereal disease stupid & unworthy of any reply. Cheeryho, Yours ever, James."

Other patients were dallying with Edinburgh women, as Butlin discovered. He accompanied "my beloved May" on June 24 to Sunday evening service at Saint Giles Cathedral in Edinburgh. Afterward, seated on a bench in "an out of the way path in the grounds of the asylum," he dared to kiss her cheek. "At the critical & epoch-making moment the CO [commanding officer, Major Bryce] . . . & my doctor appeared in full view around the corner." Nothing was said, but Bryce ordered him to his office in the morning and reprimanded him for violating hospital rules that prohibited visitors except between three and five in the afternoon. Butlin later discovered the source of Bryce's ire. A moment before the major saw him kissing May, he "came upon an officer who had brought up some harlot from Edinboro & was in the act of copulation with her which fact (or knowledge of which fact) would naturally prejudice me in his eyes."

ON JUNE 30, head gardener Henry Carmichael's youngest son, John, was in a frontline trench as a signaler with the Royal Scottish Rifles. He wrote to his mother with a light heart: "I am still jogging along in the usual way, dodging shells occasionally but one soon gets used to them." Assuring her he had enough to eat, he asked for some socks and signed, "From your loving son, Jock." Jock's brothers, Daniel and Alexander, as well as Daniel's son, John Henry, were also sending messages home that assured the family they were alive. The Carmichaels, in common with the families of soldiers on all sides, did not know when or whether their young men would return.

WHERE JAMES BUTLIN was doing his best to avoid Brock's strenuous labors, Owen took to ergotherapy with the fervor of a hound trailing a fox. He wrote essays and poems, worked on *The Hydra*, and signed up for a German course at Berlitz. Craiglockhart's other officers were taking advantage of summer to play cricket, golf, and tennis. "Probably the most exciting game played so far," *The Hydra* reported of a tennis tournament in late June, "was that played between Major Bryce and Mr Bishop." The match lasted hours, exhausting both men, "but in the end the Major laid his opponent out." Bryce's luck ran out on the golf course, when Major Bingham beat him at the last hole. The Gardening and Poultry Keeping Association's hens were "looking wonderfully strong and healthy," while Henry Carmichael's gardens "could hardly look better." Captain Bates conducted the Craiglockhart Orchestra for the last time on June 23, after which a Medical Board passed him fit to return to his battalion.

In July, Major Bryce led the charge at cricket, tennis, and billiards. When he sang an Irish love ballad, "Eileen Alannah," at the July 7 concert, the audience "loudly encored" him. Four days later, Craiglockhart witnessed the first wedding of a patient. Major S. J. Montgomery, a former divisional machine gun officer, married Miss M. Crawford at Saint Giles Cathedral. *The Hydra* offered the couple "our heartiest congratulations."

James Butlin's courtship with May Mackay was flourishing. His "complete & glorious loaf," however, was coming to an end. On July 9, a Medical Board deemed him recovered and granted him three weeks' leave before reporting to the Dorsetshire Regiment. He called on May in the evening and wrote to Burnett Hall that he would soon be in

London: "I hope you have saved up a fortune as I've spent one on girls since I've been here." If his friend could not offer him a room, "I can easily stay with one of the many ladies of easy virtue who roam the streets of our beautiful English towns." He left Craiglockhart on July 10, called on May in Edinburgh, and checked into the Royal British Hotel. Neither his diary nor his letters mentioned whether May stayed the night. He boarded the sleeper to London the next evening on his own.

Butlin returned to the Dorsetshires' camp at Wyke Regis after his London holiday. Another Medical Board concluded his health would not survive further service. He was forcibly retired from the army in March 1918. In civilian life, he recovered sufficiently to earn a double first honors degree in classics at Oxford and become a publisher. He lived until 1982.

CRAIGLOCKHART INAUGURATED A Field Club for nature studies on July 13, when its members elected Brock president. One of the founders was Wilfred Owen, who envisioned it as a version of his childhood Astronomical, Geological, and Botanical Society. "My tiny note of the first meeting of our Field Club has gone to press," he wrote to Susan of his report for *The Hydra*. "Old Brock is supposed to have written it." A measure of his growing trust in his psychiatrist was that Brock was paying him "in terms of Months, which is more than Money." The club's first lecture was "Mosses of the Craiglockhart District," which Owen's *Hydra* notice admitted "smelt mouldy with fusty suggestiveness." Yet the speaker "showed it to be one of the most beautifully interesting of living things." The club's function was as much therapeutic as scientific. Brock explained, "At the weekly meeting of our 'Field Club' he [the patient] brings his report, expounds it to those who have seen the same surroundings from a different angle, and thus the synoptic vision grows."

Six months into Owen's stay at Craiglockhart, Susan Owen took the train from Shropshire to Edinburgh to see her favorite child. They met in the vast lobby of the Caledonian Hotel, a flatiron-shaped edifice perched above the Princes Street railway station. Owen recalled their reunion in what amounted to a love letter: "I saw you gliding up to me, veiled in azure, at the Caledonian. I thought you looked very beautiful and well, through the veil, and especially on the night of the concert. But without the veil I saw better the supremer beauty of the ashes of all your Sacrifices, for Father, for me, and for all of us."

As he had planned for weeks, Owen gave his mother the grand tour of Edinburgh. The highlight was the Outlook Tower, established in 1892 by Brock's mentor, Patrick Geddes. One scholar called it "the world's first sociological laboratory." The seventeenth-century replica castle stood near the summit of the Old Town's Royal Mile. The Royal Mile, despite its exalted name, was a slum. Visitors began their inspection on the tower's crenellated roof, which boasted a camera obscura in the cupola projecting the city's image onto a vast dish. Owen led Susan down the stairs, exhibits on each floor expanding the saga of human existence from Edinburgh on the fifth floor to Scotland on the fourth, through Language, Europe, and, at ground level, the World. The tower contained a meditation cell, where Owen sometimes lounged on its single chair to read. The Outlook Tower's Open Spaces Committee, with Brock as chairman, maintained Slum Gardens for the neighborhood's poor.

As if to make an ideal day complete, Owen accompanied his mother to that evening's Saturday concert of music, drama, and comedy. The Craiglockhart Orchestra under Captain Williams opened with ragtime jazz. "But the event of the evening was 'The Bracelet,' a play in one act by Alfred Sutro," *The Hydra* noted on July 21. This was the journal's seventh issue and the first under its new editor, Wilfred Owen.

After two days with Wilfred, Susan went to Yetholm, a village about fifty miles southeast of Edinburgh, to stay with the Bulmans. Owen wrote to her there: "I have done an essay on the Outlook Tower, to be delivered in privacy to Dr. Brock this afternoon!" He read his composition to Brock as in an undergraduate tutorial. His notes for the essay began, "I perceived that this Tower was a symbol: an Allegory, not a historic structure but a poetic form . . . when I had stood within its walls an hour I became aware of a soul, and the continuity of its idea from room to room, and from storey to storey was an epic."

Owen's debut *Hydra* included the story "The Counter Attack." Written by a patient signing himself with the soldiers' slang term for fearfulness, "Windup," it described a chance meeting in Princes Street with a nurse from the hospital. She asked "Windup" to accompany her to buy silk stockings. When she found the pair she wanted, she suggested they go for tea. Lacking a pass to remain longer in the city, he took a tram back to Slateford. "Last night I slept badly," he continued. "Oh, those awful war dreams!!! It was zero minus one hour, and the barrage would start any minute now." The shells screeched through his mind. "Dear old Princes Street seemed very far away, and I wondered if ever . . . I looked up; nothing but silk stockings flying through the air towards the Hun line." He went "over the top" with his men, but "got hung up on the wire which was covered with silk stockings." As he dug in, his shovel unearthed "the same old thing—silk stockings." "Windup" concluded, "My doc has since told me to stay in bed for complete rest, and concentrate on anything except *les bas en sois* [silk stockings]." Owen, who edited the story, recognized such dreams, as did most of the journal's readers.

Susan spent two days with the Bulmans before moving to other family friends, the Newboults in Summerside Place, Leith, nearer Craiglockhart. Owen rushed there to see her. "I am glad you were eyewitness," he wrote to her later, "to the instant gravitation of Chubby Cubby into my Spheres." Cubby was the name he gave seven-year-old Arthur Newboult. The impression Owen made on Arthur was shared by his older sister, Mary. She remembered "how very easy Wilfred was to talk to. He had the gift of drawing people out of themselves."

Susan's presence was restoring her son's morale. Brock favored long stays by his patients' families, writing, "In treating people thus in families, the Medical Officer resumes once more to some extent the natural function of 'family doctor,' snatched from him temporarily by the exigences of War." Inspired by his mother and his therapist, Owen threw himself into exploring Edinburgh, studying the countryside, and, most of all, writing. He wrote to Susan in Leith that he was beginning a sonnet for Brock on "The Hercules–Antaeus Subject."

While Owen was entertaining his mother, a fresh patient strode into Craiglockhart to begin therapy with the famed Dr. William Halse Rivers. Rivers had never treated a man like him. He was, it appeared, perfectly sane.

CHAPTER SIX

A Young Huntsman

In the early afternoon of Monday, July 23, 1917, thirty-year-old Second Lieutenant Siegfried Loraine Sassoon arrived by train at Edinburgh's Princes Street Station and hired a motorized hackney carriage to drive him to Craiglockhart. The twenty-minute excursion took him through lush meadows, hedgerows, and lanes of suburban cottages. When he reached the hospital, its imposing sandstone villa struck him as "a gloomy, cavernous place even on a July afternoon." Six foot one in stature, lean and elegant, the clean-shaved subaltern with dark hair and a distinctive cleft chin looked every inch the gentleman and officer. "His nose is aquiline, the nostrils being wide and heavily arched," wrote a colleague. "This characteristic and the fullness, depth and heat of his dark eyes give him the air of a sullen falcon." Sassoon, in the words of a woman journalist, had "the springy body of an athlete and the dreamy blue-grey eyes and sensitive face of a poet." His Royal Welch—not *Welsh*, as its initiates reminded outsiders—Fusilier's uniform did not, as yet, have a medical blue band on the sleeve. Nor did his tunic bear a ribbon for the Military Cross that he had earned for "gallantry & devotion to duty in the field" on the front lines in France.

A neurologist on his Medical Board in Liverpool three days earlier had assured him, "Rivers will look after you when you get there." Sassoon allowed that Rivers was "evidently some sort of a great man; anyhow his name had obvious free associations with pleasant landscapes and unruffled estuaries." Yet the great man had resisted taking his case. Officers with real ailments had more claim on his time than a man devoid of the symptoms—trembling, frozen limbs, vacant stare—that crippled others. Sassoon had a slight stammer, but it predated the war. Anyway, Rivers had stuttered all his life. "The patient is a healthy-looking man of good physique," Rivers would write. "There are no physical signs of any disorder of the Nervous System . . . there is no evidence of any excitement or depression." What was a man like that doing at Craiglockhart?

Troubling features of Sassoon's record, however, caught Rivers's attention. On the Somme, at Arras, and elsewhere, fellow soldiers called him "Mad Jack" for his foolhardy exploits in No Man's Land. In addition, his Medical Board had concluded, "He is suffering from a nervous breakdown and we do not consider him responsible for his actions." Some men feigned neurasthenia to escape the war, but faking good health was both difficult and markedly eccentric. Rivers sensed something interesting, and, anyway, "nearly all the interesting patients floated his way."

Sassoon would recall that the hospital repelled him, "But before I'd been in it for five minutes I was actually talking to Rivers, who was dressed as an R. A. M. C. captain." Captain Rivers behaved as if he already knew him. "What he didn't know he soon found out," the patient recalled. He would write to a friend, "Rivers—the chap who looks after me, is very nice—I am very glad to have the chance of talking to such a fine man."

Sassoon had relied on fine men since the age of four to fill the vacuum left by his father's departure when his parents separated. Born in the Weald of Kent on September 8, 1886, he grew up the middle of three brothers in idyllic countryside with good books, fine paintings, horses, and servants. His mother, Theresa Georgiana Thornycroft, nicknamed Trees, dominated the household with the help of aunts, governesses, and maids. Weirleigh House, a redbrick Victorian pile that Siegfried thought vulgar, was a female world in the eyes of a boy who, while devoted to his mother, longed for male guidance.

Sassoon's paternal and maternal forebears had little in common apart from money and influence. His father, Alfred, descended from Baghdad Jewish merchants who had made fortunes trading everything from textiles to opium in such far-flung outposts of the British Empire as Bombay, Calcutta, Hong Kong, and the Shanghai settlement. Called "the Rothschilds of the Orient," they donated generously to Jewish and non-Jewish British charities. Sassoon David Sassoon, Siegfried's grandfather, moved to England in 1858, married an Iraqi Jewish girl named Farha, and established a family seat at Ashley Park near London in Surrey. When their son, Alfred, married the gentile Theresa Thornycroft in 1884, Farha, who had anglicized her name to Flora, sat shiva for seven days' mourning as if her son had died. She also put a curse on his offspring. This cut Alfred off not only from his family but his inheritance. The marriage faced other complications. Theresa was twenty-nine and Alfred twenty-two when they married. Alfred, a financier and sculptor, preferred London to Theresa's rural monotony. When he found solace in the embrace of American writer Julia Constance Fletcher, the marriage collapsed.

Theresa's family, the Thornycrofts, were English Protestants, originally farmers, more recently engineers and sculptors. The engineering firm John I. Thornycroft and Company constructed ships for the Royal Navy. Theresa was a painter, and her mother, father, and brother were well-known sculptors. Sassoon's divided loyalties tilted toward his mother's family rather than the Jewish side that had disowned him.

Both families were well connected. Theresa's brother, Sir William Hamo Thornycroft, had become the youngest member of the Royal Academy and earned a knighthood for his monumental classical statues.

Hamo, as he was known, moved in a circle of famous painters, critics, and authors. Alfred Sassoon's favorite sister, Rachel Sassoon Beer, had owned and edited England's two leading Sunday newspapers, *The Observer* and *The Sunday Times*. A cousin, Sir Philip Sassoon, was a member of Parliament and would serve as staff officer under the two successive British commanders in France, Sir John French and Sir Douglas Haig. Through both families, Siegfried dwelled in a refined milieu of intellectuals, artists, and politicians.

When Siegfried was nine, his father died of tuberculosis. The first surrogate father to enter his life was George Thomas Dixon, the family's coachman since 1890. "Tom" Dixon took young Siegfried in hand, teaching him and his brothers, Michael and Hamo, to ride and play cricket. Theresa at first had the boys tutored at home, where Siegfried studied Latin and practiced piano. While confined at age eleven for two months with double pneumonia, he wrote poetry and realized that "I had a mind with which I liked to be alone." He filled nine notebooks with poems, many dedicated to his mother, between the ages of ten and thirteen.

The Sassoon boys began formal education at the Beacon Hill School in nearby Sevenoaks. Siegfried mastered the subtleties of the golf course and perfected a loping swing that drove balls far over the fairway. From autumn 1902, he boarded at Marlborough College in Wiltshire. He played golf and cricket well, but he strained his heart on the soccer pitch. The school Cadet Corps taught him martial skills and to parade like a soldier. Aged fifteen, he succumbed again to double pneumonia. His juvenile poetry had the full support of another father figure, Uncle Hamo Thornycroft, who advised, "Let your thoughts ring true; and always keep your eye on the object while you write." The school paper rejected his poems for publication, but *Cricket* magazine published five.

Perhaps because the Sassoons had been Oxford men, Theresa sent her sons to Cambridge. Pneumonia having cost him a year, Siegfried entered Clare College, Cambridge, with younger brother, Hamo, in 1905. While there, Siegfried admitted to Hamo he was homosexual. Hamo was untroubled, telling his brother that he was too. The mutual disclosure strengthened the bond between them in an era when society viewed homosexuality as shameful, religion condemned it as sin, and the state declared it illegal. Only ten years had passed since an English court sentenced the flamboyant Irish playwright Oscar Wilde to prison for it. The Sassoon brothers were not ashamed, at least with each other. Siegfried's attraction to other men, however intense, had no physical expression.

Hamo graduated in engineering, worked in Britain for the Thornycrofts, and sailed to Argentina to construct bridges over the River Plate. Siegfried left Cambridge without a degree after two years of desultory study of law and then history. At Weirleigh with Theresa, he survived on a modest but adequate allowance for a country gentleman riding to hounds, playing cricket, and golfing. His ferocious horsemanship, vaulting the highest fences in pursuit of his quarry, made him one of the county's best young hunters. He also took up pipe smoking, collected rare books, read widely, and wrote poetry. Many of his poems went into volumes he had printed for friends. His was a life without ambition or challenge, until a family friend entered his life and a war began.

The friend was Edmund Gosse, prominent art historian, critic, author, and translator of Henrik Ibsen's plays. Siegfried found in the older man, thirty-seven years his senior, another paternal guide. Gosse, like Siegfried, had had a troubled relationship with his own father that he recounted in his acclaimed 1907 memoir *Father and Son*. His position as librarian of the House of Lords and his marriage to the Pre-Raphaelite painter Ellen Epps, with whom he had three children, shielded his discreet homosexuality from exposure. Gosse met Sassoon through his wife, a friend of Sassoon's mother. Sassoon sent Gosse some of his poems, including a pastiche of John Masefield's poetry,

"The Daffodil Murderer," that Gosse thought read "as if you had actually got into Masefield's skin."

Seeking to further Sassoon's writing career, Gosse sent the poem to
Edward Marsh. Marsh was private secretary to the First Lord of the
Admiralty, Winston Churchill, whom he had served in other government posts since 1905. Gosse advised Sassoon, "I should like you to get
into friendly relations with Mr. Marsh, who is a most charming man,
extremely interested in poetry, and the personal friend of all the new
poets." An atypical government functionary, Marsh counted among
his friends the poet Rupert Brooke; writers John Middleton Murry
and his wife, Katherine Mansfield; philosophers Bertrand Russell and
G. E. Moore; and composer Ivor Novello. He used his inherited wealth
to patronize the arts and subsidize hungry painters. He had edited the
first of five anthologies of *Georgian Poetry*, "Georgian" for the era that
began two years earlier with the accession of George V. Harold Monro
of London's Poetry Bookshop published it in December 1912. The
Georgians, in the words of one critic, sought to "come to terms with
immediate experience, sensuous and imaginative, in a language close
to common speech"—a partial break rather than outright rejection of
their elders. The first volume included poems by D. H. Lawrence,
Walter de la Mare, James Elroy Flecker, and Rupert Brooke. Marsh's
male-oriented sexual predilections, unlike Sassoon's and Gosse's, were
hardly secret. In March 1913, Marsh invited Siegfried to dinner at
London's National Liberal Club and later advised him to move to London for the sake of his poetry.

Siegfried settled into Raymond Buildings in the barristers' cloistered Gray's Inn of Court in May 1914. In June, Marsh invited him to
breakfast to meet Rupert Brooke. Brooke, probably the best-known
poet of the young generation, had been a friend of Hamo Sassoon at
Cambridge. While still an undergraduate, he had inspired Charles
Darwin's granddaughter, the poet Frances Cornford, to call him in a

short poem "A young Apollo, golden-haired." The golden boy, famously handsome, well traveled, and notoriously bisexual, wearing sandals picked up in the tropics, impressed the shy Sassoon. Neither said much to the other, despite their shared passion for poetry and Russian ballet. Sassoon wrote, "When bidding me good-bye at Eddie's outer door his demeanour implied that as far as he was concerned there was no apparent reason why we should ever meet again." They never did.

Marsh also introduced Sassoon to Robert Ross, son of a prominent Canadian politician. When Ross's father died in 1871, his mother brought two-year-old "Robbie" to England. He studied at King's College, Cambridge, where a gang of college homophobes nearly drowned the overtly camp undergraduate in a fountain. Like Sassoon, he left the university without a degree. He became a journalist and critic and was said to have been Oscar Wilde's first male lover. After Wilde went to prison for homosexual acts, Ross, unlike most of English society, who disowned the playwright, remained loyal to his mentor. Wilde accepted financial help from Ross in his post-prison penury and named him his literary executor. After Wilde's death in 1900, Ross edited his complete works for publication in 1908.

Ross befriended Sassoon and introduced him to publisher William Heinemann in the hope of seeing the young man's poetry between hard covers. Sassoon wrote of his latest almost-father, "Although seventeen years my senior, his intuitively sympathetic understanding of youth made him seem a benevolent and impulsive bachelor uncle with whom one could feel on easy terms of equality, while consenting to be guided by his astute and experienced advice." Sassoon became a regular visitor to Ross's apartment in Mayfair's Half Moon Street, where he met more young, usually homosexual, writers. Gosse, Marsh, and Ross made Sassoon a junior member of London's literary world, although he hesitated to regard himself a real poet. Friends called Marsh

"Eddie" and Ross "Robbie," but the older, more reserved Gosse was always Edmund or Mr. Gosse. Three months in the capital saw Sassoon improving his poetry with critiques from Marsh, cultivating Marsh's friends, and watching opera and Russian ballet. He went back to Weirleigh in July.

The summer's events on the Continent, plus gossip from a friend of Theresa's whose two sons were colonels, convinced twenty-seven-year-old Sassoon that war was inevitable. In late July, he cycled miles of Kent country roads imagining battles to come. He gazed at "the world of my youngness" and felt honor bound to defend it. "And, after all," he wrote, "dying for one's native land was thought to be the most glorious thing one could possibly do!" Unlike Wilfred Owen, who delayed his enlistment for more than a year, Sassoon made up his mind before war began. The romantic equestrian chose the cavalry. British horsemen had played decisive roles in Britain's previous wars, and he assumed they would again.

On August 4, 1914, the day Britain declared war, Sassoon reported to the Drill Hall in Lewes, East Sussex, for his physical. Army doctors confirmed his good health, and he signed a "Territorial Force Attestation" committing him to four years' service. The next day saw Trooper (cavalry private) Sassoon mounted and ready for duty in C Squadron of the Sussex Yeomanry.

The training was not onerous for the accomplished rider, but in October a horse fell on him and broke his arm. Recuperating at Weirleigh in Theresa's care, he wrote poetry with "newly-acquired technical control" that he later described: "My main performance had been a poem of nearly two hundred blank verse lines, vigorously impersonating an old huntsman remembering better days." He called the dying fox hunter's lament "The Old Huntsman."

Sassoon resumed cavalry instruction in January 1915. His colonel advised him to seek an officer's commission, but he did "not feel equal to the effort." The War Office asked the Yeomanry's troopers, who had enlisted on the understanding they would serve only in England, to transfer overseas. To Sassoon's dismay, 80 percent declined. He had joined to fight, not to ride the Sussex Downs. The course of the war in France convinced him that the infantry, not the vaunted cavalry, would carry the burden. Machine guns and miles of entangled barbed wire had rendered the cavalry charge obsolete. Horses were relegated to transport and reconnaissance. Sassoon decided in April to leave the Sussex Yeomanry for the infantry.

Through family connections, he obtained an officer's commission in the Royal Welch Fusiliers on May 29, 1915. The regimental motto, *Gwell Angau na Chywilydd*, Welsh for "Death Before Dishonor," suited his emotional commitment to a romantic death on the field of honor. He had a uniform tailored in London and took the train north to the Royal Welch Fusiliers' Litherland depot near Liverpool. Drill instructors taught him to fight and to lead. Uncertain he could do either, he "resolved to put up as decent a performance as I could, though dubious of my practical abilities as an amateur soldier."

While Sassoon practiced trench digging and bayonet fighting, Royal Welch Fusilier units already in France were concluding the ten-day Battle of Festubert. It was at Festubert that a broken James Butlin of the Royal Welch Fusiliers ordered his men to shoot surrendering Germans and that the British suffered sixteen thousand casualties. A friend who survived the battle wrote to Sassoon from France, "Good luck and don't come out here. It is a mug's game." The risks came home to him at the beginning of November 1915, when the War Office informed the Sassoons of the death of his younger brother, Hamo. Hamo suffered a leg wound on October 28 at Gallipoli, where Archie Carmichael had been killed five months earlier. He died soon afterward from an infection and was buried at sea on November 1, denying Theresa Sassoon the consolation of visiting her son's grave. Like many other grieving wartime relatives, she turned to spiritualism in a vain attempt to contact her son.

FRESHLY TRAINED ROYAL Welch Fusilier Second Lieutenant Sàs-soon crossed the English Channel on November 17, 1915, aboard the ship *Victoria* and disembarked at Calais. It was his first time on foreign soil. His lodging that night was the floor of a local hotel, which, un-comfortable as it was, bettered the hovels, barns, and trenches to come. A Conradian journey took him slowly south and east, passing portents of savagery in the form of razed villages and rotting corpses, toward the last zigzag of trenchworks opposite the German lines. At his first base camp in Étaples, he found himself one of 320 untested junior of-ficers awaiting assignments. Sassoon went to Company C of the 1st Battalion, the regiment's oldest and most battle scarred, in command of a sixty-man platoon. Two days later, more than a hundred miles inland at Festubert, "a ruined place, shelled to shreds," he heard his first blast of artillery in the distance.

C Company's officers were billeted in a tent, where Sassoon re-treated to smoke his pipe and read. When he left a collection of essays by homosexual poet and Catholic convert Lionel Johnson on a table, it caught the eye of a young visiting officer from the Royal Welch Fusil-iers' 2nd Battalion. Twenty-one-year-old Captain Robert Graves was impressed to see a volume "that was not either a military text-book or a rubbish novel." He opened it and saw it belonged to someone called Siegfried Sassoon. Graves looked for him among the assembled offi-cers: "He was obvious, so I got into conversation with him, and a few minutes later we were walking to Béthune, being off duty until that night, and talking about poetry."

The pair of Royal Welch Fusiliers officers marching to Béthune looked the pride of British manhood. Both were over six feet tall in an era when the British male's average height was five foot two, and army training had left them physically robust. They were otherwise a study in contrasts. Graves described himself as "six feet two inches, my eyes

grey and my hair as black. To black should be added 'thick and curly.'"
He had the burly physique of the boxer and rugby player he had been
at Charterhouse School, topped with a broken nose and two smashed
front teeth that made him "sensitive about showing them." Sassoon's
gentle brown eyes, straight auburn hair, and lithe body spoke more of
ballet than prizefighting. An officer who knew him in France recalled,
"That splendid, erect figure with the noble head, mane of dark hair,
piercing black eyes and strongly sculptured features could only belong
to a poet." Sassoon was a thoroughbred. Graves was the carthorse, albeit with a formidable intellect.

Both had joined the British Army at the outset of hostilities, but
false insinuations of pro-German sentiments hounded them. "Siegfried" sounded German, although his mother's love of Wagner's Siegfried rather than German ancestry had landed him with the name.
Graves was half German, made plain by his middle name from his
mother's family, von Ranke. Some of his cousins, with whom he had
spent childhood summers, were serving in the German Army. This
did not diminish his ardor for the British cause. He knew Germany
well, but he did not excuse its aggression against Belgium and France.

The two nascent poets had matured in different milieus, Graves
with an Anglo-Irish father who wrote poems while supporting his
family as an inspector of schools. Sassoon, for the most part fatherless,
had come of age among landed gentry. Yet their devotion to poetry and
sexual inclinations were identical. Each had written to socialist vision-
ary Edward Carpenter, Sassoon in 1911 and Graves in 1914, to praise
his sensitive and brave defense of homosexuality in his book *The Intermediate Sex*. They had friends and mentors in common, including
Eddie Marsh, whom Graves met through one of his teachers at Charterhouse. Graves was nine years younger than Sassoon, but he had seen
combat, become a captain when Sassoon was a second lieutenant, and
acted the older brother.

In the days that followed, they gave each other poems for correction

and criticism. When Graves read Sassoon's "Return to greet me, colours that were my joy, / Not in the woeful crimson of men slain . . ."
with its "eighteen-ninetyish flavour," he became indulgent: "This was
before Siegfried had been in the trenches. I told him, in my old-soldier
manner, that he would soon change his style." Sassoon wrote in his
diary about meeting "a young poet, a captain in the Third Battalion
and very much disliked. An interesting creature, overstrung and self-
conscious, a defier of convention." Graves lent him a manuscript of
poems that he was hoping to publish. Sassoon thought "some very bad,
violent and repulsive. A few full of promise and beauty."

Sassoon's platoon dug trenches under torrential rain for two nights,
"hobbling to avoid slipping, inhuman forms going to and from inhuman
tasks." Afterward, no doubt stung by Graves's criticism of his pre-battle
naivete, he wrote the first poem depicting what he saw rather than what
he felt. "The Redeemer" began in the trench he had just left:

> Darkness: the rain sluiced down; the mire was deep;
> It was past twelve on a mid-winter night,
> When peaceful folk in beds lay snug asleep:
> There, with much work to do before the light,
> We lugged our clay-sucked boots as best we might
> Along the trench; sometimes a bullet sang,
> And droning shells burst with a hollow bang;
> We were soaked, chilled and wretched, every one.
> Darkness: the distant wink of a huge gun.

The next morning's forced march took the battalion to the hamlet
of Bourecq and the shelter of a rotting, rain-soaked stable. Pensive as
ever, Sassoon wrote in his diary that he had discarded "the old inane
life" he knew before the war. Fifteen months learning to be a soldier
had matured him, and "now I must ask that the price be required of
me. I must pay my debt. Hamo went: I must follow him. I will." His
war was beginning with a death wish.

However vile Sassoon's conditions, the ordinary soldiers' were worse.

The Tommies, as British enlisted men were called, had no servants to cook and do their laundry, and their food and sleeping quarters were inferior to the officers'. Sassoon accepted the inequality, but he resolved with suitable noblesse oblige to succor his platoon as best he could. That the men reciprocated his regard found voice in the reminiscences of many he commanded. His batman, Private Molyneux, told Sassoon he loved him "like a brother," which Sassoon thought "very nice of him— he *is* a dear." Friendships, though, were with equals, other junior officers commanding 1st Battalion platoons and companies. His affection for his Litherland training-camp roommate, David Cuthbert Thomas, went beyond friendship. He loved "little Tommy." Twenty-one-year-old Thomas, a vicar's son from Wales, was like Graves nine years younger than Sassoon. Sassoon did not reveal his feelings to the heterosexual youth with a girlfriend at home. His yearnings found expression in poetry. The officer who earned his greatest respect was the company's quartermaster, Captain Joe Cottrell. Lancashire-born Cottrell was an outspoken, working-class professional soldier, who had enlisted in the Royal Welch Fusiliers as a private twenty-eight years earlier. Cottrell became another paternal figure, instructing him in regimental lore and battlefield survival. Other favorites were the Dadd brothers, Julian and Edmund, handsome and athletic subalterns in their midtwenties whose father was an artist in London.

Taking trains one day, marching forty miles another, stopping at makeshift camps to drill or dig, the 1st Battalion's officers and men tolerated indigestible food, execrable sleeping quarters, and ill-fitting boots. The battalion stopped on December 6 at Montagne in Picardy, where they remained for eight weeks. Bandsmen paraded through the camp each evening, playing fifes and drums as if on parade for the king at Windsor. "War was fifty miles away," Sassoon wrote, "though we could hear the big guns booming beyond the horizon." He drilled his platoon to keep them battle ready, taught them the military manual, and treated them to the latest football results from home.

For recreation during his off-hours, Sassoon borrowed a one-eyed "little black mare" from the transport officer, Second Lieutenant R. M. C. Ormrod. Ormrod and Sassoon shared a small cottage and rode together through the fields nearby. Sassoon's favorite sport was racing with David Thomas on pretend hunts, chasing invisible hounds and foxes as if they were riding the Southdown Hunt. Sassoon's black mare, however, balked at leaping over streams. On one occasion, Sassoon and Thomas accidentally unhorsed a brigadier general before galloping away to avoid detection.

On Christmas Day, Sassoon mounted the black mare and rode into the woods. His diary reflected his mood: "Dear are these fields and woods, dear the solitary trees against such evening skies. I am glad to be alive this Christmas, riding home in the dusk (as after a day with the hounds), the little horse stepping it out, and my heart musing in the old silly way—the heart wants to find expression and always halts on the borderlands." There was no Yuletide turkey, but, noted the *Regimental Records*, "So great was the variety of spirits, wine, and ale taken, that lunch was an impossibility." C Company spent the evening beside a log fire, where Sassoon watched "the village full of maudlin sergeants and paralysed privates." The somber anniversary of Christ's birth inspired "The Prince of Wounds":

> The Prince of Wounds is with us here,
> Wearing his crown as he gazes down,
> Sad and forgiving and austere.

Sassoon harbored no doubts about the war, "and if I had, nothing would have been gained by telling my platoon about it—apart from the grave breach of discipline involved in such heart-searchings." He had not, so far, experienced battle. The prospect of going into action diminished on January 18, 1916, when he replaced Ormrod, who had gone to England, as transport officer. Transport officers brought supplies to the rest of the battalion, but they did not fight alongside them.

On January 28, the 1st Battalion was on the march again. It took three days to reach Morlancourt, barely five miles from the front. Sassoon watched his battalion leave without him for the Bois Français trenches the next morning, bereft at losing the companionship of his beloved David Thomas.

In the evening, Sassoon and Joe Cottrell left Morlancourt for the front with C Company's rations of food, water, and rum. Their convoy of horse-drawn wagons traversed a four-mile obstacle course of shell craters, barbed wire, rubble, and mud. It took them three and a half hours. Sassoon studied the British trenches and those of the Germans a mere sixty yards away. The battalion spent six days and nights in the Bois Français, Sassoon trudging to them each evening with the supplies. At the end of their six days, they received four days' rest.

On February 23, unblooded and longing to fight, Sassoon began a ten-day leave in England. The interruption of war duty took him home to Weirleigh, where his mother remained in deep mourning for Hamo, and to London, where literary friends welcomed the brave soldier. Robbie Ross, who hosted him in London, had become a vehement opponent of the war out of antipathy toward the ruling class that had persecuted him as a homosexual and defender of Oscar Wilde. "He hated the war," Sassoon wrote, "and was unable to be tolerant about it and those who accepted it." Ross's intolerance did not extend to his guest, whose uniform marked him as one of the war's victims.

SASSOON WAS BACK in France on March 6, as C Company began one of its four-day rotations out of the trenches. Seeing David Thomas in camp inspired his poem "A Subaltern" two days later:

> He turned to me with his kind, sleepy gaze
> And fresh face slowly brightening to the grin
> That sets my memory back to summer days,

With twenty runs to make, and last man in.
He told me he'd been having a bloody time
In trenches, crouching for the crumbs to burst,
While squeaking rats scampered across the slime . . .

But as he stamped and shivered in the rain
My stale philosophies had served him well,
Dreaming about his girl had sent his brain
Blanker than ever—she'd no place in Hell . . .

The 1st Battalion's new commander was Lieutenant-Colonel Clifton Inglis Stockwell. As Captain Stockwell of the 2nd Battalion on Christmas Day 1914, he had met German captain Friedrich Freiherr of the Second (Silesian) Jaeger Battalion in No Man's Land near Frelinghien to agree the famous truce, when soldiers from both sides stopped killing one another and played soccer. The Germans gave the British barrels of beer, and the Welch Regiment sent them a Christmas pudding. Fighting resumed the next day.

Stockwell, promoted steadily for his astute soldiering, had a reputation for strict discipline and ignoring orders when a crisis demanded. Sassoon was ambivalent about his commander, whom he viewed as "the personification of military efficiency. Personal charm was not his strong point, and he made no pretension to it." Carrying rations to C Company's trenches on March 16, Sassoon was reassured that David Thomas was alive and unharmed. Two nights later, Colonel Stockwell sent Thomas's platoon into No Man's Land to reinforce the barbedwire defenses. As Thomas laid wire, a German sniper shot him in the throat. He walked to a dressing station, where a doctor bandaged him and told him not to move lest he reopen the wound.

At noon the next day, Sassoon saw Captain Cottrell in front of the quartermaster's stores. "His face warned me to expect bad news," Sassoon wrote. Cottrell told him Thomas was dead, having ruptured his throat as he reached into his pocket for a letter from his girlfriend. To

Sassoon, "No news could have been worse." That evening, he rode up to the trenches as usual with rations for the men. "The sky was angry," he wrote, but the anger was his. The chaplain conducted a nighttime service beside the trenches for Thomas and two other fallen Royal Welch Fusilier soldiers. Sassoon listened to the prayers, while machine guns fired and a mortar shell exploded a few hundred yards away. "A sack was lowered into a hole in the ground," Sassoon recalled. "I knew Death then." Robert Graves, standing beside him, felt Thomas's loss more deeply than any other in the war. But, he wrote, "It did not anger me as it did Siegfried." Sassoon craved revenge, Achilles seeking Trojan blood on the death of Patroclus. When he next brought rations to the front, Graves recalled, "he went out on patrol looking for Germans."

Colonel Stockwell, judging Sassoon's martial talents wasted in Transport, reassigned him to a platoon command. On the night of March 26, Sassoon returned to C Company's trenches, at last as a combatant. "I used to say I couldn't kill anyone in this war," he wrote, "but since they shot Tommy I would gladly stick a bayonet into a German by daylight . . . I want to smash someone's skull. I want to have a scrap and get out of the war for a bit or forever." He would prove that a poet could fight, even at the cost of his life: "And death is the best adventure of all . . ." Stockwell ordered him to capture a German for interrogation. More than taking a German prisoner, Sassoon wanted to kill one. His daring forays into No Man's Land in search of Germans earned him the nickname "Mad Jack." His mania was by this time evident even to him: "They say I am trying to get myself killed. Am I? I don't know."

He boasted to Eddie Marsh on April 3, "I did get among them in a crater with six bombs and a revolver and I don't think they liked it a bit." Three weeks later, bloodlust unsatiated, he wrote that "chasing Germans in the moonshine is no mean sport." With a trusted Welsh-born Irish corporal named Richard O'Brien, inevitably nicknamed "Mick," he hurled Mills bomb grenades at German positions. It disappointed him that he had no opportunity to use his "knobkerrie," an African-style baton with a rounded knob at one end for bashing skulls. The No Man's Land forays convinced him he would die, but he did not relent throughout eighteen nights' raiding along the front. Then came Easter Sunday, April 23, when the regiment pulled him out of the line to undertake advanced infantry training at the Fourth Army School in Flixécourt.

Two days after his arrival, Sassoon and the rest of the school's three hundred officers and noncommissioned officers assembled for Major Ronald Campbell's lecture, "The Spirit of the Bayonet," which Max Plowman would hear the following October. The Highland Scottish officer's diatribe shocked Sassoon, however much he wanted to avenge "little Tommy." "He spoke with homicidal eloquence," Sassoon wrote of the major, "keeping the game alive with genial and well-judged jokes." Campbell urged his listeners, "Kill them! Kill them! There's only one good Boche, and that's a dead one!" Sassoon left the lecture shaken, seeking his "favourite sanctuary, a wood of hazel and beeches." The major's words reverberated in his mind: "The bullet and the bayonet are brother and sister." "If you don't kill him, he'll kill you." "Stick him between the eyes, in the throat." The admonitions jibed with his craving for vengeance, but they also horrified him. In the morning, Sassoon and the other trainees jabbed bayonets into straw sacks and made "a quick withdrawal."

The erotic implications of the bayonet penetrating flesh were not lost on the poet, who penned "The Kiss" in response:

> . . . Sweet sister, grant your soldier this:
> That in good fury he may feel
> His body where he sets his heel
> Quail from your downward darting kiss.

When Sassoon returned to C Company at Morlancourt on May 21, an epic logistical operation was under way. To overwhelm the meticulously fortified German defenses in the Somme Valley, the British and French armies were moving mountains of equipment, ammunition, water, food, horse fodder, explosives, and medical supplies to the front. This meant hours of bone-crushing work for the 1st Battalion, paving roads, putting down tracks for ammunition trains, and relentless digging into swampy ground to construct more trenches. Equally important was gathering intelligence on the enemy. What was his order of battle? How deep were his trenches and tunnels? Where were his machine guns?

A German soldier might provide some of the answers. Colonel Stockwell decided to seize one in a raid on the closest enemy position in the fortified Kiel Trench opposite the 1st Battalion. His C Company raiders would also reconnoiter enemy strongpoints, destroy defenses, and kill Germans who resisted. Sassoon volunteered to lead the mission, but Stockwell selected instead a lieutenant named Stansfield. Sassoon, despite his fondness for Stansfield, feared he was too bulky and slow to conduct a lightning raid. Stansfield would, however, have the support of Sassoon's expert raiding partner, Mick O'Brien, the stout Irishman from Cardiff. Sassoon's role was to wait in C Company's trench to count in the men if and when they came back.

On the night of May 25, Sassoon watched Stansfield and twenty-five soldiers—weighed down with weaponry, faces stained in burned cork, the last section lugging ten-foot ladders—climb over the parapet into the rainy darkness. They plodded over sixty yards of wasteland laced with barbed wire and pocked with massive shell holes toward their objective. "I am sitting on the parapet," Sassoon wrote in his diary, "listening for something to happen—five, ten, nearly fifteen minutes—not a sound—nor a shot fired—and only the usual flare-lights, none very near our party." Suddenly, the din of exploding German shells broke the tension. Sassoon ran into No Man's Land with an evacuation party to rescue the wounded. In the distance, he saw most of the raiders clinging to a ridge between huge craters. Neither the

British nor the Germans moved or fired a shot. After twenty minutes, a bayonet man scrambled down from the ridge to Sassoon with a message. Sassoon followed him in silence to their trench, where the man whispered, "They can't get through the second belt of wire; O'Brien says it's a washout; they're all going to throw a bomb and retire."

When both sides resumed hurling grenades and firing rifles, some of the Fusiliers scrambled back to the trench. Sassoon counted sixteen. Lieutenant Stansfield and nine men were unaccounted for. He went out again to find them. The first he came to was Stansfield, wounded and unable to move. Two men carried him to the trench, while Sassoon searched for the rest. He found a soldier with a bleeding leg, who told him, "O'Brien is somewhere down the crater badly wounded." Sassoon slithered toward O'Brien, German rifles so close he heard the bolts click. "The bloody sods are firing down at me at point-blank range," he thought, as he crawled through a deep pit and up to the edge of O'Brien's crater.

The corporal lay motionless twenty-five feet below with another injured soldier. Sassoon slid down to them. Of O'Brien, he wrote in his diary, "He is moaning, and his right arm is either broken or almost shot off; he's also hit in the right leg (body and head also, but I couldn't see that then)." The other man said, "Get a rope." Sassoon raced back to the British trench to fetch rope and another soldier to help him. The Germans—"perhaps they felt sorry for us"—ceased firing. "Trying to lift him up the side of the crater," Sassoon recalled, "the soft earth kept giving way under one's feet: he was a heavy man too, fully six feet high. But he was a dead man when at last we lowered him over the parapet onto a stretcher." A field ambulance took O'Brien's body for burial. There was no funeral.

Sassoon missed O'Brien's "old cheeriness and courage and delight in any excitement of Hun-chasing." The death of a soldier for whom he felt responsible, added to the loss of his brother and David Thomas, etched another scar in his psyche. "But when I go out on patrol his ghost will surely be with me," his diary noted, "he'll catch his breath and grip his bomb just as he used to."

The only result of the raid was two British dead and ten wounded. Yet, noted a regimental record, "All the wounded were brought back, 'largely owing to Sassoon's bravery.'" Colonel Stockwell recommended the Military Cross (MC) for "Mad Jack," not for taking lives, but for trying to save one.

SASSOON LEARNED THE MC was his on June 30, when the medical officer, Dr. William Kelsey Fry, brought him the news. Lieutenant Fry, a twenty-seven-year-old dental surgeon, had earned his own MC saving lives under fire at Festubert. Fry removed the MC ribbon from his tunic and sewed "the white and purple portent" onto Sassoon's. The accompanying citation read "For conspicuous gallantry during a raid on the enemy's trenches. He remained for 1½ hours under rifle fire and bomb fire collecting and bringing in our wounded. Owing to his courage and determination all the killed and wounded were brought in." Sassoon's courage was about to be tested again as the biggest battle of the war, possibly of human history, began the next morning, July 1.

C Company's orders were to carry ammunition to the Manchester Regiment rather than go over the top in the initial wave. British heavy artillery pounded German defenses along a twenty-five-mile front to render the enemy incapable of halting the imminent infantry assault. Sassoon watched the Battle of the Somme unfold from a trench a mere five hundred yards behind the killing ground, writing in his diary every few minutes:

> **7.30 a.m.** Since 6.30 there has been hell let loose . . . The whole earth shakes and rocks and throbs—it is one continuous roar. Machine-guns tap and rattle, bullets whistling overhead . . . Attack should be starting now, but one can't look out, as the machine-gun bullets are skimming. Inferno—inferno—bang—smash!

7.45 a.m. . . . some Huns apparently surrendering—about three quarters of a mile away. Our men advancing steadily to the first line . . .

9.30 a.m. . . . Just been out to have another look. The 21st Division are still going across the open on the left, apparently with no casualties. The sun flashes on bayonets, and the tiny figures disappear behind the mounds of trench-debris.

9.50 a.m. Our men still advancing in twenties and thirties in file, about a mile to the left . . .

10.05 a.m. I can see the Manchesters in our front trench getting ready to go over . . . (wire gaps—which I made night before last) . . . I am looking at a sunlit picture of hell.

High-explosive artillery shells crashed onto Sassoon's dugout for a solid hour, until 2:30 p.m. When the barrage ceased, the Manchester Regiment, which Wilfred Owen would join in France five months later, sent its 20th Battalion forward. Sassoon watched them cross the desolate ground and seize the Germans' Sunken Road Trench. From there, with support from units of the 1st Royal Welch Fusiliers, they penetrated Fricourt village. Those successes coincided with positive reports reaching Sassoon from farther down the line: the British took Montauban and Mametz; the 21st Division reached Fricourt Wood; and hundreds of Germans were surrendering. Sassoon made his last diary entry at 10:45 p.m.—"Fairly quiet opposite us"—ignorant of the day's cost: twenty thousand British soldiers killed and twice that number wounded.

Sassoon woke to a clear sky. "Everywhere," he wrote, "the news seems good; I only hope it will last." It didn't. He wrote a short poem on July 3 that ended: "Tomorrow we must go / To take some cursèd wood . . . O world that God made!" When he moved into a trench facing "cursèd" Mametz Wood the next night, bodies strewn everywhere hinted at the scale of the British tragedy—first three, then another thirty corpses, "terrible and undignified carcases, stiff and contorted . . . some side by side on their backs with bloody clotted fingers mingled as if they were handshaking in the companionship of death." The stench was unbearable.

The Welch Fusiliers were as uncertain of their orders as they were of the enemy's exact location. "There was a good deal of confusion in the wood," noted a regimental history, "particularly during the night time. Groups fired on one another, mistaking one another for the enemy." Worse, on July 5, a German sniper had C Company pinned down. Although ordered to remain in position, Sassoon went ahead with Lance Corporal Gibson to stop him. Eyeing the enemy, Gibson set his Lewis automatic machine gun on its bipod, aimed, and fired. The German shot back, hitting Gibson square in the forehead. The young man's death impelled Sassoon toward "a single intention—to 'settle that sniper' on the other side of the valley." Second Lieutenant V. F. Newton took Gibson's Lewis gun to cover Sassoon's sprint with a bag of Mills bombs. At the top of the German trench, Sassoon threw two bombs at not a single sniper but "a great many Germans." Unaware that Sassoon was a lone wolf, the Germans retreated along the trench bed. Bellowing the old hunting cry, "View halloa!" he tossed four more grenades and "to my surprise fifty or sixty (I counted eighty-five packs left on the firestep) ran away like hell into Mametz Wood." He rested in the deserted trench, by then "the most advanced position held by the XV Corps."

When Colonel Stockwell learned of Sassoon's bravado, he ignored the second lieutenant's violation of orders and put his name forward to receive a bar on his MC. Sassoon's personal coup, however, did not disguise the week's costs: C Company, 2 killed and 17 wounded; the 1st Battalion as a whole, 132 casualties, 14 of them dead; and the Royal Irish Regiment, fighting nearby, 250 killed or wounded. Sassoon would be denied his second MC on the grounds that the day's attacks had failed.

On July 6, C Company left the front to rest in a camp inconveniently sited in a marsh beside the village of Heilly-sur-Ancre. Sassoon spent much of his time smoking his pipe and reading Thomas Hardy's *Tess of the d'Urbervilles* and *The Return of the Native*. The 2nd Battalion arrived a week into his interlude, affording Sassoon a reunion with Robert Graves, "as whimsical and queer and human as ever." Graves left for the front the next day. When Sassoon heard a short time later that Graves was lightly wounded, he mused on the deaths of friends. His own death, like those of soldier-poets Charles Sorley and Rupert Brooke, seemed unavoidable.

July 21 brought the worst news of all: "And now I've heard that Robert died of wounds yesterday in an attack on High Wood. And I've got to go on as if there were nothing wrong." He grieved for Graves, who could have been "a lifelong friend," and again for David Thomas, "little Tommy." His sorrow convinced him he would join them both, but the 1st Battalion denied him the luxury of death by posting him to the rear at Méricourt. A day after his arrival, Sassoon's temperature soared to 105°F. The New Zealand Hospital at Amiens treated him for dysentery. Nine days later, he was in an army hospital at Somerville College, Oxford. To Sassoon, the Victorian women's college was "Paradise." His mood improved further when he learned that Robert Graves's wounds had not killed him and the two would meet again.

Medical treatment and convalescence kept Sassoon in England for seven months. He returned to France on February 15, 1917, and reported the next night to the 5th Infantry Base Depot at Rouen. The base adjutant sent him to collect blankets from the storeroom. Disoriented in the dark, he went by mistake into a guard room. There, on his knees and stripped to the waist, a young private was wailing. A sergeant guided Sassoon to the blankets and explained that the man had attacked a military policeman "and now 'e's just had news of his brother being killed. Seems to take it to 'eart more than most would, 'Arf crazy, 'e's been tearing 'is clothes off and cursing the War and the Fritzes. Almost like a shell-shock case, 'e seems." The next day in the mess, Sassoon saw two lists on the noticeboard: one, officers ordered to the front; and the other, three private soldiers executed by firing squad for cowardice. Death was the punishment inflicted on 306 British soldiers—many of them shell-shocked—for "cowardice" or "desertion."

Sassoon fell ill again, this time with German measles, on February 18. He returned to duty nine days later, discomfited to learn he had been transferred from the 1st Battalion to the 2nd. He requested to remain with the 1st, but the regiment turned him down. He presented himself at Chipilly to the 2nd Battalion's B Company, whose company commander, Captain W. W. Kirkby, was unwelcoming. The regular soldiers, however, received him well. Private Frank Richards, a Welsh former coal miner who had enlisted in the Royal Welch Fusiliers in 1901 and served in India, recalled, "Two new officers had just arrived and seemed a far better stamp than some we had during the last few months, and one named Mr. Sassoon, who was wearing the ribbon of the Military Cross, was soon very popular with the men of the Company he was posted to." Captain Kirkby, who had followed battalion custom in referring to the new subaltern as "wart," took time to accept his new second-in-command as more or less an equal.

Kirkby led the company forward on horse with Sassoon at the rear on foot. The 2nd Battalion, which heavy casualties had reduced to 270 men, marched toward their position for another "big push." This would be the Battle of Arras, where Wilfred Owen and Max Plowman also fought. The undernourished rank and file struggled to keep up, some so weak that a sergeant carried their rifles. When they arrived at Villers Bocage, Sassoon bandaged the men's blisters and sent their boots for repair, cursing the war profiteers who had unloaded inferior goods on the army. Six more days of marching took them to the village of Saulty, where Sassoon bought twelve dozen packs of Woodbine cigarettes "for the future consolation of B Company." The next day, Easter Sunday, Sassoon pondered his role in the war. The prospect of impending battle elated him, but he wondered, "Was it some suicidal self-deceiving escape from the limitless malevolence of the

Front Line?" The war had lost all justification. "All I knew was that I had lost my faith in it, and there was nothing left to believe in except 'the Battalion spirit.'"

At 5:30 the next morning, April 9, the Arras offensive erupted across a twelve-mile front stretching from Vimy south to Bullecourt. British guns bombarded German trenches and British infantrymen charged into German machine-gun fire. Sassoon waited in reserve with other officers in a comfortable château for his turn to fight. They were playing cricket the next day, when a whistle interrupted play—the signal to move out. The clear sky turned black, and snow pelted B Company on its eight-mile slog to the rough bivouac where they camped for the night. At first light, they were on the march again. At 9:00 p.m., they reached their destination, a German reserve trench that the British had captured on Easter Monday. Sassoon, afflicted with gastritis and hands covered in festering sores, went to the dressing station in a tunnel deep below the trench. There, doctors awash in blood and guts struggled to save wounded men groaning in agony. Sassoon left them to it.

The British-occupied trenches and tunnels were as forbidding as Piranesi's hellish eighteenth-century Roman "Imaginary Prisons": "The dead bodies lying about the trenches and in the open are beyond description—especially after the rain. Our shelling of the line—and subsequent bombing etc—has left a number of mangled Germans—they will haunt me till I die." He made that diary entry on Sunday night, "fully expecting to get killed on Monday morning."

Going outside to peer over the trench parapet, he watched the unfolding battle, "aware of its angry beauty." It frustrated him to be a passive observer for two days in his "cramped little trench." B Company at last went out, following guides from the 13th Northumberland Fusiliers uphill until, at midnight, they were lost. Sassoon went ahead to reconnoiter and found a group of sappers in a sunken road. One of the sappers led him to the rendezvous point in a portion of the Germans' Hindenburg Trench that had fallen to the British. "Now we groped and stumbled along a deep ditch to the place appointed for us in that zone of human havoc," Sassoon wrote. "The World War had got our insignificant little unit in its mouth; we were there to be munched, maimed or liberated." The time was four in the morning.

Captain Kirkby told Sassoon to post sentries, but B Company's sixty men barely covered the nine-hundred-yard front. Their objective was unclear, and no one from the company they replaced had remained to put Sassoon in the picture: "I didn't even know for certain that we were in the front line." He moved along the trench to find the company to his left, but they were running in panic through a doorway to a fortified tunnel deep underground. One of them gasped that "the Germans are coming over." There were no Germans, and Sassoon returned to his company.

He spent the next day with his platoon carrying mortar bombs under lashing rain through trenches that were "like glue." A human face detached from its skull floated in the wet ground, the remains of a German, with "two mud-clotted hands protruding from the wet ashen soil like the roots of a tree turned upside down." Back in his hovel, Sassoon received an order to command a bombing party of one hundred men in reserve for the 1st Battalion of the Cameronians (Scottish Rifles) in the morning. The objective was to penetrate a barrier in the trench separating the British from the Germans and trap German forces in the tunnel below.

Sassoon selected twenty-five men from each of the battalion's four companies and posted them on the steps between the Cameronians' underground command post and the jumping-off point. At zero hour, 3:00 a.m., the Cameronians moved out. Sassoon waited in suspense to know whether he would be called upon. Three hours passed. Communications with the Cameronians' headquarters broke down. A messenger ran in with the unwelcome news that the Germans were driving the Cameronians back. "I got up stiffly," Sassoon wrote, "aware that my moment had arrived." A Cameronian colonel and his adjutant were silent, but Sassoon imagined them thinking, "Well, old chap, I suppose you're for it!"

Sassoon took the first twenty-five men, all from A Company, on what he believed to be a suicide mission. "I hadn't the slightest idea what I was going to do, and my destination was in the brain of the stooping Cameronian guide who trotted in front of me." They stumbled through a narrow trench to the main trench, where the Cameronian raiders were retreating. They said they had run out of grenades and Germans were swarming around them. "But where *are* the Germans?" he asked. "I can't see any Germans."

With the prestige of the Royal Welch Fusiliers at stake, Sassoon led his men with self-confessed swagger past the Cameronians toward the trench barrier. A hundred yards on, he told his sergeant to collect the Mills bombs all around and bring them to him. At the next turn in the trench, a Cameronian corporal named Smart was waiting with a bagful of grenades. The two of them ran past a wounded Cameronian private lying in his own blood and, farther on, a dead German officer. Angry about the wounded Briton, Sassoon hurled bombs in the direction of the Germans' position. "I went on throwing bombs and advancing, while the corporal, who was obviously much more artful and efficient than I, dodged up the saps at the side," Sassoon wrote. He followed the corporal's example, dodging in and out of the trench wall's recesses and throwing grenades. They continued forward, sighting an occasional German running away, until the corporal told Sassoon they had reached their objective. "I had no idea where our objective was," Sassoon admitted.

The battle zone went quiet. Sassoon stood and raised his head to inspect the landscape. Suddenly, he felt a massive blow between his shoulders. He thought a grenade had hit him from behind. It hadn't. A sniper's bullet had pierced his shoulder from the front. Falling against the trench wall, he closed his eyes. When he opened them, the only thing that prevented him from renewing the attack was an order from the Cameronian colonel to pull back.

One of Sassoon's twenty-five raiders told Private Frank Richards, "God strike me pink, Dick, it would have done your eyes good to have seen young Sassoon in that bombing stunt . . . It was a bloody treat to see the way he took the lead. He was the best officer I have seen in the line or out since Mr Fletcher [Second Lieutenant W. G., killed by sniper fire in March 1915] and it's wicked how good officers get killed or wounded and the rotten ones are still left crawling about. If he don't get the Victoria Cross for this stunt I'm a bloody Dutchman; he thoroughly earned it this morning." Sassoon did not receive the VC or any other decoration for his "stunt," but Richards thought he had won "the respect of every man that knew him."

CHAPTER SEVEN

The Protest

Sassoon's bullet wound was healing in the early summer of 1917, when he came down with gastroenteritis. Doctors moved him from Oxford to Chapelwood Manor, a Sussex house that Lord and Lady Brassey had opened to recovering officers. Guilt at enjoying "the graciously-organized amenities of Chapelwood Manor" gnawed at him. While still in France, he had been too busy to question the war. Resting at the Brasseys' from May 12 to June 4, he had time. Was there any justification for his brother Hamo's loss at Gallipoli in 1915, for "little Tommy," for all the other friends whose lives were cut short? The war's goals could not be worth the cost. "My mind," Sassoon wrote, "had dwelt continually on the battalion with which I had been serving. Since I left it, ten officers had been killed and fourteen wounded."

Robbie Ross visited him at Chapelwood and drove him to Garsington Manor, an impressive, ramshackle country house near Oxford. Its chatelaine, Lady Ottoline Morrell, had sought Sassoon out the year before after reading in *The Times* his unsigned sonnet "To Victory" ("I would have hours that move like dancers / Far from the angry guns that boom and flash"). Edmund Gosse told her the unsigned poet's name, and she wrote to him. A steady exchange of letters followed. When Sassoon arrived at Garsington, Ottoline looked at his face and thought, "He could be cruel." She fell in love with him, knowing he was thirteen years younger but unaware of his homosexuality. As he departed, she gave him a peacock feather.

Sassoon, while not reciprocating her infatuation, befriended her and her husband, Philip Morrell. As a Liberal Party member of Parliament, Philip had observed with dismay His Majesty's Government's rejection of a German peace proposal. On December 12, 1916, German chancellor Theobald von Bethmann Holweg declared to the Reichstag that his government had offered to negotiate an end to the war with Britain, France, and Russia. Kaiser Wilhelm II informed his generals on the same day that "I have made an offer of peace to the enemy. Whether it will be accepted is uncertain." France rejected it at once, and Britain's new prime minister, David Lloyd George, followed suit on December 19. Philip Morrell's insights into tensions within the Liberal Party over the possibility, however remote, of a negotiated peace left Sassoon "feeling that I was at last learning the truth about what was happening behind the political scenes."

Sassoon confided his doubts about the war to the Morrells. Ottoline supported his instinct to refuse to serve. Philip advised against: "'It would only be a nine-days' wonder,' he said, foreseeing "the pathetic absurdity of a solitary second-lieutenant raising his voice against the architecture of a world conflict." Sassoon sought the advice of Ottoline's lover, the philosopher Bertrand Russell. Russell had become acting chairman of the No-Conscription Fellowship when its original committee was imprisoned. Russell, grandson of a Whig prime minister and England's leading philosopher since his publication with Alfred North Whitehead of *Principia Mathematica* in 1910, had become the war's most prominent critic. In Sassoon, he discovered a champion for the antiwar cause: a brave officer, holder of the Military Cross, and a poet. Russell helped him to compose a letter stating his reasons for refusing to serve any longer.

In London, Sassoon sat for a "Byronic" portrait by Glyn Philpot during the day and worked on his "Soldier's Declaration" at the Reform Club by night. He conferred with leading members of Britain's antiwar movement on visits to Garsington. The manor was a refuge for conscientious objectors, attracting writers like D. H. Lawrence and the painter Augustus John. Garsington's home farm provided the "conchies," as their detractors called them, with agricultural work as an alternative to military service. They were among sixteen thousand men registered for exemption from conscription under the January 1916 Military Service Act. Sassoon felt his army uniform imposed an unbridgeable gulf between him and the civilian pacifists. Yet the encounters with men who shared his beliefs made him more adamant that a war neither side was winning while both hemorrhaged men was evil. The agony would end only if the war did. He believed with Russell that people of conscience had a moral duty to stop it.

Sassoon finished a draft of his protest on June 15 with the regret that fellow officers would misunderstand his motives: "Some of them would regard my behaviour as a disgrace to the Regiment. Others would assume I had gone a bit crazy. How many of them, I wondered, would give me credit for having done it for the sake of the troops who were at the Front?" He sent the draft to literary luminaries he knew, including Thomas Hardy, Arnold Bennett, and H. G. Wells. The protest dismayed most of his mentors, including Edmund Gosse. Arnold Bennett wrote a furious letter to Sassoon condemning the statement for its futility: "The Army will ultimately lay it down that you are 'daft.' You aren't of course, but that's how it will end. What is the matter with you is spiritual pride." Robbie Ross was "quite appalled." Eddie Marsh, who had moved with Winston Churchill to the

Ministry of Munitions, wrote that "I do think you are intellectually wrong—on the facts." Marsh urged him, "Don't be more of a martyr than you can help."

The war tormented Sassoon's thoughts and dreams. He rejected outright the government's insistence that peace could come only with "the destruction of Kaiserism and Prussianism." He wrote in his diary on June 19, "I only know, and declare from the depths of my agony, that these empty words (so often on the lips of the Jingos) mean the destruction of Youth." His diary called the army "dumb," while revealing empathy for soldiers "entrapped by the silent conspiracy against them." The entry continued,

> Poor heroes! If only they would speak out; and throw their medals in the faces of their masters; and ask their women why it thrills them to know that they, the dauntless warriors, have shed the blood of Germans. Do not the women gloat secretly over the wounds of their lovers?

His anger at women who encouraged husbands, sons, and lovers to fight was matched by his disgust with England's ruling class: "If the crowd could see into those cynical hearts it would lynch its dictators." He summed up the difference between soldiers and civilians:

> Soldiers conceal their hatred of war.
> Civilians conceal their liking for it.

Five days later, his diary picked up the theme of "the present conditions under which humanity is suffering and dying." Sassoon was in full revolt against the politicians and the press for preventing negotiations to end the war. "Will Englishmen be any happier because they have added more colonies to their Empire? The agony of France! The agony of Austria-Hungary and Germany? Are not those equal before

God?" While staying with his mother at Weirleigh, he heard the cannons' roar from across the English Channel. The noise inspired him to
begin a poem that he would not complete for many months:

> You're quiet and peaceful, summering safe at home;
> You'd never think there was a bloody war on! . . .
> O yes, you would . . . why, you can hear the guns.
> Hark! Thud, thud, thud,—quite soft . . . they never
>   cease—
> Those whispering guns—O Christ, I want to go out
> And screech at them to stop—I'm going crazy;
> I'm going stark, staring mad because of the guns.

Sassoon's medical furlough ended in late June. Rather than return
to duty, he stayed at Weirleigh. On July 4, after a week's absence without leave, he received a telegram from the 3rd Battalion, Royal Welch
Fusiliers: "Join at Litherland immediately."

Sassoon wrote to his commanding officer, Lieutenant-Colonel H.
Jones-Williams, at the Royal Welch Fusiliers' Litherland base on July
6, "I am writing you this private letter with the greatest possible regret.
I must inform you that it is my intention to refuse to perform any further military duties. I am doing this as a protest against the policy
of the Government in prolonging the War by failing to state their
conditions of peace." His defiance was a clear breach of the King's
Regulations, for which the punishment might be imprisonment at hard
labor. He enclosed a single-page, typed statement, which he also circulated to the press:

> I am making this statement as an act of wilful defiance of military
> authority, because I believe the war is being deliberately prolonged
> by those who have the power to end it. I am a soldier, convinced
> that I am acting on behalf of soldiers. I believe that this war, upon
> which I entered as a war of defence and liberation has now become
> a war of aggression and conquest . . .

I have seen and endured the suffering of the troops, and I can no longer be a party to prolong these sufferings for ends which I believe to be evil and unjust. I am not protesting against the conduct of the war, but against the political errors and insincerities for which the fighting men are being sacrificed . . .

Among the many recipients of Sassoon's declaration was *The Cambridge Magazine*, the antiwar journal that had been publishing his poems. An accompanying letter to editor Charles Kay Ogden asked him to disseminate the statement "after it has appeared in Hansard." Hansard, the official record of parliamentary debates, would print it when a member of Parliament cited it in the House of Commons. Sassoon and Russell had given a copy to antiwar Liberal MP Hastings Lees-Smith for that purpose. Sassoon wrote the next day to Ogden, "This is a bloody performance, but I suppose someone has to do it." He was daring the army to court-martial him and thus put the war on trial.

Court-martial was the standard response to a soldier's refusal to fight, but Sassoon was not a standard officer. He held the Military Cross for rescuing a wounded soldier under fire. His commanding officer had recommended him for the empire's highest military honor, the Victoria Cross, after he captured a German trench. In May, William Heinemann had published a collection of his verse, *The Old Huntsman and Other Poems*, to critical applause and strong sales. Moreover, his first cousin, Sir Philip Sassoon, was an MP and private secretary to Douglas Haig, by this time promoted to field marshal and commander of British Forces on the Western Front. Siegfried's court-martial would not go unnoticed.

Lady Ottoline encouraged Sassoon, writing from Garsington about his statement, "It really couldn't have been better, I thought. Very condensed and said all that's necessary." In her journal, however, she was skeptical: "Siegfried is terribly self-centred, and it seems almost as if when he does a valiant action, such as this protest, that he watches himself doing it, as he would look into a mirror."

His fellow poet and Royal Welch Fusiliers comrade, Robert Graves, whose wounds and damaged lungs had taken him out of the war, wrote, "I entirely agreed with Siegfried about 'political errors and uncertainties'; I thought his actions magnificently courageous. But there were more things to be considered than the strength of our case against the politicians." His concern was Sassoon's health, which he believed would not withstand trial and imprisonment. Graves approached Welsh poet Evan Morgan, a friend and private secretary at the Labor Ministry: "I explained to Morgan that I was on Siegfried's side really, but that he should not be allowed to become a martyr in his present physical condition." Graves urged Morgan to persuade the War Office to convene a Medical Board that would attribute Sassoon's protest to a nervous breakdown. The next potential advocate he approached was Major A. R. P. Macartney-Filgate, deputy commander of his and Sassoon's battalion, whom Graves described as a "humane Irishman." To Graves's letter stating that Sassoon was mentally unbalanced, the major sent Graves "a most kind and sympathetic letter in reply." Sassoon's politically connected literary friends conspired to prevent his court-martial. Ross wrote to Gosse, "I have promise of powerful help if necessary at the War Office."

Sassoon reported on July 12 to the Royal Welch Fusiliers at Litherland, ready for punishment. Instead, Major Macartney-Filgate, having read Graves's letter, shook his hand and offered him a cigar. "I can honestly say I have never refused a cigar with anything like so much regret," Sassoon wrote. "To have accepted it would have been a sign of surrender." The major pleaded with him to reconsider what he called the "ultimatum." Sassoon was too weary to explain that his letter was not an ultimatum, but a protest. "So I gazed fixedly at the floor and said, 'Hadn't you better have me put under arrest at once?'" The major exclaimed, "I'd rather die than do such a thing!" He sent Sassoon to the Exchange Hotel in Liverpool to "await further instructions."

Three days later, an assistant adjutant handed Sassoon orders to appear before a Medical Board in Crewe, about an hour south of Liverpool. The board might deny him a court-martial and airing of his protest by declaring him mentally unbalanced. Sassoon pondered the "opportunity to avoid martyrdom," but he tore up the papers and skipped the review. He wrote that night to Graves, "Dearest Robert . . . I hate the whole thing more than ever—and more than ever I know that I'm right, and shall never repent of it." The next day, Monday, was devoted to memorizing poems to help him endure prison, which he assumed would have no books. While he was studying the poetry, a colonel arrived to ask why he had missed his Medical Board. The colonel berated Sassoon, telling him "you surely must be wrong when you set yourself against the practically unanimous feeling of the whole British Empire." Sassoon stood his ground, and the colonel departed in a bad temper. The following two days saw Sassoon languishing alone in the hotel with "the haggard clarity of insomnia."

On Saturday afternoon, July 14, he took a tram to the suburb of Formby, where he used to play golf. Avoiding the links, he stumbled through sand dunes feeling "outlawed, bitter, and baited." The walk south must have taken more than two hours, because he remembered reaching the mouth of the River Mersey. He tore off the Military Cross ribbon that Dr. Kelsey Fry had sewn to his shirt and cast it into the current. That decoration had nearly cost him his life, and most young officers would have given much to win one. "As it was," he wrote, "the poor little thing fell weakly on to the water and floated away as though aware of its own futility."

The next morning, Sunday, Robert Graves strutted into the Exchange Hotel to find a demoralized Sassoon slumped in a chair in the smoking room. "Thank God you've come!" Sassoon exclaimed. Graves was stern: "I've come to tell you that you've got to drop this anti-war business." Sassoon answered that he wouldn't. He had assumed wrongly that Graves came as "prisoner's friend" for the court-martial. Graves, who thought Sassoon looked "very ill," said that "the only possible course for us to take was to keep on going out to France till we got killed." Graves told Sassoon how the men in the trenches would react: "They would say that he was ratting, that he had cold feet, and was letting the regiment down by not acting like a gentleman."

The two young officers argued all morning, had lunch, and walked along the shore at Formby. Graves told him resistance was pointless. It would not shorten the war. The debate raged, until Sassoon said, "Can't you understand that this is the most difficult thing I've ever done in my life? I'm not going to be talked out of it just when I'm forcing them to make a martyr of me." Graves snapped, "They won't make a martyr of you."

Sassoon was stunned. Graves had been maneuvering behind his back. The regiment's colonel had told Graves that Sassoon's refusal to appear before a Medical Board would force the military to "shut me up in a lunatic asylum for the rest of the war." There would be no court-martial, no public airing of his protest. Anyway, Graves said, Sassoon's declaration had not been and would not be publicized because Sassoon was ill. Sassoon relented, writing, "So that was the end of my grand gesture."

Graves accompanied his friend to the Medical Board five days later, on July 20. Sassoon waited in an anteroom while Graves testified. Graves pleaded that his comrade's combat experiences had affected his mind. "The irony of having to argue to these mad old men that Siegfried was not sane!" Graves wrote. "It was a betrayal of truth, but I was jesuitical." Twenty-one-year-old Graves was so emotional that he broke down three times, prompting one of the three board members to comment, "Young man, you ought to be before this board yourself." He was not mistaken. Graves in later years would accept that he suffered from shell shock, a condition that he believed affected much of his war poetry.

When Sassoon's turn to testify came, the board's president, a colonel, asked whether his objections were religious. "No, sir; not particularly." More questions followed. Sassoon felt defeated. He knew the verdict before he heard it. The board declared him not "responsible for his actions as he was suffering from a nervous breakdown." The judgment spared the War Office the embarrassment of prosecuting a war hero, prominent poet, and first cousin of a member of Parliament.

THE BOARD DEPUTED GRAVES to accompany Sassoon to Craiglockhart, but he missed the train. Sassoon arrived alone, feeling he was there under false pretenses—a political dissident masquerading as a lunatic. This was one of many subjects he hoped to clarify in discussions with Rivers, the first of which was scheduled for the morning.

Sassoon moved into a double room that faced east from an upper floor, affording a view of Wester Craiglockhart Hill. His roommate was "a cheerful young Scottish captain who showed no symptom of eccentricity . . . a thoroughly nice man." The tartan-wearing captain, however, was experiencing paranoid hallucinations. Such was life in, as Sassoon called it, "Dottyville." At night, he discovered, doctors "lost control and the hospital became sepulchral and oppressive with saturations of war experience. One lay awake and listened to feet padding along passages which smelt of stale cigarette-smoke; for the nurses couldn't prevent insomnia-ridden officers from smoking half the night in their bedrooms, though the locks had been removed from all doors." The patients had seemed almost normal during the day. "But by night each man was back in his doomed sector of a horror-stricken Front Line, where the panic and stamp of some ghastly experience was re-enacted among the livid faces of the dead. No doctor could save him then."

Morning brought Sassoon's first therapeutic session with Dr. Rivers. Rivers's orders were to cure Sassoon, not of neurasthenia, but of pacifism, to change his mind rather than fix it. The consultation was more political than psychiatric. Yet both men felt a growing affinity. "In an hour's talk," Sassoon wrote, "I told him as much as I could about my perplexities." Rivers listened sympathetically, his method as much a "listening" as a "talking" cure. Sassoon appreciated his psychiatrist's informality, writing, "Forgetting that he was a doctor and that I was an 'interesting case,' I answered his quiet impartial questions as clearly as I could with a comfortable feeling that he understood me better than I understood myself."

Rivers, unlike Brock with his prescription of vigorous work for Wilfred Owen and his other patients, imposed no obligations on his charges. Apart from consultations, Sassoon was free to do whatever he liked: go into Edinburgh, roam the hills, read, or do nothing at all. Sassoon found in the fifty-three-year-old doctor a "father confessor," the latest in a sequence of paternal surrogates dating to his childhood. The rapport between psychiatrist and patient was evident to Robert Graves, who arrived at Craiglockhart a day late with apologies for missing Sassoon's train. When Sassoon introduced him to Rivers, he observed, "Siegfried was interested in Rivers' diagnostic methods and Rivers in Siegfried's poems."

Sassoon and Graves left Rivers to celebrate Graves's twenty-second birthday. The reunion with Sassoon in Scotland on July 24, despite its being Sassoon's first day in a mental hospital, delighted them both. Their shared experience of poetry, battle wounds, and the anguish of Sassoon's protest strengthened a friendship marred on occasion by fraternal rivalry. Graves declaimed some of his new poems, which Sassoon thought were "very good." "It was really jolly seeing Robert Graves up here," Sassoon soon wrote to Robbie Ross. "We had great fun on his birthday, and ate enormously."

After Graves's departure, Sassoon's protest became public knowledge. The Independent Labour Party's *Bradford Pioneer* published the statement on July 27, Sassoon's fourth day of therapy with Rivers. *The*

Workers' Dreadnought, the crusading London newspaper edited by suffragette and socialist Sylvia Pankhurst, ran it on page one the next day. On July 30, Scotland Yard's Criminal Investigation Department (CID) confiscated copies of the statement during raids on the *Dreadnought* and Bertrand Russell's No-Conscription Fellowship—revealing the depth of official fear of Sassoon's dissidence and its potential effect on morale at home and at the front.

The seizures, however, failed to contain the story to readers of two small, radical publications. The Liberal MP for Northampton, Hastings Lees-Smith, rose in the House of Commons at seven o'clock that evening, July 30. With Sassoon's declaration in hand, he detailed the creditable war record, "one of the first 1,000 men to enlist . . . wounded and awarded the Military Cross . . . formal recognition from the General Commanding for distinguished service." He then recited Sassoon's protest word for word, rebuking His Majesty's Government for refusing to state its war aims or consider negotiating peace with Germany.

Lees-Smith's next revelation was that the government had used a Medical Board to pronounce on the gallant officer's sanity rather than a court-martial to judge his arguments on their merits. "This young officer is known to Members of this House," Lees-Smith intoned to the chamber. "I myself had a long interview with him only a few weeks ago, and he certainly impressed me as a man of most unusual mental power and most extraordinary determination of character." Yet the board had judged him mentally unbalanced, "not based on health, but based upon very easily understood reasons of policy." The policy was to destroy the growing antiwar movement, whose gatherings the government had used armed troops to suppress. "The letter," the MP continued, "is worth reams of articles in the newspapers, and it is worth hundreds of soldiers got together in order to break up a meeting without knowing what the meeting is about. That is why it is necessary in the House to prevent the action of this officer being stifled and discredited by the absurd doctrine that it has been due to the effects of nervous shock."

The Deputy Secretary of State for War, Ian MacPherson, answered for the government. Calling Sassoon "this gallant young officer," he said the Medical Board had determined he was "not responsible for his actions, suffering from a nervous breakdown." He then condemned the No-Conscription Fellowship for taking advantage of his emotional fragility. Lees-Smith intervened to condemn the army, the Medical Board, and the government for "colluding in this farce . . . They sent a sane man to a psychiatric hospital because he spoke the truth and that truth did not fit their plans."

Sassoon feared he had been forgotten, until word of the debate reached him. He wrote, "But at the end of my first week at Slateford my career as a public character was temporarily resuscitated by my 'statement' being read out in the House of Commons." On July 31, *The Times* reported Lees-Smith's speech, quoting Sassoon's statement in full. Reading the article, Sassoon felt detached. He had registered his protest, and it had made no difference. As *The Times*'s Parliamentary Report noted, soldiers egged on by the government had broken up a pacifists' meeting in Islington, north London, the previous Saturday, while the police stood by. The war would go on, no matter the cost.

Sassoon had failed to achieve the cause célèbre of a military trial, but he refused to retract what he had written. The only result of *The Times* article was "a batch of letters from people who either agreed or disagreed with my views." He needed a holiday from the controversy, reflecting, "The intensity of my individual efforts to influence the Allied Governments had abated." Meetings with Rivers, which had taken place each morning at first, settled into a routine of three evenings a week.

Sassoon took long, lonely treks though the Pentland Hills, "which really did seem unaware that there was a war on," remembering that the great Scottish author of *Kidnapped* and *Treasure Island*, Robert

Louis Stevenson, had walked the same green knolls thirty years before. At Rivers's suggestion, he asked his mother to send his golf clubs. They arrived the next day, and he played on the nearest greens at the Merchants of Edinburgh Golf Club. Watching his tee shots slice into the long grass, he realized he didn't know what he was doing—"referring to my swing and not to my recent political activity."

CHAPTER EIGHT

Poet by Day,
Sick by Night

Every summer before the war, Siegfried Sassoon had gloried in playing cricket. Yet, at Craiglockhart, he shunned team sports and clubs. His only athletic pursuits were golf and leaping alone "like a young ram" over the Pentland ridges. At the end of his first week, he wrote to Ottoline Morrell, "My fellow-patients are 160 more or less dotty officers. A great many of them are degenerate looking." One had committed suicide. Estranged from the other inmates, Sassoon cherished his time with Rivers, "a sensible man who doesn't say anything silly." Rivers assured him he was sane, albeit with one abnormality: opposition to the war. Yet, Sassoon wrote to Ottoline, the doctor's pro-war arguments "don't make any impression on me."

He used the evening sessions with Rivers "to give my anti-war complex an airing." Doctor and patient debated the war's rights and wrongs, neither making headway with the other. Among discussion topics were European politicians' declarations as translated in *The Cambridge Magazine*. Sassoon maintained the statesmen, far from waging defensive war, sought to annex territory from Germany and its allies. France wanted Alsace and the portions of Lorraine that Germany had seized in the 1870 Franco–Prussian War. The Kingdom of Italy had joined the war in April 1915 to acquire chunks of Austria-Hungary. Britain coveted German colonies in Africa. The May 1916 Sykes–Picot accord dividing the Ottoman Empire among France, Britain, and Russia would have bolstered Sassoon's case had it not been an official secret. Rivers argued that Germany would not negotiate. Its military and political leaders were as determined as Britain's to fight until victory, despite the stasis of the trenches, the daily death toll, and the calamitous offensives. Like the belligerent nations, Rivers and Sassoon stuck to their positions without breakthrough or compromise.

Rivers accused Sassoon of inconsistency: his intellect was "suffering from trench fever" and his protest's inspiration was more emotional than moral. Moreover, peace without Germany's outright defeat would "nullify all the sacrifices we had made." Sassoon answered, "It doesn't seem to me to matter much what one does so long as one believes it is right!" As soon as the words were out, he regretted his "particularly fatuous" remark.

Rivers diagnosed Sassoon's anxiety as stemming from the deaths of friends and of men in his platoon: "His view differs from that of the ordinary pacifist in that he would no longer object to the continuance of the War if he saw any reasonable prospect of a rapid conclusion."

Sassoon suggested articles and books to Rivers, among them one of the first novels by a frontline soldier, Henri Barbusse's *Sur le Feu*. The English translation, *Under Fire*, had just appeared in Britain. Barbusse fought in a French regiment for seventeen months as a *poilu*, "hairy" enlisted man, until gas-damaged lungs took him out of the war. His novel exposed the degradation of working-class troops caught between their officers and the enemy in a "troglodyte world." Barbusse became a pacifist, whose works circulated in antiwar circles. *Under Fire* enlightened Rivers, who had not experienced life and death in the trenches as Sassoon had.

What struck Sassoon more than Rivers's politics was the man himself. "All that matters is my remembrance of the great and good man who gave me his friendship and guidance," he wrote, adding,

> I can visualize him, sitting at his table in the late summer twilight, with his spectacles pushed up on his forehead and his hands clasped in front of one knee; always communicating his integrity of mind; never revealing that he was weary, as he must have been after long days of exceptionally tiring work on those war neuroses which demanded such an exercise of sympathy and detachment combined.

If Brock classified Owen's poetry as therapeutic, Rivers recognized Sassoon's as art. Literary creativity fascinated him as much as Melanesian languages. Poetic images, he felt, "are symbolic expressions of some conflict which is raging in the mind of the poet, and that the real underlying meaning or latent content of the poem is very different from that which the outward imagery would suggest." He conjectured that poems and dreams were alike in their hidden meanings, a point he could not prove "for the obvious reason that, unfortunately, I am not a poet."

Sassoon was earning acclaim with Heinemann's publication in May of *The Old Huntsman and Other Poems*. Many verses were shocking for their stark rendering of the soldier's existence in this bloodiest of wars. No less a critic than Virginia Woolf wrote in *The Times Literary Supplement*, "What Mr. Sassoon has felt to be the most sordid and horrible experiences in the world he makes us feel to be so in a measure which no other poet of the war has achieved." Woolf also praised Sassoon's pastorals, quoting as an example "South Wind":

> You have robbed the bee, South Wind, in your adventure,
> Blustering with gentle flowers; but I forgave you
> When you stole to me shyly with scent of hawthorn.

Such passages in Woolf's view constituted "evidence not of accomplishment, indeed, but of a gift much more valuable than that, the gift of being a poet, we must call it; and we shall look with interest to see what Mr. Sassoon does with his gifts." Sassoon was struggling with those gifts at Craiglockhart, as new poems true to his experience of conflict, comradeship, and fear eluded him. The daily diary he kept most of his life had come to an abrupt halt. He was "marking time," no closer to recanting.

WILFRED OWEN, unlike Sassoon, immersed himself in the Craiglockhart regime. He edited *The Hydra*, wrote articles for it, studied the region's rocks and flora, investigated conditions in Edinburgh's slums, took a Berlitz course in German ("It's a vile language to learn."), and acted in plays at the Saturday concerts. This was the university life that his family's lack of money had denied him. He called it "a free-and-easy Oxford," where he exercised mind and body. Swimming, he wrote, "never fails to give me a Greek feeling of energy and elemental life."

Brock suggested he visit a munitions factory and then a brass foundry, where he spent the morning of July 13 "beating out a plate of copper into a bowl." He was also pounding words together, melding memory and nightmare into verse. The Hercules–Antaeus poem Brock had asked him to compose began as a sonnet before outgrowing the fourteen-line form and becoming a blank verse Homeric epic. Owen took "The Wrestlers" to Brock and, despite his nervous stammer, read it aloud. It began,

> So neck to neck and obstinate knee to knee
> Wrestled those two; and peerless Heracles
> Could not prevail nor catch any vantage . . .

Heracles/Hercules, whose "huge hands which small had strangled snakes," exhausts himself through hours of failing to gain hold of "slim Antaeus's limbs." The sinewy Libyan evades Heracles's grasp again and again, "While Heracles,—the thews and cordage of his thighs / Straitened and strained beyond the utmost stretch." Young Hylas, Heracles's servant, divines the source of Antaeus's strength. As night approaches, Hylas runs to his master with sponges to wipe away his sweat and whispers, "If thou could'st lift the man in air—enough / His feet suck secret virtue of the earth / Lift him, and buckle him to thy breast and win." Heracles leaps up, recalling "how he tore the oaks in Argos," and wraps his arms around Antaeus. He uproots him, crushes "his inmost bones," parades his corpse through the town, and drops him at the altar of his earth goddess mother, Gea/Gaia. The poem does not end with Antaeus's death. Owen has Gea causing the ground to erupt and rouse her son back to life. The two wrestlers feast, and Heracles "on the morrow passed with Hylas / Down to the Argo, for the wind was fair."

Owen's depiction of muscle resisting muscle, pantings "like the sighs of lions at their meat," and the struggle of each contestant to kill the other mirrored his own grappling with the demons of his dreams. The war machine, like Hercules, had ripped him from his earth and metaphorically killed him. In the poem, earth redeems Antaeus, as Owen's growing connection to the world was rehabilitating him. For Brock, the poem demonstrated Owen's understanding of the myth depicted on his office wall. Yet "The Wrestlers" was more than that: Owen, as much as a recovering neurasthenic, was a maturing poet. His Hercules sailed away, but the war machine that crippled him did not. It lurked in beastly fury, awaiting Owen's cure to ambush him again.

Owen made his stage debut with a small part in the trial scene of *The Merchant of Venice* during July 28's Saturday concert. Four other cast members were professional actors, patients Lieutenant John Leslie Isaacson, Second Lieutenant James Walter Graham Pockett, and their wives. Owen wrote to his mother two nights later that Mrs. Isaacson as Portia forgot her lines and Mrs. Pockett, "fresh from the vast London stage, prompted her at the top of her voice!" Owen assured Susan, who disapproved of actresses, that "both these ladies are model wives, no less than model women." *Hydra* critic Peas Blossom praised the actresses' "charming" elocution, but his sole allusion to Owen, his editor, was the quip, "The remaining characters were of course only background." Owen wrote to Susan that Peas Blossom's review had arrived too late for him to edit. After finishing his letter to her, he readied *The Hydra* to hand to the printers in the morning.

Owen wrote to his cousin Leslie Gunston, with whom he and Gunston's sisters, Vera and Emma, had organized their childhood nature society, that he was preparing an imaginative lecture for Craiglockhart's Field Club: "My subject has the rather journalese Title of 'Do Plants Think?'—a study of the Response to Stimuli & Devices for Fertilisation, etc. I have no books yet, but I remember a number of useful points from your big Cassell's [Encyclopedia] (I think it was Cassell's) studied in 1911." On Monday evening, July 30, the Field Club assembled to hear Owen argue that "plants have all the elements of perception, and if not consciousness, at least *sensience*: that they have the glimmerings of sight; that vaguely and sleepily, they feel; they feel heat and cold, dryness and damp, and the contact of bodies, that they are even able to smell." His novel theory compared soldiers with their tin helmets and bayonets to a plant that "produces special protective coverings, sharpens its spines, wastes its young substance in riotous colours, allows those colours to fade immediately fertilization is accomplished." The question-and-answer session went on until 10:20. At eleven, he wrote to Susan from his room upstairs, "The lecture was a huge success . . . I have only once since getting through the Barrage at Feyet [Fayet] felt such exultation as when winding up to my peroration tonight!" He wrote a full report on his lecture for *The Hydra*, again modestly remaining anonymous in print.

Editorship of *The Hydra* entitled Owen to a seat on the General Committee of Officers. Its monthly General Meeting convened on August 3 and approved Owen's proposal to make *The Hydra* free for patients. The committee elected Major Bingham chairman; Owen's therapy partner, Charles Mayes, treasurer; Pockett, head of Entertainment; and other officers, chiefs of tobacco, golf, cricket, Field Club, etc. After the meeting, Owen wrote to his mother that his second edition of *The Hydra* was ready and he would "plunk the copies outside the Breakfast Room Door tomorrow morning, where they will be given away to all the Club."

At breakfast on Saturday, August 4, the patients could read Owen's facetious editorial: "The results of the story and verse prize competition . . . took the eloquent form of the schoolboy's essay 'On the results of idleness'—a blank page . . . The competition is still running on the old lines—like the Edinburgh tramways." Next came a conversation ostensibly overheard on a tram about the meaning of "Hydra": "A 'ydra's a 'undred 'eaded serpent, and the 'eads grew again as fast as cut off, signifyin' these 'ere officers at Craiglockhart; for as soon as one gets too uppish, like, they cut 'im off the strength, an' another comes up in 'is place." There followed accounts of societies and clubs, as well as criticism of the cricket squad: "The bowling of our eleven is decidedly weak." That weakness did not prevent Craiglockhart from defeating Edinburgh Academy "in glorious sunshine" with 215 runs for eight wickets to the academy's 134 for two. *The Hydra* of August 4 included short stories by patients. One was "Elise," a macabre tale about a young Frenchwoman whose soldier husband "gave up his soul to God for you and for France" and miraculously appeared to her as she wept beside his grave. A poem of equal banality, "Why Worry!," by a Guards officer who signed himself "SYNJIN," graced the issue, Owen admitted, because it was the only poem submitted. He was not bold enough to print his own verse.

That evening's musical program opened with the Craiglockhart
Orchestra's rendition of Tchaikovsky's *Chant sans Paroles* and "Glow
Worm" from the German operetta *Lysistrata*. While commending Captain Williams's conducting, Peas Blossom lamented, "It was perhaps
unfortunate that so many of the songs touched on death." The concert
concluded with Second Lieutenant Pockett's production of the operetta *The Lady Lawyer*, which Peas compared favorably with Gilbert
and Sullivan. Mr. Gage's "light-hearted dancing and his free and easy
'gags'" delighted Peas as much as Miss Goldie Scott's singing.

Owen kept a rendezvous on August 8 with Second Lieutenant
James Bell Salmond. Until he checked into Craiglockhart on June 25,
a day before Owen, Salmond had served in the 7th Fife Battalion of
the Black Watch Regiment. The garrulous six-foot twenty-five-year-
old was the professional journalist Owen needed on *The Hydra*.
Salmond's late father had been editor and coproprietor of northern
Scotland's *Arbroath Herald*. His own journalism began with editing
College Echoes at Saint Andrew's University, where he graduated in
1912. He spent the following two years in London on the national
press and writing for *The Boy's Own Paper*. Salmond accepted Owen's
offer to become his deputy editor. Owen thought he was just the man
to "talk our printer into shape." Salmond had fought on the same front
lines around Beaumont Hamel as Owen and suffered the same shell
shock. The two officers had something else in common: both aspired
to be poets. They discussed "many mighty things and men" until they
had nothing left to say and "went upstairs to the Cinema, & so finished
a very pleasant afternoon."

After the film, Lieutenant Pockett offered Owen a larger role than
he had in *The Merchant of Venice*. Owen would play Arthur Wallcomb,
"a fashionable young fellow, whose chief business in the play is in introducing people," in Wilson Barrett's 1904 four-act melodrama *Lucky
Durham*. Owen had only four days to learn his lines and rehearse

before performing on August 11, when, he crowed to Susan, "I shall know what it really feels like to be on the stage." Despite his excitement, he confessed mental confusion: "At present, I am a sick man in hospital, by night; a poet for a quarter of an hour after breakfast; I am whatever and whoever I see while going down to Edinburgh on the tram: greengrocer, policeman, shopping lady, errand boy, paper-boy, blind man, crippled Tommy, bankclerk, carter, all of these in half an hour."

Owen paid regular visits to his mother's friends the Newboults, reading poetry to Mrs. Newboult and dedicating two poems to Chubby Cubby, seven-year-old Arthur. "Winter Song" began,

> From off your face, into the winds of winter,
> The sun-brown and the summer-gold are blowing;
> But they shall gleam with spiritual glinter,
> When paler beauty on your brows falls snowing,
> And through those snows my looks shall be soft-going.

His second poem to Arthur Newboult, "To Your Antique Body," continued the theme of youth and beauty soon to fade, ending,

> Your smile shall dull, because too keen aware;
> And when for hopes your hand shall be uncurled,
> Your eyes shall close, being opened to the world.

Owen's fascination with young males found its way into many other poems. An Edinburgh newspaper boy inspired "Six O'Clock in Princes Street":

> Dared I go side by side with you;
>
> Or be you in the gutter where you stand,
> Pale rain-flawed phantom of the place,
> With news of all the nations in your hand,
> And all their sorrows in your face.

Owen began a poem about a shirtless working-class boy he had seen by the River Thames in London's East End. He called it "Lines to a Beauty Seen in Limehouse." "I saw thee siting carven like a god, / That may have cared for such as barefoot trod." The poem praised the boy's vermilion lips and "smooth, smooth naked knees," before descending to the reality of the boy's life:

> And yet shall thy brows be given to a soiled pillow at night
>   (Thy hands shall be gloved with?)
> Because you are poor.

The poor lad in the London slums, like a god, was unapproachable. Calling him "half-god, / Immortal clay, incomparable clod," Owen sighed,

> So shalt thou take thy pleasures with thy kind,
> Where love is cast, where I cannot go,
> What image I have garlanded what throne,
> What sacrifice wherewith I lie and moan.

Owen labored over "Limehouse," which he left incomplete, and other poems in his first weeks at Craiglockhart. Brock made little of passages that implied sexual frustration, love of young soldiers, and the effect on him of their suffering. Owen's upbringing had excluded sex, which his brother Harold wrote "belonged to one of the great mysteries which were never talked about in our house." Homoerotic yearnings in an era when law and custom combined to conceal them went unexplored. The purpose of Brock's therapy was to restore Owen's confidence as a soldier. Reconnecting to the environment excluded consideration of romantic attachments to other males. Brock appeared not to acknowledge that to love, after all, is to connect and, rejecting Freud's emphasis on the sexual in psychological analysis, missed or chose to disregard the symbols of manly love in poems like Owen's "Has Your Soul Sipped":

To me was that smile,
Faint as a wan, worn myth,
Faint and exceeding small,
On a boy's murdered mouth.

Though from his throat
The life-tide leaps
There was no threat
On his lips.

But with the bitter blood
And the death-smell
All his life's sweetness bled
Into a smile.

Charles Mayes was becoming a kind of younger brother to Owen, who showed him the concern he lavished on his real younger brothers, Harold and Colin. Mayes took charge of the accounts at *The Hydra*, and Owen appointed him the new "Peas Blossom" theater critic. Mayes/Peas Blossom covered August 11's Saturday concert. He wrote that the first half of *Lucky Durham*—the second was scheduled for the following Saturday—was "produced and produced well; the stage setting was very pretty, and the stage staff are much to be congratulated upon their work." The review praised all the cast save Owen, the self-effacing editor who "cancelled reference to myself."

Owen's varied pursuits did not arrest his nightmares or prevent him from slipping into melancholy. A biography of Victorian-era poet laureate Alfred Lord Tennyson told him that tragedy had haunted the poet throughout his life. "But as for misery," Owen wrote to Susan on August 8, "was he ever frozen alive, with dead men for comforters." The biographer quoted a friend who claimed Tennyson had always been "like a great child, simple and self-absorbed."

"So should I have been," wrote Owen, "but for Beaumont Hamel.

(Not before January 1917 did I write the only lines of mine that carry the stamp of maturity: these:

> (. . . But the old happiness is unreturning.
> Boys have no grief so grievous as youth's yearning;
> Boys have no sadness sadder than our hope.)"

Owen's dreams featured claustrophobic images redolent of his time trapped in cellars and in the hole astride the railroad track next to the maggot-eaten lumps of Cock Robin's flesh: caves, pits, and dugouts rocking to the shock of exploding shells. Yet his treatment was progressing, nowhere more evident than in his poetry. Brock was satisfied with Owen's poetic achievements, which he viewed as signs of health more than of artistic maturing. The doctor was not illiterate. He quoted from memory the poetry of Dante and Tennyson in his sessions with Owen, but he insisted art needed a purpose outside itself. That purpose was to find and remove the causes of Owen's nightmares, shakes, and stammering. Poetry's aid to the process was all the justification Brock needed to encourage it. Owen was more ambitious.

CHAPTER NINE

High Summer

C raiglockhart defeated the Merchants of Edinburgh Golf Club six to three in August's opening tournament, but a rainstorm the following week robbed the Merchants of their chance for revenge. Team competitions bored Siegfried Sassoon, who preferred golf on his own or with another patient, a shell-shocked RAMC physician, who had survived the sinking of the troopship *Transylvania* by a German U-boat on May 4, 1917. Sassoon recalled, "His temper wasn't quite normal when things went wrong, and he looked like losing his half-crown, but that may have been a peace-time failing also." Despite many "enjoyable games" with the doctor, all the while improving his iron shots, Sassoon felt himself "a healthy young officer, dumped down among nurses and nervous wrecks."

He remained convinced that he was different from the other patients. "I am perfectly free, and there is no pretense made of anything being wrong with my health," he wrote on August 1 to Roderick Meiklejohn, a Scotsman and homosexual who had served as private secretary to Prime Minister Herbert Henry Asquith until David Lloyd George replaced Asquith in December 1916. If some of Sassoon's friends were blaming his insubordination on a nervous breakdown, Sassoon was having none of it. He insisted to Meiklejohn, "Anyone who says I'm 'not responsible for my actions' is a sanguinary liar."

On the day he wrote that letter, police in London seized another hundred printed copies of his protest from Russell's No-Conscription Fellowship. With his statement suppressed and his world circumscribed, Sassoon felt he had become "a complete back-number." Letters of support ceased to arrive at Craiglockhart. He feared his brother officers in the Royal Welch Fusiliers regarded his *beau geste* as nothing more than shirking duty. He was right, as the Royal Welch Fusiliers' medical officer, Captain James Churchill Dunn, confirmed, "Sassoon's quixotic outburst has been quenched in a 'shell-shock' retreat. He will be among degenerates, drinkers, malingerers, and common medical cases, as well as the overstrained . . . I have not heard any stop-the-war talk among front-line troops." Sassoon believed he spoke *for* them, if not with them, but a comfortable hospital was not as convincing as prison.

During Scotland's long summer daylight hours, Sassoon escaped the hospital's "nervous wrecks" with excursions to golf courses, the Pentlands, and Scottish mansions where he had introductions. At night, he tried to write despite his omnipresent, verbose Scottish roommate. On Monday morning, August 8, he ventured out to North Berwick, a pretty beach about twenty miles north of Craiglockhart beside a golf course he knew, and "sat by the sea which was clear & cold, & splashed around, & sat in the sea among rocks and sand."

That evening, he wrote to his friend Graves, "What do you think of the latest push? How splendid the attrition is! As [former Liberal government minister] Lord Crewe says, 'We are not in the least depressed.'" The "latest push" at Pilckem Ridge in Flanders raged from July 31 to August 2. The Royal Welch Fusiliers distinguished themselves, killing 50 Germans and capturing 150. The British, however, paid a high blood price. An American surgeon at the front, Dr. Harvey

Cushing, noted in his journal for Thursday, August 2, "*10.30 p.m.* We're about through with this particular episode. Around 30,000 casualties, I believe—a small advance here and there, and that's about all." The final toll was 31,000, and the gain was three thousand yards of desolate, swampy ground. Pilckem Ridge fired the starting pistol for what British historian A. J. P. Taylor called "the blindest slaughter of a blind war." Officially, it would be the Third Battle of Ypres, remembered by the name of a ruined Belgian village in its midst, Passchendaele.

Sassoon felt a deserter's guilt. "To wake up knowing that I was going to bicycle off to play two rounds of golf," he wrote, "was not a penance." Yet he felt penitent when he studied the newspapers' daily casualty lists. One Royal Welch Fusilier who fell at Pilckem was thirty-one-year old Corporal James Llewellyn Davis, who earned a posthumous Victoria Cross for capturing a machine-gun position, killing most of its crew and bringing back a prisoner under fire. Another Welshman lost in the battle was Corporal Ellis Humphrey Evans, a farmer, former pacifist, and Welsh-language poet under the name Hedd Wyn, "Blessed Peace." One of his last poems, "War," as translated into English, spoke of hope hanging from willow boughs, "Drowned by the anguish of the young / Whose blood mingled with the rain."

Passchendaele led at least a few soldiers to reconsider Sassoon's dissidence. Edmund Gosse, despite having opposed Sassoon's protest, wrote, "There was a mysterious circulation of some of Sassoon's poems among others about the time (1917) that the battle of Passchendaele made many of the fighting men wonder if any good ever came of such increasing bloodshed." A junior officer in the Royal Welch Fusiliers, Vivian de Sola Pinto, was recovering from battle wounds at a hospital in France when he chanced upon a Sassoon poem in a magazine. "It was an attractive piece of verse expressing something felt by many sensitive spirits amid the drabness of trench warfare," he wrote. The poem was "To Victory":

Return to greet me, colours that were my joy,
Not in the woeful crimson of men slain,
But shining as a garden, come with streaming
Banners of dawn and sundown after rain.

When Pinto recovered and transferred to a base camp in Rouen, a poem in *The Old Huntsman* resonated with him: "It was called 'Blighters' and its burning sincerity made every other 'war poem' that I had seen pale into insignificance." The second verse made a particular impression:

I'd like to see a Tank come down the stalls,
Lurching to rag-time tunes, or "Home, sweet Home,"
And there'd be no more jokes in Music-halls
To mock the riddled corpses round Bapaume.

Sassoon's poetry, if not his protest, was reaching a wider military and civilian public as the war dragged on. Antiwar militant Bertram Lloyd wrote to ask Sassoon's permission to reprint two poems, "In the Pink" and "The Dead Boche," in an anthology he was editing. Sassoon agreed and urged Graves to send Lloyd "anything new you have done which is against the 'honour and glory' stunt." Graves, however, refused to see himself as an antiwar poet, and none of his poems appeared in Lloyd's collection.

Sassoon's next letter to Graves, on August 10, mentioned a few short poems he was writing for Charles Kay Ogden's *Cambridge Magazine*. He congratulated Graves on the impending publication by William Heinemann of his book of verse, *Fairies and Fusiliers*, advising him to insist on a smaller typeface than Heinemann had used for *The Old Huntsman*: "The 'Sassoon' one is only fit for latrine work, like its author." He assured Graves, who remained dubious about Sassoon's antiwar posture, "My opinions remain four-square." A scrawl across the top of the letter reflected a deepening bond between Sassoon and his psychiatrist: "We go to New Zealand & Polynesia apres la guerre. Rivers gives noble accounts of both regions."

Sassoon's life was improving, but it was about to take a knock: "I am sorry to say that Rivers is going to Cambridge for a month." Rivers, always short of stamina, had not had a break from duty since coming to Craiglockhart ten months earlier. Rivers must have informed Sassoon about his leave, which was not scheduled until late September, to allow him to prepare for the interruption of their conversations.

RIVERS AND SASSOON were less physician and patient than friends by August 1917. Their quarrels about the war progressed in an amicable fashion. Sassoon, not always sure of his ground, reinforced his arguments by pressing assorted publications on his "father confessor." Rivers read them for insights into Sassoon's state of mind. The antiwar literature, however, was having an unexpected effect: Rivers became less certain about the justice of prolonging the war. One day after he and Sassoon lunched together, Rivers went back to reading the trench life novel Sassoon had given him, Henri Barbusse's *Under Fire*.

When he finished it, he picked up a journal Sassoon had recommended, *The English Review*. An article in the August issue, "War and Reconstruction: An International Magna Carta," made the case for a diplomatic resolution of the war. The author, signed only "001," proposed that "Wise Men and Elders of the peoples" hold conferences around the globe to agree an "International Magna Carta representing the world's Justice." Admitting that many complex problems needed attention, he asked, "Does the death or wounding of a single German soldier bear any relation to the solution of any of these problems?" Germans faced food shortages, lack of clear wartime objectives, and the imminent arrival of American troops that would force them to heed the demands of an "International Magna Carta" requiring all nations to abide by the same standards of law and justice. It was a utopian essay, but no more outlandish than slaughtering thousands of men every day.

Reading *The English Review*, Rivers realized "that I had found myself in a frame of mind more favourable to peace by negotiation than I had ever known before." It led him to imagine "the situation that would arise if my task of converting a patient from his 'pacifist errors' to the conventional attitude should have as its result my own conversion to his point of view." Sassoon said they often joked "about the humorous situation which would arise if I were to convert him to my point of view." The main blocks to Rivers's denunciation of the war were his uniform and the obligations it implied. Rivers, like Sassoon, felt overwhelmed by "a definite mental conflict." In writing about the dilemma, he protected Sassoon's identity by calling him "Patient B":

> As a scientific student whose only object should be the attainment of what I supposed to be the truth, it was definitely unpleasant to me to suspect the opinions which I was uttering might be influenced by the needs of my position, and I was fully aware of an element of constraint in my relations with B on this account. So long as I was in uniform I was not a free agent, and though no one can be a free agent in a war, it was a definite element in my situation at the time that my official position might be influencing the genuineness of the views I was expressing in my conversation with B.

When Sassoon appeared for another nightly medico-political discussion, Rivers kept his inner turmoil to himself. The uniform was prevailing over the scientist who wore it.

SASSOON'S TROUBLED CONSCIENCE marred his solitary walks through the Pentland Hills, but Owen's rural excursions with the Field Club were pure pleasure. On August 13, Owen accompanied Brock, a local clergyman, an officer named Captain Mackenzie, and Mackenzie's thirteen-year-old son over the Pentlands. Owen boasted to Susan that "I held my own in the matter of Water Plants, and my ancient chippings at Geology came in useful." They ate a picnic lunch, wandered past streams and waterfalls, and stopped at teatime for "scones and jam and fresh eggs in the shepherd's cottage at the head of the reservoir." The lengthy trek made them fifteen minutes late for dinner and left Owen "very fatigued." He managed after dinner to perform in the final rehearsal for the second half of *Lucky Durham*. He wanted Susan to see the play, "for I am fairly sure of my part, and the more so, being with professionals, who can't let one down by any false cues or anything."

Owen's frequent letters to his mother expressed feelings other men reserved for their diaries or their confessors. Religion was a recurring theme in the intimate correspondence between the son and his evangelical mother. Susan had long supported missions in Africa, but the war and her son's role in it were turning her sympathy to her country's soldiers. "I'm overjoyed that you think of making bandages for the wounded," he wrote after his *Lucky Durham* rehearsal. "Leave Black Sambo ignorant of Heaven. White men are in Hell. Aye, leave him ignorant of the civilization that sends us there, and the religious men that say it is good to be in that Hell." He asked her to remind the archbishop of Canterbury that Saint John's Gospel said, "Ye have heard that it hath been said: An eye for an eye, and a tooth for a tooth: But I say that ye resist not evil, but whosoever shall smite thee on thy right cheek, turn to him the other also." The Church of England in wartime preached the opposite, forcing Owen to confront the contradiction between Christianity as he understood it and the forms prescribed by church and state.

The Hydra, the Field Club outings, and stage acting kept Owen busy, but what he called "bellicose dreams" persisted. Letters referring to nightmares did not describe them, but they may have resembled those of another patient who, like Owen beside the remains of Gaukroger, had seen a fellow officer's "body blown to pieces, with head and limbs severed from the trunk." The man was under the care of Rivers, to whom he confided that the dismembered corpse plagued his dreams. Like Owen, he dreaded sleep.

Owen penned an editorial for the next *Hydra* that urged readers to send more copy: "You don't get someone else to fill your pipe and smoke it at you. *Yet you allow others to fill your own magazine?*" Along with the usual news about golf, bowls, billiards, tennis, and the Model Yacht Club, Owen included an item on his special interest, the Field Club. His unsigned report of the July 30 meeting reprised his "Do Plants Think?" Sticking to anonymity, he referred to himself as "the lecturer," who "touched on the similarity of plant-respiration and digestion with our own; on their secret power of utilising light-energy for building up foods from crude elements; on their remarkable contrivances for effecting cross-fertilisation, and the dispersal of seeds." At the Field Club's next meeting on August 6, Captain Hyland spoke on "Geology in Flanders." Many of the patients knew Flanders' earth only too well, having sheltered in its bowels and buried comrades in its clay.

Late summer brought with it a few days of what Sassoon called "beastly fog," but Craiglockhart enjoyed enough sun for cricket, bowls, tennis, and croquet on Henry Carmichael's pristine lawns. For Carmichael, the war loomed as a permanent threat to his family. He had lost one son, Archie, at Gallipoli two years before. On August 16, his brother's son, Donnie Bayne Carmichael, died at Ypres with the Royal Field Artillery in the Passchendaele fighting. With his sons Alexander and Henry, a grandson, and a nephew still at the front, the devoted gardener toiled in Craiglockhart's acres dreading another of the War Office's unwelcome telegrams.

"I HAVE JUST BEEN READING Siegfried Sassoon," Owen wrote to Susan on August 17, "and am feeling at a very high pitch of emotion.

Nothing like his trench life sketches have ever been written or ever will be written." *The Old Huntsman* reduced to irrelevance the patriotic doggerel by civilian poets who had not been near the front. Poems glamorizing the war appalled Owen. Poetry, alongside newspapers, theater, film, music, fine arts, and music, had been reduced to propaganda. Three days after declaring war on Germany, Britain established a government press bureau to censor the news. Control of literature followed a few weeks later with the establishment of the War Propaganda Bureau (WPB). Its chief, Liberal MP and social reformer Charles Masterman, invited twenty-five of the country's most popular writers—among them J. M. Barrie, Arthur Conan Doyle, Ford Madox Ford, John Galsworthy, Rudyard Kipling, and H. G. Wells—to a conference on September 2, 1914, at his headquarters in Wellington House, near Buckingham Palace. The meeting's purpose was "to discuss how they could defend civilisation against the invading Hun." All attended, except Kipling, who sent a message of support. The writers went on to produce books and pamphlets demonizing the Germans and sanctifying British arms. Robert Graves believed they aimed "to make the English hate the Germans as they had never hated anyone before." Oxford classics scholar Gilbert Murray, although cooperating with the WPB, called it the "Mendacity Bureau."

The disinformation campaign infuriated Sassoon. "They all know how to win the war—in their highly paid articles!" he wrote. "Damn them." No aspect of British culture escaped the onslaught of nationalist zeal. Patriotic songs like "Keep the Home Fires Burning" and "It's a Long Way to Tipperary" roused audiences in Britain's music halls. War artists romanticized the noble British soldier on canvas and in stone, while novels portrayed him as the embodiment of all that was honorable in the British character. Poetry too succumbed to the mass mobilization of art.

Rudyard Kipling, John Masefield, and other poets of a generation too old to fight stimulated nationalist fervor among civilians in verse that left soldiers unmoved. Thirty-nine-year-old Masefield was one of the few who had been to France, but as a hospital orderly rather than as a soldier, before touring the United States to propagate the British cause. Unlike Sassoon and Owen, Masefield had not rotted underground with rats and lice, had not killed other men, and had never seen friends' bodies decomposing on barbed wire. Masefield poems like "August 1914" romanticized English warriors who left the "fields of home,"

> And died (uncouthly, most) in foreign lands
>   For some idea but dimly understood
> Of an English city never built by hands,
>   Which love of England prompted and made good . . .

Similar poems achieved wide circulation, but none portrayed the experience Owen knew. He had a particular distaste for one of the most popular poets of the day, Jessie Pope. Her *Daily Mail* contributions seemed as remote from reality as that newspaper's jingoist news reports:

> War-worn, khaki-clad figures lie,
>   Their faces rigid and grey—
> Stagger and drop where the bullets swarm,
>   Where the shrapnel is bursting loud,
> Die, to keep England safe and warm—
>   For a vigorous football crowd!

Patriotic myth and paeans to war heroes, not least by Poet Laureate Robert Bridges, enraged Owen. Typical of the official poetry was Bridges's homage to War Secretary Lord Kitchener, who had drowned on June 5, 1916, when a German mine sank the ship carrying him on a mission to Russia:

> Unflinching hero, watchful to foresee
> And face thy country's peril wheresoe'er,

Directing war and peace with equal care,
Till by long toil ennobled thou wert he
Whom England call'd and bade "Set my arm free
        To obey my will and save my honour fair" . . .

Sassoon was more dismissive of the fallen warrior, writing, "When will someone write the true life of Lord Kitchener, Britain's syphilitic hero?" Owen admired Sassoon's refusal to pay homage to the High Command, the clergy, and the politicians. Sassoon satirized and ridiculed them all for dispatching young men to death or the living death of permanent, disabling wounds:

The Bishop tells us: "When the boys come home,
They will not be the same; for they have fought in a just
     cause . . ."

"We're none of us the same!" the boys reply.
"For George lost both his legs; and Bill's stone blind;
"Poor Jim's shot through the lungs and like to die;
"And Bert's gone siphilitic: you'll not find
"A chap who's served that hasn't found *some* change."

And the Bishop said: "The ways of God are strange!"

Sassoon was a revelation, the first poet to capture the war that had caused Owen's breakdown. One Sassoon poem, "Died of Wounds," ended with the couplet "I fell asleep . . . next morning he was dead / And some Slight Wound lay smiling on his bed." Another, "The Death-Bed," depicted a scene familiar to every survivor of the trenches:

Light many lamps and gather round his bed.
Lend him your eyes, warm blood, and will to live.
Speak to him; rouse him; you may save him yet.
He's young; he hated war; how should he die
When cruel old campaigners win safe through?

But Death replied: "I chose him." So he went,
And there was silence in the summer night;
Silence and safety; and the veils of sleep.
Then, far away, the thudding of the guns.

Owen promised to send *The Old Huntsman*, of which he had bought several copies, to his mother. He added, "I think if I had the choice of making friends with Tennyson or with Sassoon, I should go to Sassoon." Sassoon had been at Craiglockhart more than three weeks. Shyness had so far prevented Owen from approaching him, but he was steeling himself to seek out his new idol and would let Susan know "what kind of pow wow we've had."

CHAPTER TEN

Mentors and Novices

T he War: 4th Year: 15th Day" headlined *The Times* on August 18, 1917, above its daily rundown of battles on land and sea from France to Africa to the Middle East. England's newspaper of record updated its regular roll call of men killed in action with the names of ten officers, most in their twenties. One, Second Lieutenant Frederick Charles Westmacott, would have turned twenty in a few days. He was the third of nine brothers to die. Five others had been wounded. News from France began, "Sir Douglas Haig last night reported the situation unchanged." With the Western Front yielding more than eighty thousand British casualties in August, *The Times* declared, "The war has brought new opportunities of heroism to us all. Every Briton in the full strength of manhood is a soldier, and the business of fighting is his duty."

At Craiglockhart, those who had done their duty were basking in summer sun on a peaceful Saturday far from the guns and the blood. Preparations were under way in the Recreation Hall for the weekly concert. The tennis courts and bowling greens were drawing men outdoors for their medically recommended exercise. For Wilfred

Owen, there was much to do. Before breakfast, he deposited the latest *Hydra* at the dining hall entrance. Evening would see him donning costume and makeup for the final two acts of *Lucky Durham*. In the meantime, the reticent subaltern faced a daunting task. Gathering a bundle of books, he marched up the hospital's marble staircase and along a dark, windowless corridor and tapped on a door. The man inside barely looked up from the golf clubs he was polishing. "The sun blazed into his room," Owen recalled later, "making his purple dressing suit of a brilliance—almost matching my sonnet." It was his first sight of the living poet he admired above all others, Siegfried Sassoon.

"Short, dark haired, and shyly hesitant," Sassoon described his visitor, "he stood for a moment before coming across to the window, where I was sitting on my bed." Owen was immediately in awe: "He is very tall and stately, with a fine firm chisel'd (how's that?) head . . . He himself is 30! Looks under 25!" He handed Sassoon his books, copies of *The Old Huntsman*, to sign for friends and himself. As Sassoon was about to autograph the last, he asked the young man his name. That was their introduction. "I had taken an instinctive liking to him," Sassoon would write, "and felt that I could talk freely." Their talk lasted for more than a half hour, mainly about Sassoon's poems and their connection to the war. Sassoon averred that his visitor's questions showed "reticent intelligence." As Owen departed, he mentioned that, although unpublished, he too was a poet.

The rapport born that afternoon was not between equals. Owen played disciple to Sassoon's master. Sassoon was six years older, a half foot taller, an established poet, a decorated warrior, and a Cambridge man. Owen had never published, harbored fears that senior officers suspected him of cowardice, and could only dream of Cambridge. The social gap separating them was tempered by commonalities: devotion to poetry, loyalty to their regiments, dependence on their mothers, and chaste homosexuality. Sassoon thought at first that Owen was "an interesting little chap but had not struck me as remarkable" and "a rather ordinary young man, though unobtrusively ardent in his responses to my lordly dictums about poetry." Owen's provincial, lower-middle-class accent grated on Sassoon's patrician ears, but it was not long before he appreciated "the velvety quality of his voice, which suggested the Keatsian richness of his artistry with words. It had the fluid texture of soft consonants and murmurous music." Meeting a poet in the hospital, especially one who admired his poems, pleased Sassoon. Pleasant for himself, Sassoon realized, but "momentous" for Owen. Owen had met only two published poets, Laurent Tailhade in France and Harold Monro at London's Poetry Bookshop, neither of whose writing he venerated as he did Sassoon's.

In the evening, Owen joined the cast of *Lucky Durham* in the Reception Hall. The concert program began with the march from Wagner's *Tannhäuser*. "Mustard Seed," replacing Peas Blossom as *Hydra* drama critic, praised the music for "the powerful work of the piano and first violin which made good the lack of wind instruments in our orchestra." Next came *Lucky Durham* with Owen in the part of "fashionable young" Arthur Wallcomb. "The scenes are frankly melodramatic," Mustard Seed wrote, "but melodrama at its best." The review lauded all the actors—the Pocketts, the Isaacsons, Major Bingham, and Lieutenant Davidson—except Owen. The omission was easily explained. Mustard Seed was Owen, still unwilling to name himself in print.

In the morning, Sassoon went to Glasgow by car and "lunched ponderously." A letter he wrote from the city's Central Station Hotel to Lady Ottoline Morrell praised the novel he had recommended to Rivers, Henri Barbusse's *Under Fire*, and thanked her for sending a volume of Keats. He was working at new poems while devoting more time to "slogging golf-balls on the hills above Edinburgh." Having been at Craiglockhart almost a month, he reflected, "A month ago

seems like a bad dream. 'And still the war goes on, *he* don't know why.'"
The quote was from his 1916 poem "In the Pink": "To-night he's in the
pink, but soon he'll die; / And still the war goes on; *he* don't know
why." The letter did not mention Wilfred Owen.

Owen's gushing letters home were all about Sassoon. He recounted
a second, more intimate encounter to his cousin Leslie Gunston: "Last
night when I went in he was struggling to read a letter from [H. G.]
Wells; whose handwriting is not only a slurred suggestion of words,
but in a dim pink ink!" Wells wanted to visit Sassoon, "not about Sassoon's state of health, but about *God the Invisible King* [a denunciation
of Christianity that Wells was writing]." Owen ventured his opinion
of *The Old Huntsman*, telling Sassoon "The Death-Bed" ("But Death
replied, 'I chose him.'") was "the finest poem." Sassoon, to Owen's
satisfaction, agreed. Owen then dared to show him "The Dead-Beat,"
a poem he had written in "Sassoon's style" just after their first meeting.
It concerned a soldier whose breakdown, like so many at Craiglockhart, elicited contempt from his peers:

> He dropped, more sullenly, than wearily,
>   Became a lump of stench, a clot of meat,
>   And none of us could kick him to his feet.
> He blinked at my revolver, blearily.

The fifth and final stanza read:

> We sent him down at last, he seemed so bad,
>   Although a strongish chap and quite unhurt.
>   Next day I heard the Doc's fat laugh: "That dirt
> You sent me down last night's just died. So glad!"

Sassoon considered the poem with care, telling Owen that the
middle stanzas were too facetious to fit with the first and last. This
made Owen feel that the entire poem was worthless, not what Sassoon

had said. Owen handed him "The Wrestlers" and some sonnets. Sassoon liked Owen's rendering of the Antaeus myth, but he pronounced another poem "perfect." Its Old Testament title was "Song of Songs":

> Sing me at morn but only with thy laugh
> Even as Spring that laugheth into leaf;
> Even as Love that laugheth after Life.

The near rhyming, in this instance alliterative, of each three-line stanza (laugh/leaf/Life) was a device Owen had been trying out with other poems and was a rarity in English poetry. Sassoon, while not commenting on the technique, asked Owen to copy the poem out for him. At the end of the improvised tutorial, Sassoon ordered, "Sweat your guts out writing poetry!" Owen muttered, "Eh?" Sassoon repeated, "Sweat your guts out, I say!"

That was the benediction Owen, consciously or not, needed to overcome the fear of making his poetry public. Sassoon recommended Martin Secker as future publisher "for a small volume of 10 or 20 poems" when Owen's work improved. He later admitted, "I have an uncomfortable suspicion that I was a bit slow in recognizing the exceptional quality of his poetic gift."

Flattered by Sassoon's attention, Owen was oblivious to his new teacher's emotional state. That morning, *The Times*'s register of the fallen had stunned Sassoon: "Killed in action, on the 14th Aug., Lt. (Temp. Capt.) STEPHEN GORDON HARBORD, M.C., R.F.A., third son of Rev. H. and Mrs. Harbord, Colwood Park, Bolney, aged 27." The Harbords were close family friends and neighbors from Sassoon's childhood. Sassoon had often hunted with Gordon Harbord and maintained a jocular wartime correspondence with him and his brother, Geoffrey. He had been writing a "cub hunting poem" for Gordon that he would now not be able to send. The shock revived the one he suffered when his brother Hamo died at Gallipoli in 1915. Owen might fill the void left by their deaths, but Sassoon had not grown close enough to his youthful admirer to confide his sorrow.

OWEN, anxious to show his early work to Sassoon, wrote to his cousin Leslie Gunston asking for manuscripts he had entrusted to him. A few days later, he sent *The Old Huntsman* to his father, Tom, with the comment, "There is nothing better this century can offer you." Several pages were marked for his father's attention, including a prewar poem that Virginia Woolf had praised in *The Times Literary Supplement*: "'Morning Express,' page 56 is the kind of thing that makes me despair of myself; everyone says 'I could have done that myself!' Only no one ever did."

Sassoon's "Morning Express," about the mundane departure of a passenger train, included the lines:

> Boys, indolent eyed, from baskets leaning back,
> Question each face; a man with a hammer steals
> Stooping from coach to coach; with clang and clack,
> Touches and tests, and listens to the wheels . . .

Owen missed his family. Therapy, poetry, and Sassoon's friendship were lifting his spirits, but recovery was a long way off. "I was make-believing that I was a free creature here," he wrote to his father, "but it is only that my chain has been let out a little. I should only hurt myself with tugging at it."

Developments on the battlefield tormented him—"the Russians panicking and getting out of the war, and ourselves deeper and deeper into it." Writing to his sister, Mary, he blamed the war for this "snappy" editorial he was about to publish in *The Hydra*:

> Many of us who came to the Hydro slightly ill are now getting dangerously well . . . In this excellent Concentration

Camp we are fast recovering from the shock of coming to England. For some of us were not a little wounded by the apparent indifference of the public and the press, not indeed to our precious selves, but to the unimagined durances of the fit fellow in the line.

Discouraged as he was, he told Mary, he received occasional solace: "But a word from Sassoon, though he is not a cheery dog himself, makes me cut capers of pleasure."

The *Hydra* of September 1 achieved a breakthrough for Owen with the publication of two original poems. The first was "Dreamers" by the great Sassoon. Signed only "S. S.," it contrasted the men's misery at the front with their longing for the lives they had left and to which some would not return:

> I see them in foul dug-outs, gnawed by rats,
> And in the ruined trenches, lashed with rain,
> Dreaming of things they did with balls and bats,
> And mocked by hopeless longing to regain
> Bank-holidays, and picture shows, and spats,
> And going to the office in the train.

Sassoon had agreed to let Owen publish it in *The Hydra* on condition that Owen published a poem of his own in the same issue. This was "Song of Songs," the poem Sassoon had pronounced "perfect." Its four three-line stanzas ended:

> Sing me at midnight with your murmurous heart!
> Let youth's immortal-moaning chords be heard
> Throbbing through you, and sobbing, unsubdued.

Sassoon sent *The Hydra* to Ottoline Morrell, scribbling under Owen's poem, "The man who wrote this brings me quantities & I have to say kind things. He will improve, I think!" Owen mailed the issue to his cousin Leslie Gunston, writing under "Song of Songs," "My first printed poem!" His debut as a published poet signaled growing self-confidence. Brock's therapy and Sassoon's friendship were dissipating his shyness and uncertainty.

OWEN'S FRIENDSHIP WITH Charles Mayes mirrored his developing attachment to Sassoon. As Sassoon was six years his senior, Owen had five years on Mayes. Sassoon was his mentor, the role Owen assumed with Mayes. Brock's occasional treatment of Owen and Mayes together gave each patient insights into the other's trauma. At *The Hydra*, Owen provided Mayes a forum for his written work. Mayes repaid the favor by introducing Owen to a glittering avant-garde milieu unlike any he had known.

The two young men in khaki officers' uniforms and blue armbands left the hospital on Saturday, September 1, for Stockbridge, a suburb just beyond Edinburgh's elegant New Town. There, in a magnificent Georgian house at 21 Saint Bernard's Crescent, Owen entered an unfamiliar world of what he called "some 'modern' people." "Modern" meant bohemian. Two married couples, the Grays and the Steinthals, shared the residence. The drawing room with its "black carpetless floor, white walls, solitary superb picture, grand piano, Empire sofa" was nothing like the respectable rugs, wallpaper, and Bibles among which Owen had grown up.

Saint Bernard's Crescent was the epicenter of an Edinburgh Bloomsbury, where artists, sculptors, and intellectuals mixed with the upper and lower reaches of society. Twenty-four-year-old Leonard Gray and his alluring twenty-nine-year-old wife, Maidie, had rented the house from a married couple of painters, Eric Robertson and Cecile Walton. Robertson, a Quaker, was serving with the Friends Ambulance Service in France. To save money while he was away, Cecile, who was then twenty-six and a blossoming painter, had moved into her parents' house with their young son and given the Grays a three-year lease. Leonard Gray, a captain in the Royal Scots Regiment, had been relieved of combat duty in order to run the family's arms factory in Edinburgh. The Grays invited a sculptress, Maria Sophia Zimmern, and her husband, Paul Cuthbert Steinthal, to move in with them and share costs. Maidie and Maria, a mere month apart in age, were both mothers. Maria had two children, a year-old girl, Pixie, and a newborn son, Martin. Maidie's daughter, Deirdre, was three. Maria worked in her studio each day, leaving Maidie to manage the household and the maid.

When Owen and Mayes arrived that afternoon, the cohabiting couples appeared to be holding court. Paul Steinthal was home on a leave from France, where he was serving with the Royal Artillery. His wife, the German-born Maria, was nursing their infant son. The Grays lavished hospitality on the two junior officers. Such was Owen's excitement that he wrote to Susan, "I think they are genuine people— the moreso because they adore their progeny than because they profess to admire my poetry." He sketched the women's short hairstyles, fashionable among liberated *femmes fatales*, and complimented their "decorative gowns."

Owen's one note of deprecation was that "the women think themselves artists." That was unfair to Maria Steinthal, a talented sculptress, who had studied with Aristide Maillol in Paris and exhibited in both Paris and Brussels. Maidie had modeled for Eric Robertson, whose portrait of her with her sister, *Miss Maidie and Miss Elsie Scott*, had been exhibited at the Royal Scottish Academy in 1912. The portrait of two handsome young Scotswomen with ruddy, voluptuous features draped in long skirts, furs, and caps could have been of Russian countesses. Robertson's usual subjects, to genteel Edinburgh's disdain, were nudes.

At Saint Bernard's Crescent, Owen began negotiating a maze of social complexities in a class radically different from that of his Shropshire family and the sturdy Newboults and Bulmans in Scotland. That world nonetheless welcomed the young provincial whom

Mayes brought into their midst. Maidie thought her daughter adored him, "and the tacit understanding between him and the child was almost uncanny." Amid cries of babies that suited the general chaos, they discussed the "solitary superb picture" that caught Owen's eye: *Avatar* by Henry John Lintott. The large oil painting was an ethereal, William Blake–like image of the war that depicted something Owen was attempting with words. Two barefoot men, possibly angels, in diaphanous sheets bore a stretcher heavenward. The pale head of a soldier protruded from a black shroud, oblivious to his journey through milky, sun-soaked clouds. It symbolized martyrdom and release from terror, themes that attracted Owen. Lintott, who lived with his wife, Audrey, opposite the Grays and Steinthals, had loaned it to his neighbors prior to its exhibition at the Royal Scottish Academy. Owen did not know Lintott's name, only that he was "the painter of the finest picture now in the Edinburgh Gallery." *Avatar* affected him, but the house's inhabitants impressed him more.

Owen and Mayes left the Grays and Steinthals in time for Saturday's concert. Franz von Suppé's overture, "Morning, Noon and Night in Vienna," opened the program to much applause. Craiglockhart's repertoire, despite the war, often featured music by German and Austrian composers. The hospital's musicians clung to a culture that defied borders, just as Rivers and Brock championed the Austrian Freud. Next to the stage came, in Mustard Seed's words, "some charming dances by Miss Jackson." The lithe, thirteen-year-old girl inspired Owen to write to his mother, "When I see a Ballet Dance, I surrender half my kingdom, lose my head, and put it on a charger." The evening continued with comedians and popular tunes. Mustard Seed commented on one that revealed a regrettable if common prejudice among Englishmen of the era, "Mr. Baylis scored a success with his coon songs."

Brock and Owen met after the concert at eleven o'clock for an hour's therapy. Owen wondered when a Medical Board might release him. Brock asked, wasn't he happy at Craiglockhart? Owen realized that he was. Life at the hospital was not only healing him, it was transforming his poetry and advancing him socially. Lacking Sassoon's agonies over separation from comrades at the front, he felt no urgency to leave.

He returned with Mayes to Saint Bernard's Crescent on Thursday, September 6, for "a perfect little dinner." Paul Steinthal's Oxford history degree intimidated him, as did Leonard Gray's ownership of a munitions factory. Yet his ready acceptance by social superiors reassured him. He reconsidered his opinion that their wives "thought themselves artists": "The ladies have more effusiveness, but are genuine. One is really witty and the other is a sculptor of great power." At the end of dinner, his hosts "showered books upon me." The witty one, Maidie Gray, invited him to explore Edinburgh with her and meet an Italian street singer she liked. It was the kind of outing that Brock encouraged.

Having overstayed at Saint Bernard's Crescent, Owen and Mayes reached Craiglockhart after curfew and crept in to avoid detection. Owen was settling into bed at midnight, when a nurse burst in. "Dr. Brock will see you at once Mr. Owen!" she announced. Fearing a reprimand, Owen did not bother to change out of his pyjamas and was in a sweat when he reached Brock's office. Brock told him only that he was expected the next day for lunch in Edinburgh with a woman who would guide him through the Outlook Tower's Slum Gardens. The guide would be Miss Wyer, a member of the Open Spaces Committee and one of "Brock's ladies," who had volunteered to help the doctor's patients.

Owen turned up for lunch with Miss Wyer and her sister at their elegant house in Rothesay Place. Miss Wyer took him to the Slum Gardens, Patrick Geddes's green land that afforded the poor healthy work and a little fresh air. There he met some of "Edinburgh's submerged tenth" that Brock wanted him to know. Owen feared his officer's uniform distanced him from a shabbily dressed pauper, "but I

cannot tell him that." At the end of the excursion, the maiden Wyer
sisters gave Owen tea at home. "Then," he recalled, "in sailed an enor-
mous old lady of the type of old lady I have but once or twice met—
outside Thackeray—intellectual, witty, vigorous: told some good stories
and eat a huge tea." With these older, educated women, as with the
artists at Saint Bernard's Crescent, Owen was discovering "'kultur' in
its universal sense" and his changing views of "sculpture, state-craft,
ethics, etc., etc., in these strange beings and places were enough to
make the day memorable in itself."

When he returned to Craiglockhart in the evening, Sassoon invited him to his room. The older man disparaged some of Owen's
verses, "amended others, and rejoiced over a few." Sassoon then declaimed some of his own recent work, which was flowing more freely
since he met Owen. Owen thought they were "superb beyond anything
in his Book." One struck Owen as "the most exquisitely painful war
poem of any language or time. I don't tell him so, or that I am not
worthy to light his pipe." He suggested improvements, and Sassoon
made changes. The disciple was leveling up with the master.

Sassoon lent him Barbusse's *Under Fire* and advised him to read
The Cambridge Magazine.

Owen's eager embrace of ergotherapy involved him in so many pursuits that he worried whether he could finish the latest *Hydra* on time.
With the help of his deputy editor, John Bell Salmond, he did. Yet
amid poetry writing, studying with Sassoon, visiting Saint Bernard's
Crescent, and talking to Brock, he missed a Field Club outing on September 7 to the Astronomer Royal for Scotland, Ralph Allan Sampson. Sassoon made up for it by inviting Owen to pay a personal call on
the scientist at his observatory. "So," wrote Owen, "I shall see much
more than what I missed!"

Saturday brought his rendezvous with Maidie Gray. Like Miss
Wyer, she would guide him through the poorer quarters of Edinburgh.
Meticulous about his dress, Owen appeared in civilian garb—"a hooli-

gan manner and cap, but unimpeachable gloves, boots and tie." Mrs. Gray, as he always referred to her, wore what he called "weird clothes and some priceless rings." They carried food for Tomaso, a one-eyed Italian street singer "with a most tragic history and a fine personality." Owen recalled, "Tomaso was out, but we found a suitable object of compassion in his (unmistakably Italian) boy who had impaled his leg on a railing spike."

As they promenaded through the squalid streets, Maidie observed in Owen a rare compassion for the inhabitants. She would not have known that this dated to his youthful reading of Shelley, and his work among the indigent of Dunsden parish that had alienated him from its vicar. Brock wanted Owen to know the Edinburgh underclass, who were as much victims of the social order as the soldiers dying at the front. Owen felt sympathy for them, but he was like a tourist in their midst. He felt he belonged among the higher reaches of society, the Grays and Steinthals, and spent more time with them than with "Edinburgh's submerged tenth." That did not negate his sympathy for the poor, which brought Maidie closer to the handsome young officer. She wrote, "The bond which drew us together was an intense pity for suffering humanity—a need to alleviate it, wherever possible, and an inability to shirk the sharing of it, even when this seemed useless." Maidie saw Owen gravitate to people in need and noticed that he "was adored—there's no other word for it." Prime among the adorers was Maidie herself.

Their next stop was "a delightful dark and filthy curiosity shop," where Owen bought a Roman vase for far less than it was worth. Maidie's purchase was a bronze lamp that Owen thought was "doubtful Roman." When Maidie presented it to him as a token of affection, he had little choice but to give her his Roman vase. They went on to Princes Street to see Maria Steinthal and find a present for Charles Mayes. Mayes was appearing that evening in *The Marriage of Kitty*, the theatrical production for the evening's concert. They purchased a laurel wreath

with which to crown him at the end of the performance. Owen ate dinner at Saint Bernard's Crescent and caught a taxi to Craiglockhart.

Despite the normality of the day, the evening's theater brought a
reminder of why he, Mayes, and the others had been sent to Craiglockhart. "Poor Mayes overdid himself and has lost his speech," Owen
wrote, as Mayes's muteness rendered the laurel superfluous. In the
morning, Mayes came to Owen's room and woke him up. The teen-
aged soldier still could not speak. With his eyes and shaky gestures, he
appealed to Owen for help. "I thought he was mad," Owen wrote, "and
have yet to get over it! He has been often seized thus, and will soon get
right again." Later that Sunday, the two attended the General Meeting
of Officers. It voted to extend Owen's tenure as *Hydra* editor and
Mayes as treasurer.

SASSOON SENT AN APOLOGY on September 5 to Lady Ottoline for
not having answered her recent letters, explaining that he had "been
knocked flat once again by the best sporting friend I ever had getting
killed on August 14—in France. He was indeed my greatest friend
before the war." Gordon Harbord's love of horses, hunting, and the
outdoors prompted Sassoon to reflect, "When the <u>un</u>intellectual people go it is much the worst—one feels they've so much to lose." He
enclosed the poem he had written for Harbord, "A Wooden Cross (To
S. G. H.)," with its mournful yet enraged final stanza:

> Come back, come back; you didn't want to die;
> And all this war's a sham, a stinking lie;
> And the glory that our fathers laud so well
> A crowd of corpses freed from pangs of hell.

IN EARLY SEPTEMBER 1917, a United States Army psychiatrist in a
newly minted major's uniform reported to Craiglockhart. His credentials

more than qualified him to be the first American military psychoanalyst sent overseas. Thirty-eight-year-old Dr. Arthur Hiler Ruggles had graduated Phi Beta Kappa from Dartmouth College in his native New Hampshire in 1902 before taking his doctorate of medicine at Harvard three years later. Like his prospective colleagues Rivers and Brock, he studied psychology in Germany. His instructor at the University of Munich in 1912 and 1913, Professor Emil Kraepelin, had taught Rivers in Heidelberg twenty years earlier. Ruggles believed "the beginning of psychiatry as an independent science" was the professor's classification of mental illnesses into two distinct categories: those caused by external influences and others due to a damaged brain. On his return to the United States in late 1913, Butler Hospital in Providence, Rhode Island, appointed him "first assistant physician." He was treating mental cases there when, on April 6, 1917, the United States declared war on Germany. Unprepared in every way for the clash of forces in Europe, the U.S. Army was expanding from a strength of one hundred thousand to two million men, and upgrading basic services, including medical care. Ruggles joined the Sanitary Corps, so called by the War Department "for want of a better name," just after its establishment on June 30. Of the thousands of new army physicians, only 108 were psychiatrists or psychologists. None had experience of shell shock.

The army issued Dr. Ruggles a major's oak leaf insignia only a few weeks before he embarked for Britain. Ruggles found a congenial environment in Scotland, whose early autumn leaves were turning the woods into varied hues of crimson and russet as in his native New England. Moreover, Craiglockhart's psychiatric methodology corresponded to his own. Rivers and Brock shared his disdain for painful practices like electric-shock therapy, cold-water ducking, and convulsion-producing drugs. All three doctors relied on forms of Freudian analysis. Ruggles had Professor Kraepelin's teaching in common with Rivers, and his belief in the importance of purposeful work put him in accord with Brock. "If the work that the therapist assigns to the patient has some meaning," Ruggles wrote in words Brock himself might have used, "and is not merely a device to kill time, it will give the patient a feeling of dignity, self-respect, and accomplishment." An admirer called Ruggles "this humane healer." One patient wrote, "Major Bryce & Capt. Rivers sallied forth quite often like two schoolboys, gibing at each other, and when Major Ruggles arrived he joined in & they made a cheery trio."

Craiglockhart's overworked physicians welcomed the extra pair of hands, but Ruggles's primary mission was to obtain what the Butler Hospital Annual Report called "preliminary training." When American boys hit the battlefield in the coming spring, the conditions their British allies had endured since 1914 would affect them as well. No one was immune to mental stress. Ruggles admired Rivers and Brock as, in his words, "outstanding British psychiatrists." With more than a year treating shell shock, the Britons had much to teach him. So too did the shattered British soldiers he was about to meet. "While there," Ruggles wrote, "I began to learn why men, both weak and strong, suffered breakdown." That knowledge would prepare him to assume command of a base hospital's psychiatric unit in France when the first American doughboys fell victim to the unavoidable mental shocks of war.

CHAPTER ELEVEN

Who Die as Cattle

Britain, in common with its allies and enemies, faced a manpower shortage as the war entered its fourth year. With four million British men in uniform, civilian work fell to women, conscientious objectors, prisoners, and other noncombatants. When Scottish farmers called for labor to bring in the autumn harvest in September 1917, officers from Craiglockhart leapt at the challenge. Rising at 5:30 each morning to work at three local farms led one volunteer to quote comedian Harry Lauder that "it's nice to get up in the morning, but it's nicer to lie in your bed!" The volunteers cut wheat and oats, tied them into sheaves and set them at angles to one another, pointing skyward like rifle stacks, in "stooks." One officer-laborer recalled, "We were all very shy of it for the first day or two, but we soon learned the gentle art of 'stooking' . . . there is a knack in this job, as in most others, as was proved to us when the first gust of wind came—only those 'stooks' with plenty of 'leg' survived the efforts spent over them." Harvesting served a dual purpose: helping farmers to feed the nation and giving mentally distressed men the healthy, purposeful work that Brock and Ruggles prescribed.

While some officers were "bringing in the sheaves," others constructed miniature sailboats to race in the Model Yacht Club regatta on September 3. Twelve patients entered their crafts in a fierce competition on Craiglockhart's pond. Only one boat made it over the finish line without being disqualified for "fouling." The hospital's golf team competed against the Mortonhill Club in early September, when it suffered a "rather heavy defeat." Sassoon, a member of Mortonhill, did not play for either side.

ON SUNDAY MORNING, September 9, an overworked Wilfred Owen rose at ten o'clock—too late for breakfast. Anticipating a hearty lunch at Sassoon's golf club, he arrived famished at one o'clock. Sassoon, however, was absent. "My discipleship was put to a severe trial," Owen admitted. It was 2:15 when Sassoon trudged in from the eighteenth hole and offered him lunch. Owen, in his words, then put Sassoon "to the test of writing a poem in three minutes in the manner of the *Graphic*, etc. He produced 12 lines in 4 minutes. Absolutely indistinguishable from the style of thing in the Magazines." Afterward, the pair walked to Edinburgh's Observatory for the meeting Owen had missed with Ralph Allen Sampson, Scotland's Astronomer Royal. As they had tea, Owen, ever sensitive to the young, noticed Sampson's children were "dumfounded with boredom." Sassoon was oblivious to the youngsters until Owen "took courage" and spoke to Sampson's son. Then, wrote Owen, "the only stars Sassoon saw were in the electric-blue eyes of little Tom."

Craiglockhart's theater company staged an unusual event the next evening—a stand-alone play on a Monday rather than as one element of the regular Saturday concert. Mrs. Pockett directed *Sweet Lavender*, a sentimental comedy, with her husband, Lieutenant J. W. G., as a corrupt banker redeemed in the final act. Owen attended the performance and probably wrote the unsigned review that lauded his friend Charles Mayes: "Mr. Mayes, as the adopted son and lover of Lavender, had a very difficult part, and, despite a little obvious nervousness, carried it through with pleasing success." That Mayes at last played his role without becoming speechless pointed toward recovery.

In a letter written to his mother after the curtain fell, Owen complained that brother officers were not writing enough for *The Hydra*. The shortage obliged him to fill much of the journal himself. Yet his finished compositions gave him a measure of satisfaction. He boasted to Susan, "My pen is wet from an amusing contribution to myself: Extracte from the Chronicles of Wilfred de Salope, Knight: describing the Hospital Life in mediaeval jargon":

> For indeed it is an abode of much invitingness, where men may well repose from the noise of battle; where hunger is but seldom endured; where no strong liquors tempt the heart to sin, and where all dangerous arms may be laid aside—nay, perforce must be surrendered. For myself, when taking up lodgement herein, did lay my firearm by my pallet-side, as it had long been my wont; but lo! At morn it was utterly vanished away . . .

The saga lauded "the Chief Lord of the Castle, the Knight out of Fife," obviously Commandant Bryce. "Both doughty and courteous is he, of noble aspect and right jovial demeanour, and beloved by all that have dealings with him. Seldom doeth he administer rebukes." While staff and patients alike shared Owen's admiration for "the Major," War Office traditionalists looked askance at the hospital's unmilitary practices.

Bryce's regime was relaxed, but Brock's wasn't. The rigorous clinician kept Owen tethered to a hectic schedule—*Hydra*, poetry, Field Club, Outlook Tower, teaching, learning German, and visiting the poor. More was on the way, as Owen wrote to Susan:

> Brock wants me to get busy with Scouts now!
> Chase wants a Lecture on "Soil" for the Field Club.
> I just want to get home.

⬦⬦⬦⬦⬦⬦⬦⬦⬦⬦

SASSOON'S ATTACHMENT TO "proud isolation" emerged in his correspondence and his disdain for fellow patients. When he assembled
with the other "failures" at dinner, he cast a critical eye. Most of the
men around him were "average types," and some "wouldn't have had
much success in life at the best of times." At one dinner, Sassoon sat
between two "bad stammerers—victims of 'anxiety neurosis' as the
saying went." The dining hall resembled a university senior commons
room with a high table for doctors and refectory tables below for patients. Sassoon gazed up at Rivers, who looked weary and ignored his
food. A year of working to heal mental wounds was pushing Rivers to
the limit of his endurance. Any psychiatrist hearing accounts of incon-
solable suffering could not shake them off at day's end, and Rivers was
more sensitive than most. It would soon be time for his first leave in a
year at Craiglockhart. The prospect worried Sassoon. How would he
cope without his "father confessor" for three weeks?

Friends on the outside compensated for Sassoon's self-imposed
separation from the Craiglockhart community. Robert Graves, Robbie
Ross, Roderic Meiklejohn, and others visited, and he maintained a
lively correspondence. He and Graves exchanged poems and arguments about the war. Graves, who was at the Royal Welch Fusiliers'
Litherland headquarters, sent him proofs of his upcoming poetry collection from publisher William Heinemann, *Fairies and Fusiliers*. The
letter he enclosed with the book complained about "the worse people
than ever" in the Litherland mess.

> You are much better off: at least, Sassons, I'd like you to tell me
> honestly are these shell shock fellow-patients of yours getting
> on your nerves? I'd be very unhappy if I thought they were:
> you talk of golf with lunatics, but I hope to God it's not as bad
> as that. Damn Rivers, why should he go and get ill like that and
> leave you?

Graves added that their friend Second Lieutenant Julian Dadd, had been discharged from the army with "brainfever," a euphemism for shell shock. Dadd and his brother Edmund, both subalterns in the Royal Welch Fusiliers, had lost another brother, Stephen, at Gallipoli. Like the men at Craiglockhart, Julian cracked under pressure of battle. Sassoon's guilt intensified. Why didn't he, as Graves urged, go back to the regiment and share the men's suffering?

Sassoon wrote to Ross on September 17 praising Graves's poetry volume as "a wonderful expression of him." Just as Sassoon had dedicated one of his poems in *The Old Huntsman*, "Letter Home," to Graves, Graves addressed "Letter to S. S. from Mametz Wood" to Sassoon. The poem imagined the two veterans traveling after the war from Graves's Welsh hills to the exotic Orient:

> So then we'll kiss our families,
> And sail away across the seas
> (The God of Song protecting us)
> To the great hills of Caucasus.
> Robert will learn the local *bat*
> For billeting and things like that,
> If Siegfried learns the piccolo
> To charm the people as we go . . .
>
> In old Baghdad we'll call a halt
> At the Sâshuns' [Sassoons'] ancestral vault . . .
>
> And doing wild, tremendous things
> In free adventure, quest and fight,
> And God! What poetry we'll write!

Graves's poetry, like Owen's, was flowing at this time, but lack of privacy hindered Sassoon's. His Scottish roommate's hearty interruptions frustrated him until, in mid-September, the man was discharged from the hospital. Sassoon at last began to write undisturbed, but the solitary idyll was short-lived. "I was rejoicing in getting a room to myself—my late companion having gone—" he wrote, "but after two days a man of forty-five with iron-grey hair, an eyeglass and an aquiline nose has floated in." Sassoon called the monocle-wearing officer "the Theosophist, since he was of that way of thinking (and overdid it a bit in conversation)." The man's constant presence, pompous elocution, and affected manner prevented Sassoon from thinking, let alone writing. Sassoon conceded, however, that he was avuncular and tolerant and had "come back from the front suffering from not being quite young enough to stand the strain."

The poems Sassoon managed to produce were falling short of the quality he had achieved in *The Old Huntsman*. On September 22, the pacifist *Cambridge Magazine* published one, "Editorial Impressions," probably more for political content than artistic merit. The poem savaged war correspondents as mere propagandists:

> "One can tell
> You've gathered big impressions!" Grinned the lad
> Who'd been severely wounded in the back
> In some wiped-out impossible Attack.
> "Impressions? Yes, most vivid! I am writing
> A little book called *Europe on the Rack*,
> Based on notes made while witnessing the fighting . . .
> I watched one daring beggar looping loops,
> Soaring and diving like some bird of prey.
> And through it all I felt that splendour shine
> Which makes us win."
> The soldier sipped his wine.
> "Ah, yes, but it's the Press that leads the way!"

"Autumn was asserting itself, and a gale got up that night," wrote Sassoon of a storm during the autumnal equinox, September 23. "I lay awake listening to its melancholy surgings and rumblings as it buffeted the big building." Nature's lament turned his thoughts to the Ypres salient, "that morass of misery and doom." His almost-wish to be there with the regiment "meant that the reality of the War had still got its grip on me." At the approach of dawn, he awoke from "an uneasy slumber" to see someone standing near the door. Could he be a sleep-walking patient? Staring at the figure, Sassoon recognized a beige greatcoat worn by a fellow subaltern in his Royal Welch Fusiliers' company, Second Lieutenant Edward Leslie Orme. But Orme was dead, killed in battle the previous May. Sassoon turned to his Theosophist roommate, who was staring at him from his bed across the room. When he looked back at the door, Orme had gone. "Did you see anyone come into the room?" Sassoon asked. "He hadn't seen anyone. Perhaps I hadn't either." He wanted to discuss it with Rivers, but by the time he went downstairs Rivers had left for his three-week leave.

For Maidie Gray's thirtieth birthday on September 19, the Grays invited Owen, Mayes, Maria Steinthal, Cecile Walton, and Edinburgh University's librarian, Frank Nicholson, to dinner in the Caledonian Hotel's grill. At seven o'clock that evening, Maidie paraded from Queensferry Street into the lobby of the "Caley," as Scots called their capital's grandest hotel. Owen was on her arm, with Leonard Gray, Maria, and Mayes in train. Nicholson met them in the opulent, chan-deliered grill, where waiters guided them to a table. Cecile Walton thought the occasion had the "most piquant air," until Maidie slipped her a note asking her to be nice to the young officer on her left, "a dear, a real dear." The officer was Owen. Cecile made an effort, but the only responses she received from the reserved subaltern were "Oh, rather" and "I should think so." Maidie, infatuated with Owen and woozy with drink, confided her romantic woes in Nicholson. She drank more wine as the evening progressed, sighing that she "never had had such a happy birthday." Dinner was ending as Craiglockhart's curfew hour approached. Owen and Mayes bade farewell, and the others decamped on foot to 21 Saint Bernard's Crescent to prolong the celebration.

Leonard Gray took Maria's hand and led the group homeward beside the Water of Leith. With Leonard and Maria well ahead on the moonlit path, Maidie blurted, "Owen is so charming you can't help loving him, don't you love him Mr. Nicholson? Don't you Cecile?" A sobbing Maidie then declared that her husband and Maria had fallen in love, stressing the affair was "all quite spiritual there's no sex about it." Captain Gray's reputation and subsequent propositioning of Cecile Walton made that unlikely.

In the sitting room at Saint Bernard's Crescent, the raucous soirée would have had Shropshire lad Owen blushing. Cecile stripped off her clothes and donned a flimsy, translucent shift she fashioned from one of Maidie's silk tunics and Maria's scarf. The young, attractive artist danced for the assembled company to gramophone recordings of Wagner. As her gyrations became more lascivious, Maidie joined to the rhythm of Hungarian rhapsodies. When the music paused, Cecile, suddenly embarrassed at her nakedness, sobered up, dressed, and fled to her parents' house.

She feared her behavior had upset Frank Nicholson, but the librarian remembered her less than he did Owen. The two men had met briefly at the Grays' on a previous occasion, when, Nicholson recalled, "even before I had exchanged a word with him, I was conscious of that immediate attraction which his presence seems to have exercised on a great number of people." More than youth and comeliness, he felt, "it was rather that the youth and comeliness were so strongly expressive of the personality behind them." At Maidie's birthday dinner, Owen told Nicholson, a German scholar, that he had been studying the language at Berlitz in Edinburgh. With the course completed, he asked Nicholson to tutor him.

Owen appeared two days later at the university library for his first lesson. Nicholson found him "a delightful pupil," who grasped the essentials of grammar as they studied a German novel. The tutor soon understood why Owen had chosen German:

He had brought with him from the Front a very keen realization of the agony which the combatant nations, one and all, were enduring, and his sense of pity, which must have been strong in him by nature and had been intensified by his experiences, enabled him to regard Germany as a fellow-sufferer with the rest and made him wish, I think, to prepare himself for any future opportunities of holding intercourse with the Germans.

Owen's compassion for suffering enemies was not universal at Craiglockhart. An unsigned reminiscence in the September 15 *Hydra* epitomized a more common view. The author described seeing German prisoners of war under armed guard in France with "their trousers and breeches bearing the well-known letters painted as large as possible in healthy black paint—P.G. [*Prisonnier de Guerre*]—one letter on each leg." As the prisoners unloaded potatoes from a captured German tramp steamer, a "large lazy Uhlan," German cavalry trooper, heard the wheels of caissons laden with French artillery shells scraping the cobblestones. Then,

> A grim smile passes across his ugly face as he pauses to think with some satisfaction of the barbarous and wanton cruelties he has perpetrated on his way from Germany—the homes he has demolished, the helpless girls and women he has violated, the little children whose irreparable injuries cry to heaven for vengeance and whose prayers are being heard by the arrival of these countless munitions of war.

Hatred of the Germans was anathema, not only to Owen, but to the Craiglockhart psychiatrists who had studied in Germany. Rivers, Brock, and Ruggles counted German scholars among their friends and utilized Germany's medical advances. German psychologist colleagues appeared in Rivers's dreams, and he regretted the academic rupture wrought by war. In his book *Conflict and Dream*, he took exception to "the fact that several recent writers in the English medical press had regarded Freud's nationality as good evidence for the worthlessness of his views." Sassoon recalled that "it pained him deeply to feel he was 'at war' with German scientists." To Rivers, fighting "German militarism" may have been necessary, but hating Germans was wrong.

THE MEDICAL BOARD that consigned Wilfred Owen to Craiglockhart on June 25 had declared him unfit even for light duty for three months. With the three months elapsing, Owen's first board at the hospital was scheduled for September 25. The doctors might return him to the trenches, post him to a noncombatant job in Britain, or, if they judged him incurable, discharge him. Owen was determined to stay in the army in some capacity, writing, "S. [Sassoon] wants to get me a green-tab job in England. I think he could." "Green-tab" implied intelligence, for which Owen's proficiency in French and study of German qualified him. Nothing came of the suggestion. Brock warned Owen the board was likely to keep him at the hospital. While some of his symptoms, especially the trembling, had vanished, the stammering and the nightmares lingered.

On the morning of September 25, Owen lectured thirty-nine boys at Edinburgh's Tynecastle High School—part of the Craiglockhart Boys Training Club inaugurated on September 18 to provide pupils with ten classes each week. It was another Brock project to bind his patients to a community as well as to educate boys whose parents could not afford private-school fees. *The Hydra* commented that "the boys seem very keen, and the Headmaster is pleased at the work." While other officers taught "map-reading, signalling, first aid, and physical culture," all military-related subjects, Owen chose English literature. He told the boys about Robert Louis Stevenson, who had lived in and written about Scottish terrain that the boys knew. "I think one of the most humanly useful things I am doing now is the teaching at Tynecastle School," he wrote to his mother. "Did I tell you what a great time

I had on Tuesday with the 39 boys. Their 'Teacher' [Mrs. Edward Fullerton] is a charming girl—wife (of course) of an Army Doctor. She had the exquisite tact to leave me alone, but I requested her company for the lesson." More lessons were to come in the classroom and on field trips, as Owen weaved teaching into his schedule. A verse by one of his pupils in the school's magazine charmed him so much that he quoted it to Susan:

> Mr Seaton bought a motor car
> And had it painted yellow.
> In goggles and a big fur coat,
> He looked a handsome fellow.

"Observe the astonishing conciseness of the thing," he urged. "I called for the poet—a wizened little pinch-face, about two feet high!"

The board that met that day did not inform Owen of its decision, and he was unsure which outcome he preferred. The uncertainty itself was a sign that he was not ready to resume his duties at the front. On the one hand, he wanted to believe his sanity had been restored. Yet an extension of his confinement would not have been unwelcome. It allowed him to meet artists in Edinburgh, improve his German, and satisfy his boyish curiosity. He wrote to his mother on the day the board convened, "Last week has been a pretty full one. I might if I wanted become mildly 'lionized by Edinburgh society.' The best visit I made was to John Duncan, a pretty great artist, living near the Grays. He is 'one of the ones' in the [Royal Scottish] Academy." Maidie Gray had taken him to meet Duncan, who lived with his wife, Christine, and their two children at 29 Saint Bernard's Crescent. The fifty-one-year-old painter had illustrated *The Evergreen* magazine for Brock's mentor, Patrick Geddes, and was a pillar of Geddes's Celtic Revival. He had tutored Maidie's landlady, Cecile Walton, at the Edinburgh College of Art and introduced her to the artist she would marry, Eric Robertson. A woman's downcast face in one of Duncan's Pre-Raphaelite-like paintings saddened Owen, but Duncan enchanted him. Owen lingered so long into the afternoon that he missed a rendezvous with Henry Lintott, whose mystical painting *Avatar* had impressed him on his first visit to the Grays. He visited Lintott a few days later, finding the artist to be "an excellent gentleman, blessed by nature with a club foot, for he is still 'of age.'"

Owen's burgeoning social life and embrace of myriad projects pointed toward recovery, but war dreams featuring bleak images of caves, bulging eyes, demons, and blood implied the cure was incomplete. Brock viewed the nightmares as Owen's unconscious grappling with the experiences that had brought him to Craiglockhart. Owen's most assiduous biographer, Dominic Hibberd, found a note Brock made in the margins of a book of poems by Edgar Allan Poe: "*Nightmares—* Note that Strindberg . . . came to realise the *utility* of a period of nightmare for the purgation of the soul." The useful period had not ended, as Owen wrote to Susan about his most recent nightmare, enclosing "my two best war Poems."

Both poems drew on his dreams. The first was "The Next War," in which the narrator dined with Death and "sniffed the green thick odour of his breath":

> Oh, Death was never an enemy of ours!
>   We laughed at him, we leagued with him, old chum.
> No soldier's paid to kick against his powers.
>   We laughed, knowing that better men would come,
> And greater wars; when each proud fighter brags
> He wars on Death—for Life; not men—for flags.

The second was a sonnet that he had redrafted often that month and shown to Sassoon before sending it home. Sassoon thought the poem demonstrated "that my little friend was much more than the minor poet I had hitherto adjudged him to be. I now realized that his verse, with its sumptuous and large-scale imagery, its noble naturalness and depth of meaning, had impressive affinities with Keats, whom he took as his supreme exemplar. This new sonnet was a revelation." Sassoon suggested what he called "one or two minor alterations," but Owen accorded him more credit than that. "Sassoon supplied the title 'Anthem': just what I meant it to be," he wrote to Susan. The sonnet became "Anthem for Doomed Youth," a landmark elegy for a betrayed generation.

> What passing-bells for these who die as cattle?
>   Only the monstrous anger of the guns.
>   Only the stuttering rifles' rapid rattle
> Can patter out their hasty orisons.
> No mockeries for them from prayers or bells,
>   Nor any voice of mourning save the choirs,—
> The Shrill, demented choirs of wailing shells;
>   And bugles calling for them from sad shires.
>
> What candles may be held to speed them all?
>   Not in the hands of boys, but in their eyes
> Shall shine the holy glimmers of good-byes.
>   The pallor of girls' brows shall be their pall;
> Their flowers the tenderness of silent minds,
> And each slow dusk a drawing-down of blinds.

Owen incorporated some, not all, of Sassoon's suggestions in the final draft. "Only the solemn / Monstrous anger of our guns" became "the monstrous anger of the guns." And "tenderness of silent / Sweet white minds" changed to "tenderness of silent minds." While not the exhaustive rewriting that Ezra Pound would devote to Eliot's *The Waste Land* a few years later, Sassoon's alterations heightened the emotional force of "Anthem." Sassoon promised to send the sonnet to *The Nation*, which declined to publish it. He did not give up, recommending Owen's work to other publishers and to influential friends. Owen still saw himself, he told Sassoon, as Sancho Panza to his Don Quixote. Yet Sassoon had come to regard the younger poet as his equal.

Brock saw Owen's poetic achievements from a psychiatrist's point of view. Poems like "Anthem," he wrote, represented "the heroic testimony of one who in the most literal sense 'faced the phantoms of the mind' . . . they still appear in his poetry but he fears them no longer." Owen used words to confront fear, translating the very images that tormented his sleep into poetry and purging his dread of memory and nightmare. The dreams still came, he wrote to Susan, but they were developing a "civilian character." Sassoon remembered Owen at this time as "consistently cheerful."

When Owen at last published "The Next War," unsigned and at Sassoon's insistence, in *The Hydra*, he prefaced it with a fragment from his mentor:

> War's a joke for me and you,
> While we know such dreams are true.
> SASSOON.

OWEN MET SASSOON almost daily throughout September. Sassoon's morale, however, was plummeting. He wrote in one of his many memoirs, "During my second month at the hydro I think I began to feel a sense of humiliation." War was a forbidden topic with his "fellow breakdowns." He recalled, "Most of them had excellent reasons for disliking that theme. Sometimes I had an uncomfortable notion that none of them respected one another; it was as though there were a tacit understanding that we were all failures, and this made me want to reassure myself that I wasn't the same as the others." His presence among them was tenable on the pretext that he had not "broken down" so much as "broken out."

Sassoon's estrangement from the Craiglockhart fraternity did not strike Rivers as a symptom of neurasthenia so much as a political dissident's reluctance to accept the status of mental patient. Brock, however, viewed avoidance of the hospital's societies and clubs as symptomatic of an impaired psyche. In common with Sassoon, some of his patients frowned on weaklings with whom they supposedly had nothing in common. That attitude, Brock wrote, was unhealthy: "Undoubtedly, the criticising of other people does tend to raise one relatively in one's own self-esteem, and therefore can to some extent replace the self-satisfaction normally gained by actual positive function of one's own."

Brock believed "a good grumble" was "a form of self-drugging, of preserving one's self-confidence; it is a protective neurosis, which in war-time at least, must not be too harshly judged." Brock's analysis of "protective neurosis" could have applied as much to Sassoon as to the other Craiglockhart men who suppressed or "submerged" thoughts that they shared their comrades' mental impairment:

> They suffer terribly if a neighbour should, either by word or look, help to unshackle the "submerged complex." Realising the danger of this happening, they tend to withdraw themselves from their neighbours and assume a position of "proud isolation" (it is this which is technically known as "standing on one's dignity").

Sassoon stood firm on his dignity, avoiding the exercises and good works that Brock prescribed for his patients. He had known since his confinement for double pneumonia at the age of eleven that he "had a mind with which I liked to be alone." Owen, despite his attachment to Brock and ergotherapy, admired Sassoon's emotional self-restraint. He wrote to Susan, "In this he is eminently English. It is so restful after the French absurdities and after Mrs. Gray who gushes all over me." He had sent Susan one of his signed copies of *The Old Huntsman* as proof of Sassoon's greatness. Her reaction did not surprise him. The strong language, the common soldier's slang, shocked the prim matron. Blasphemous passages like "O Jesus, send me a wound to-day, / And I'll believe in your bread and wine, / And get my bloody old sins washed white!" could only offend her puritan sensibilities. Owen reassured her that Sassoon "doesn't swear conversationally" and stressed the older man's importance in his life:

> Sassoon I like equally in all the ways you mention, as a man, as a friend, as a poet.
>
> The man is tall and noble looking . . . I quote from a publication: "very slim and shy, with eyes which may be blue or brown when you come to examine them closely."

His deepening affection for Sassoon coincided with the waning of his connection to his cousin Leslie Gunston. He wrote that Sassoon "is already a closer friend than, say, Leslie." Gunston's poetry had not matured as his own was doing, leaving them less in common. Moreover, Gunston had not endured his and Sassoon's "seventh hell." Some mildly disparaging comments about his cousin in letters to Susan hinted at Owen's distance from the old friendship. Putting childhood behind, Owen was evolving under the combined influence of Sassoon and Brock into a self-confident soldier and poet. Craiglockhart was having an effect.

CHAPTER TWELVE

The Celestial Surgeon

By late September, Sassoon was, in his words, "full of poetry, but rather hampered by the constant presence of an iron-haired Theosophist in my room all the time." The Theosophist was not his only worry: "I hear an R.W.F. friend of mine has had one arm amputated, and will probably lose the other. As he was very keen on playing the piano this seems a little hard on him, but no doubt he will be all the better in the end. At least the Theosophist thinks so."

The friend was Lieutenant Ralph Greaves, whom Sassoon would call "Ralph Wilmot" in his lightly fictionalized autobiography, *The Complete Memoirs of George Sherston*. "Wilmot," he wrote, "was a dark, monocled young man, mature for his years." Greaves/Wilmot, a popular officer in the Royal Welch Fusiliers' 2nd Battalion, had served at Gallipoli and survived "a long spell" in France. Sassoon recalled the night when Greaves hosted his comrades in "a sparsely furnished little parlour on the ground-floor of a wine-merchant's house." His piano playing, pieces from *La Bohème* and *Tosca*, delighted the company. They all drank heavily and joined in singing the chorus of a popular ballad. Greaves "couldn't tear himself away from that piano" and "caressed the keys with lingering affection."

Greaves's loss inspired Sassoon to write the poem "Does It Matter?" in which the pianist is transformed into a fox hunter:

> Does it Matter?—losing your leg? . . .
> For people will always be kind,
> And you need not show that you mind
> When the others come in after hunting
> To gobble their muffins and eggs.

ON THURSDAY, SEPTEMBER 27, the Medical Board that reviewed Owen's case two days earlier confirmed Brock's prediction: "Unfit G.S. [General Service] four months. Unfit Home two months. Unfit light duty one month . . . Requiring indoor Hosp. treatment." At ten o'clock that evening, Owen wrote a letter to his mother that expressed no regret at the outcome. He was about to attend a meeting on the funding of *The Hydra*, and he had asked for Sassoon's help with the publication. Unfortunately, he wrote, "Sassoon is too much the great man to be bothered with it, and I wish I had back again the time I have wasted on it. I was cajoled into promising to act in the next big play, but had the fortitude to get out of it again." For poetry's sake, some things had to go.

BY THE END of Craiglockhart's first year in October 1917, it had admitted 556 shell-shock patients. With as many as 170 residents at any time, pressure on clinicians intensified. Dr. Ruggles observed, "No one psychiatrist, nor a psychiatric team, can be expected to deal with more than three or four new patients in the course of a half day." Treating each entailed, Dr. Rivers explained, not only "the restoration of the patient to health" but also "fitness for military service." Therapies developed over the year depended on patients' resurrecting their most distressing memories and revealing them to psychiatrists. Thus, wrote

Rivers, they were "enabled to return to some form of military duty with a degree of success [that was] very unlikely if they had persisted in the process of repression."

The War Office, despite Commandant Bryce's disdain for petty regulations, could not fault an institution that was sending more officers to the military than to county mental hospitals. Craiglockhart was earning a creditable reputation for treating the causes of nervous collapse rather than, as in hospitals using electro-shock therapy, the symptoms.

October brought torrential storms that inundated head gardener Henry Carmichael's lawns, beech groves, and flower beds. At night, lightning and thunder mimicking artillery fire drove patients quaking in fear under their beds. During the day, a kind of normality prevailed. The hospital had settled into a predictable routine: Saturday concerts, Sunday morning services for Anglicans at eight thirty and for Presbyterians at ten, Field Club lectures on Monday evenings at seven, and debates on Wednesdays at eight.

The Hydra failed to appear in October. Wilfred Owen's other preoccupations left him so little time for the magazine that he handed the editorship to James Bell Salmond. Salmond used the October hiatus to solicit articles, poems, short stories, and jokes, and to redesign the journal as a monthly with a new cover. Relieved of what had become a chore, Owen delivered "an interesting paper on the classification of soils, soil air, soil water, root absorption and fertility" to the Field Club. He devoted his energies to Sassoon, poetry, German lessons, and lecturing the Tynecastle boys. His latest text for them was Longfellow's *Song of Hiawatha*, which he brought to life by erecting teepees in the woods. Reading the poem around a campfire made a greater impression than recital in a classroom: "Listen to this Indian Legend, / To this Song of Hiawatha! / Ye whose hearts are fresh and simple, / Who have faith in God and Nature."

Owen was flourishing under Brock's tutelage, but Sassoon grew more morose in Rivers's absence. "While Rivers was away," he would recall, "only one event occurred which now seems worth recording." What happened was less an event than two encounters, the first after breakfast at the beginning of October. Sassoon was polishing his golf clubs in preparation for the day's play, when an orderly delivered "a mysterious message" from a man waiting to meet him in the hall. Sassoon went down and saw an elderly civilian holding a brown, broad-brimmed hat. Dr. Macamble—a doctor of philosophy rather than medicine—took Sassoon's hand and declared in thunderous voice, "I am here to offer you my profoundest sympathy and admiration for the heroic gesture which has made your name such a . . . such a bugle-call to your brother pacifists."

While Sassoon's golfing partner waited impatiently outside, Macamble said he wanted to discuss his "Stop the War" campaign. Lest they be overheard, he proposed a walk. Sassoon declined, lying that he had an appointment with his doctor. "Ah," said Macamble, "the famous Dr. Rivers!" Sassoon consented to a rendezvous the next day in Edinburgh, where he was going anyway for a haircut. Arriving early at the Caledonian Hotel for the five o'clock appointment, Sassoon eavesdropped on a "well-dressed yellow-haired woman with white eyelashes" called Mabel and "an unemphatic-looking major with a sandy moustache." Mabel condemned antiwar Labor members of Parliament Ramsay MacDonald and Philip Snowden as worse than the Germans. Snowden had defended Sassoon on the night Hastings Lees-Smith read his statement to the House of Commons. "I only hope," Mabel declared, "that if they do start their beloved revolution, they'll both be strung up to the nearest lamp-post by the soldiers they are now trying to betray."

Macamble arrived and launched into a tedious oration. "After listening to him for about an hour and a half," Sassoon wrote, "I could be certain of one thing only—that he believed himself to be rather a great man." The great man made the mistake of disparaging Dr. Rivers, whom he accused of diverting Sassoon from the cause. Matters deteriorated when Macamble urged Sassoon to desert the hospital, take a train to London, and have an "alienist" certify his sanity. The military would then have no option but to court-martial him. "Good Lord," Sassoon thought, "he's trying to persuade me to do the dirty on Rivers!" Politely avoiding further discussion, he departed "with the heartiest of handshakes."

Owen called on Sassoon most evenings, compensating in part for Rivers's absence. Sassoon appreciated that "in a young man of twenty-four his selflessness was extraordinary. The clue to his poetic genius was sympathy, not only in his detached outlook upon humanity but in all his actions and responses towards individuals." Owen's companionship, however, did not dispel Sassoon's frustration. "I have great difficulty in doing any work as I am constantly disturbed by nurses etc and the man who sleeps in my room—an awful bore," he complained to Robbie Ross on October 3. "It is pretty sickening when I feel like writing something and have to dry up and *try* to be polite (you can imagine with how much success!)." His Theosophist roommate's obtuse observations irritated him as much as his affected diction. When Sassoon told him Britain's official casualty toll for September was 102,000, the Theosophist replied, "Yes, Sassoon; it is the Celestial Surgeon at work on humanity." Rivers would be back on October 5 and "may be able to get me a room to myself (or get me away from these imbeciles)."

Sassoon was able to read if not to write. After Barbusse's graphic trench novel *Under Fire*, he turned to a war memoir by his friend and fellow Royal Welch Fusiliers subaltern Bernard Pye Adams. Adams explained his title, *Nothing of Importance*, in the preface: "There was one phrase in the daily communiqués that used to strike us rather out there; it was, 'Nothing of importance to record on the rest of the front.'" Like a later book from the German side, Erich Maria Remarque's *All Quiet on the Western Front*, it mocked the militarists' disparagement of the blood-drenched intervals between major engagements. Grinding attrition and mounting casualties after the Verdun battle of September 1915 and before Haig's July 1916 Somme offensive may have seemed unimportant to the High Command, but the dangers were of supreme importance to the men who faced them. Waiting in rat- and lice-infested underground hovels for shells, bullets, or poison gas to kill or obliterate them exacted a high physical and mental toll. Cambridge-educated classicist Adams did not live to see his book in print, having been wounded on the Somme on February 26, 1917, and dying the next day. Sassoon, as he had recommended Barbusse to Rivers and Owen, encouraged Ross, Graves, and Owen to read *Nothing of Importance*. He wrote to Graves, who had also served with Adams, "I am reading Bill Adams's book. If you and I had re-written and added to it it would have been a classic; as it is it is just Bill Adams—and a very good book—expressing his quiet kindliness to perfection."

Adams's saga reminded Sassoon, who appeared in its pages as "Scott," of their time together at the front. It played on a conscience divided between commitment to ending the war and duty to lead "his" men in the field. For him, as for Hamlet, "conscience does make cowards of us all." His comrades were suffering, while he basked in the "luxury" of clean sheets and rounds of golf. He did not discuss the dilemma with Owen. Their conversations dwelled on poetry rather than war. "At Craiglockhart," wrote Sassoon, "he and I talked very little about our experiences of the disgusting and terrible, as seen in France. I discouraged him from reviving such memories, knowing that they were bad for him." It was only after the war that "I discovered that Wilfred had endured worse things than I had realized from the little he told me." Apart from Owen, Sassoon continued to shun the other patients, refusing to be seen—or to see himself—as another mental case. Only golf provided an "escape from the truly awful atmosphere of this place of wash-outs and shattered heroes. Result: go to bed every night tired and irritable, and write querulous peace-poems." The person in whom he needed to confide his inner turmoil was Rivers, whose arrival he awaited with growing impatience.

Sassoon managed to write short antiwar poems—he called them "cameos"—that *The Cambridge Review* printed in nearly every issue. Yet they failed to measure up to what he demanded of himself. He wrote on Thursday, October 4, that his attempt to compose a long poem in blank verse was failing, because "I can't get a room alone, and 8–11 p.m. is my brainy time, so I am rather hung up at present." He pinned his hope for privacy on Rivers, due back the next day.

During afternoon visiting hours on Friday, October 5, Sassoon was in an unusually exuberant mood. His "father confessor" was returning. Deprived of his regular golf game by an autumn gale, he was "indulging in some horse-play with another young officer who happened to feel 'dangerously well' at the moment" in the entrance hall. A visitor's unattended hat caught his eye, and he booted it across the foyer. The prank made him laugh, until, suddenly, he saw Rivers at the door. The doctor, suitcase in hand, had been observing him. "Standing there in the failing light of that watery afternoon, he had the half-shy look of a middle-aged person intruding on the segregative amusements of the young," Sassoon recalled. Rivers told him, "Go steady with that hat," and walked through the corridor to his consulting room. Sassoon picked up the hat, molded it back into shape, and thought "it might have belonged to Doctor Macamble."

Sassoon enjoyed a rare moment alone in his room that afternoon. He reached into his pocket for a fire opal on a gold chain that Lady Ottoline had sent him as a talisman to protect him in battle. "I had derived consolation from its marvellous colours during the worst episodes of my war experiences," he wrote of the stone. Its fiery colours flickered between his fingers, resurrecting, madeleine-like, memories that had remained dormant at Craiglockhart. "Had I really enjoyed," he asked himself, "those tours of the trenches, up to the Bois Français sector?"

Sassoon's melancholy reminiscences pushed him toward going back into battle. Yet, he wrote, "Everything would be different if I went back to France now—different even from what it was last April." One difference was the surge in deaths from poison gas. His latest golfing partner had lost half his company in a chemical attack that drove him mad and brought him to Craiglockhart. Sassoon imagined an endless column of men on the march singing, "It's a Long Way to Tipperary":

> I saw them filing silently along ruined roads, and lugging their bad boots through mud until they came to some shell-hole and pillar-box in a landscape where trees were stumps and skeletons and no quartermaster on earth could be certain of getting the rations up . . . "From sunlight to the sunless land" . . . The idea of going back there was indeed like death.

Death, however, was no deterrence. He had both wished for and expected death in France. More shameful was living in a comfortable Scottish hydro, while the men he loved were dying in the chalk and clay of Picardy. Like Jacob wrestling the angel, Sassoon struggled all night with memory and conscience. The mental conflict approached an inevitable resolution. He needed to prove to critics who accused him of being "not quite normal" that he was willing to die: "Killed in action in order to confute the Under-Secretary for War, who had officially stated that I wasn't responsible for my actions. What a truly glorious death for a promising young pacifist!" By the time the sun rose, he had put down his fire opal talisman, convinced "that going back to the War as soon as possible was my only chance of peace."

When he went downstairs for his evening consultation, he would tell Rivers.

CHAPTER THIRTEEN

A Grand Gesture

No contemporary account of the Rivers–Sassoon consultations has survived, due to Sassoon's neglect of his diary and the disappearance of psychiatric case notes. Sassoon came to regret the loss: "I would give a good deal for a few gramophone records of my 'interchanges of ideas' with Rivers." Yet the decisive exchange that followed his conscience-stricken night imprinted itself on his memory: "As I went along to see Rivers that evening, I felt rather as if I were about to make a grand gesture." Sassoon prefaced his gesture by telling Rivers about Second Lieutenant Edward Orme's apparition at his door early on the morning Rivers went on leave. Aware of Rivers's skepticism about "psychic phenomena," Sassoon played down the incident as a probable "delusion." To his surprise, the story distressed Rivers, who went silent, removed his glasses, and cleaned them as if suppressing tears. Regaining his composure, the psychiatrist waited for Sassoon to come to the point.

What would happen, Sassoon asked, if he refused to recant his pacifist stance? "Then," Rivers answered, "you will be kept here until the end of the War." And if he applied to the Medical Board for reconsideration of his mental condition? "I could only tell them that you are not suffering from any form of psycho-neurosis." The board, Rivers added, might release him for noncombat service in Britain. Sassoon wanted more, explaining, "I was getting things into focus a bit while you were away and I see now that the only thing for me to do is to get back to the front as quick as I can." He insisted on the front, not "some home-service job."

Rivers advised Sassoon to reconsider. If he remained certain, "We could then discuss our plan of campaign to wangle things with the War Office." This was the opposite outcome of what Rivers had achieved with Max Plowman, whose anxiety neurosis he successfully treated but who turned to pacifism. With Sassoon, Rivers had won a partial victory: his charge wanted to return to the war but refused to withdraw his antiwar protest. The war's purpose was anyway becoming a mystery to Rivers himself.

THE WEEKLY SATURDAY concert for October 6 featured a theatrical presentation that strayed beyond the usual bounds of Shakespeare, light comedy, and melodrama. *The Silver Box*, *Forsyte Saga* author John Galsworthy's first play, had premiered in 1906 at London's Court Theatre. An overtly political piece, it contrasted the law's indulgence of the rich with its callousness toward the poor. The play's portrayal of class conflict seemed timely during a war in which regular soldiers resented and suffered the decisions of their "betters." Staging the controversial drama at Craiglockhart risked inflaming class antagonisms in a country that was desperate in wartime to suppress them. The theater troupe was making a bold statement, which Major Bryce did not censor.

Most of the patients, including Owen but not Sassoon, attended the production. The plot revolved around a petty theft and its consequences for two families, the upper-middle-class Barthwicks and the working-class Joneses. The curtain opened on the Barthwicks' dining room as young Jack Barthwick, son of Liberal member of Parliament John Barthwick, entered holding a woman's handbag that he had stolen during a drunken night out. A man named Jones, whose wife worked there as charwoman, followed him in. When Jack passed out, Jones left with money from the handbag and a silver box. The next scenes depicted the two households' differences in social status and attitudes to the thefts. The Barthwicks, despite their liberal pretensions, dismissed Mrs. Jones from her job, leaving her family without an income, while ignoring their son's boyish prank. Police arrested Jones and brought him to trial. The magistrate upbraided Jones for using drunkenness as an excuse for stealing. When Jack testified that he drank so much champagne that he did not remember taking the woman's handbag, the magistrate gave him a conspiratorial smile. Jones remonstrated, "I've done no more than wot he 'as. I'm a poor man; I've got no money an' no friends—he's a toff—he can do wot I can't." Jack was not prosecuted, and the magistrate sentenced Jones to a year at hard labor.

The clear injustice had an effect on the audience, *The Hydra* commenting that the play "has turned us all into Socialists. I saw one man in tears about the vulgar rich and their power." Sassoon wrote to Robbie Ross, "I didn't see it, but I hear a dotty padré who is here was most upset and said 'Such a play is pernicious, and calculated to set class against class.' Aren't people wonderful?"

Sassoon was biding his time, waiting for Rivers to lobby the War Office and hoping for a room of his own. Luck intervened, when a Medical Board discharged his Theosophist roommate and assigned him to light duty in Britain. "I shall sit in an office," the Theosophist proclaimed to Sassoon, "O man of little faith, wearing blue tabs upon my tunic and filling in Army Forms whereof no man knoweth the mysterious meaning." Rivers gave Sassoon a single room upstairs that he called "the garret." At last "free from theosophy and conversation," although "somewhat chilly," he produced poems that had been gestating for weeks.

One, "Death's Brotherhood," expressed both guilt at abandoning his comrades and uncertainty that Rivers would succeed with the War Office:

> When I'm asleep, dreaming and drowsed and warm,
> They come, the homeless ones, the noiseless dead.
>
> . . .
>
> "Why are you here with all your watches ended?"
> "From Ypres to Frise, we sought you in the Line."
> In bitter safety I awake, unfriended;
> And while the dawn begins with slashing rain
> I think of the Battalion in the mud.
> "When are you going back to them again?"
> "Are they not still your brothers through our blood?"

His new garret afforded privacy for more intimate conversations with Owen: "Almost every evening he would visit me and there was much comfort in his companionship. For I was enduring the difficult and distressing experience of making up my mind to withdraw from my 'stop the war' attitude and get myself passed for service abroad." Owen's sympathy tided him over his "inevitable moods of bitterness and depression."

Sassoon invited Robert Graves, still at the Litherland base recovering from the battle wounds that nearly killed him, to visit. "You will find me playing golf at a place called Baberton," he wrote. "You walk to Juniper Green.—(2¾ miles from the Hosp.)" Graves caught the overnight train, at Sassoon's expense, to Edinburgh on Friday evening, October 12. On his arrival in the morning, Wilfred Owen was waiting to guide him to Baberton Golf Club. Graves had no idea who the youngster was, remarking only that he appeared to be "a quiet, round-faced little man." Having read Graves's poetry, Owen was surprised to see only "a big, rather plain fellow, the last man on earth apparently capable of the extraordinary, delicate fancies in his books." Owen and Graves ambled out in the rain, crossing a footbridge over the Water of Leith, to find Sassoon at the golf course. "It was a wet day, I remember," Sassoon wrote. "W. O. was modest and shy, and regarded R. G. as a great man, because he'd published two books. No doubt R. G. did most of the talking."

At Baberton, under a gray sky and drizzling rain, Graves and Sassoon discussed war, poetry, and mutual friends as if Owen were not there. Then Owen showed Graves a draft of his poem "Disabled." Reading it, Graves realized the little Manchester Regiment subaltern was a poet of rare promise:

> He sat in a wheeled chair, waiting for dark,
> And shivered in his ghastly suit of grey,
> Legless, sewn short at elbow. Through the park
> Voices of play and pleasure after day,
> Till gathering sleep had mothered them from him.

The seventh and last stanza portrayed the wounded veteran, like thousands of others, receiving condescension rather than acclaim:

> Tonight he noticed how the women's eyes
> Passed from him to the strong men that were whole.
> How cold and late it is! Why don't they come
> And put him into bed? Why don't they come?

While Owen had approached Sassoon the previous July as a disciple, he felt on a more equal footing with Graves. That coincided with his growing self-confidence as a poet, itself the result of Sassoon's encouragement as well as the high regard in which the Saint Bernard's Crescent grandees held him. He wrote to his mother about Graves, "No doubt he thought me a slacker sort of sub. S.S. when they were together showed him my longish war-piece 'Disabled' (you haven't seen it yet) & it seems Graves was mightily impressed, and considers me a kind of <u>Find</u>! No thanks, Captain Graves! I'll find myself in due time."

Much of the conversation between Sassoon and Graves at Baberton and later at dinner in Edinburgh emerged in letters the two wrote soon afterward. Sassoon must have worried about his mental health, because Graves wrote to him, "Don't be silly about being dotty: of course you're sane. The only trouble is you're too sane which is as great a crime as being dotty and much more difficult to deal with." He reminded Sassoon of the advice he had given him that day, "The Bobbies and Tommies and so on, who are the exact people whom you wish to influence and save by all your powers, are just the people whose feelings you are going to hurt the most by turning round in the middle of the war, after having made a definite contract, and saying 'I've changed my mind.'" The regiment's men would respect him only if he shared "all their miseries as far as you possibly can" even while "denouncing the principles you are being compelled to further." Graves's admonition made clear that Sassoon had yet to tell him, as he had Rivers, of his decision to go back to the war. Their relationship was under strain, due to Sassoon's unflinching opposition to the war and to Graves's infatuation with a woman he would soon marry, Nancy Nicholson. Graves was abandoning his youthful homosexuality, while Sassoon clung to his.

One outcome of the Baberton rendezvous, the only occasion all three soldier-poets met together, was a burgeoning friendship between Graves and Owen. Graves saw potential in Owen's poetry, even if some of it was "too Sasso[o]nish in places." The two began a correspondence in which Graves suggested, as Sassoon had earlier, minor changes to Owen's work. Graves wrote at first with praise, "Do you know, Owen, that's a damn fine poem of yours, that 'Disabled.' Really damn fine!" Owen's sense of sound and use of words enhanced the effect of "the occasional metrical outrages." But Graves discouraged phrases like "They cheered him home but not as they would cheer a goal" and urged Owen to avoid the clichés "Girls glanced lovelier" and "scanty suits of grey." Overall, his letter was an endorsement from a serious, acclaimed poet who knew the trenches and their miseries as Owen did: "Owen, you have seen things; you are a poet; but you're a very careless one at present."

Owen had more faith in his own talent than Graves realized, deliberately ignoring rules that Graves the classicist revered and incorporating few of his suggestions in subsequent drafts of "Disabled." At this time, he was waiting for his next Medical Board, scheduled for the end of October, to order his release or to keep him as a patient for another month. "Both issues are acceptable," he wrote to his mother. "I could do a lot with another month here, but I feel a growing homesickness." His longing for home contrasted with Sassoon's burning desire to get back to the war.

Owen made the most of what might be his last days with Sassoon, Brock, the Saint Bernard's Crescent bohemians, the Tynecastle students, and the Field Club. His poetry was flourishing, evidenced by the "gas poem" he wrote on October 15 and sent to Susan the next day. "Dulce et Decorum Est" turned on its head Roman poet Horace's *Dulce et decorum est pro patria mori* (It is sweet and proper to die for one's country). It revealed a poetic imagination at the height of its powers as well as a mind that had struggled through the tunnel of madness:

> Bent double, like old beggars under sacks,
> Knock-kneed, coughing like hags, we cursed through sludge,
> Till on the haunting flares we turned our backs,
> And towards our distant rest began to trudge.
> Men marched asleep. Many had lost their boots,
> But limped on, blood-shod. All went lame, all blind;
> Drunk with fatigue; deaf even to the hoots
> Of gas-shells dropping softly behind.

Gas! GAS! Quick, boys!—An ecstasy of fumbling
Fitting the clumsy helmets just in time,
But someone still was yelling out and stumbling
And flound'ring like a man in fire or lime.—
Dim through the misty panes and thick green light,
As under a green sea, I saw him drowning.

These opening stanzas resembled in form a Shakespeare sonnet, but for the jarring lack of rhyme in the final two lines. The second verse drew on one of his most harrowing moments in the trenches, when a soldier under his command failed to get his mask on before the gas hit him. The poem moved from the past tense of the experience itself to the present of its nocturnal recurrence at Craiglockhart:

In all my dreams before my helpless sight
He plunges at me, guttering, choking, drowning.

His shell shock more or less exorcised, his shaking and stammering under control, Owen stated the truth it had taken him months in France and at Craiglockhart to realize:

If in some smothering dreams, you too could pace
Behind the wagon that we flung him in,
And watch the white eyes writhing in his face,
His hanging face, like a devil's sick of sin,
If you could hear, at every jolt, the blood
Come gargling from the froth-corrupted lungs
Bitter as the cud
Of vile, incurable sores on innocent tongues,—
My friend, you would not tell with such high zest
To children ardent for some desperate glory,
The old Lie: Dulce et decorum est
Pro patria mori.

It was in praise of such verse that Sassoon wrote, "He pitied others; he did not pity himself." Owen explained, "My subject is War and the pity of War. The poetry is in the pity." He was shedding illusions about the war. "I am no longer neurasthenic," he wrote to Susan, "though I may be neurotic."

Owen took his students to Swanton Cottage, the farmhouse on the Pentland Hills slopes where Robert Louis Stevenson had spent childhood summers. His research into the Scottish storyteller's life took him to the Constable printing works to meet Walter Blaikie, who knew Stevenson as a boy and had the same nurse, Alison "Cummie" Cunningham, in infancy. "So it was an interesting afternoon," he wrote, "tho' old Blaikie affects a contempt for R. L. S." Owen reveled in the notion that his pupils knew Stevenson better "than this person who played with him before even Treasure Island was dreamed of."

In his newfound maturity, Owen played confidant to Charles Mayes and Sassoon. Each came to his room to discuss problems well into the night, Sassoon disclosing his qualms about returning to the war. His Medical Board was due to meet on October 23. While he believed Rivers would convince the War Office to release him for General Service abroad, he "confessed he didn't know what to do about his 'show.'"

Profound guilt over the separation from his "brothers in blood" oppressed Sassoon, but there was also regret that he was betraying the pacifist friends who had supported his protest. He justified himself to Lady Ottoline Morrell in a letter on October 17:

I am afraid I cannot do anything "outrageous." They would only say I had a relapse and put me in a padded room. I am at present faced with the prospect of remaining here for an indefinite period, and you can imagine how that affects me . . . I have told Rivers that I will not withdraw anything that I have said or written, and that my views are the same, but that I will go back to France if the War Office will give me a guarantee that they really will send me there.

Because his protest had been on behalf of fellow soldiers, he wrote, "the fittest thing I can do is to go back and share their ills." If the War Office tried to assign him to light duty in Britain rather than to the front lines, he "would do a bolt for London—and see what course they adopt." Ottoline clung to the hope he would not surrender his ideals, reading the final lines of his poem "Glory of Women" as evidence of his confusion:

> Oh, German mother, dreaming by the fire,
> While you are knitting socks to send your son
> His face is trodden deeper in the mud.

She judged him harshly, writing in her journal, "It did not seem to dawn on him that in going back to the War he was going to kill young Germans." Sassoon wrote also to his parliamentary advocate, Hastings Lees-Smith, to explain why he was taking up arms again. The letters to Ottoline and Lees-Smith constituted attempts to convince them he was not betraying their faith in him. He needed also to convince himself.

CHAPTER FOURTEEN

Fight to a Finish

Sassoon's and Owen's Medical Boards drew closer, October 23 for Sassoon and Owen a week later. Late October's foul weather limited Sassoon's golf time and left him to rehearse again his interior dialogue on the morality of fighting an unjust war. Owen meanwhile was profiting from a recovery that Sassoon attributed to Dr. Brock, who "had been completely successful in restoring the balance of his nerves."

No longer trembling and stammering, a self-assured Owen ventured out of the hospital daily to see the many friends he had made over the previous four months. He charmed everyone he met, especially his friends' children and the Tynecastle students. Maria Steinthal, the German artist who lived at 21 Saint Bernard's Crescent with Leonard and Maidie Gray, invited him to sit for a portrait on October 17. Owen was surprised when she completed a charcoal sketch of his features in five minutes. As was his custom, he played with Maria's year-old daughter, Pixie, "the most exquisite bit of protoplasm that age I have handled." He entertained Pixie, Maria painted, and "before tea the complete rough likeness was done in oils!" The portrait would need more sittings, but even its incomplete form pleased Owen. A water-color that Maria's mother-in-law made of him did not.

While Owen was writing and socializing, Sassoon brooded. He wrote to Graves on October 19, "My position here is nearly unbearable, and the feeling of isolation makes me feel rotten." His friend Quarter-master Joe Cottrell wrote to him from Polygon Wood that the regiment's circumstances were appalling. Friends were dying. Miles of mud, shell holes, and human and equine corpses covered the ground that Cottrell crossed each evening to bring up the rations. It was, he told Sassoon, worse than anything he had seen thus far. This as much as anything else afflicted Sassoon's conscience. At last, he told Graves about his decision to return to France "if they will send me (making it quite clear that my views are exactly the same as in July—only more so)." Yet he felt he would be "returning to the war with no belief in what I was doing." The letter contained a note of desperation: "O Robert, what ever will happen to end the war?"

The War Office was looking at Craiglockhart, in Sassoon's words, "with a somewhat fishy eye." Rivers told him that the army's local director of Medical Services disapproved of the hospital and "never had and never would recognize the existence of such a thing as shell-shock." The director must have shared the conventional opinion that mental patients were malingers feigning illness and that Craiglockhart was coddling them. It was no secret that Major Bryce permitted offi-cers to wear slippers in the common rooms and did not prevent the staging of a dangerously socialist play. A full War Office inspection was inevitable, and Bryce received several weeks' notice to prepare for one.

Forewarned, commanders of military hospitals, as of army bases, saw to it that staff scrubbed every surface and that the men polished brass buttons, shined shoes, and stood to attention for the examiners. Major Bryce, who Sassoon maintained "had won the gratitude and affection of everyone," took the opposite approach. He believed that War Office inspectors should see the hospital as it really was. "He did this as a matter of principle," wrote Sassoon, "since in his opinion a shell-shock hospital was not the same thing as a parade ground."

The War Office sent a general, who found Craiglockhart in its usual state of managed disorder. The kitchen pans did not shine like mirrors. Bathroom floors were not clean enough to eat off. Patients' uniforms lacked the required waist-to-shoulder Sam Browne belts. Doctors and nurses did not line up before the general to pay homage. Instead, they went about the business of caring for patients. The general, furious at the absence of discipline, decided that Major Bryce had to go. When the medical staff learned of their commandant's dismissal, Rivers and other staff members submitted their resignations pending reassignment elsewhere. The patients were not told what was happening. Sassoon wrote that if he had been aware of Rivers's intentions, he would not have done what he called "the stupid thing" when his Medical Board met.

SASSOON HAD GOOD news for Owen when he appeared in the garret for tea on October 22: there was no reason, as he had previously advised, to delay publishing a collection of his poems. He urged Owen to "hurry up & get what's ready typed" so he could send the typescript to publisher William Heinemann. Owen would type his work, including six poems he had written that week, and give it to Sassoon. Sassoon's gesture strengthened their mutual bond.

Rivers returned from the War Office in London to inform Sassoon that "two influential personages" would support his demand to serve at the front. Sassoon might at last return to what he called the "regions where bombs, mustard-gas, box-barrages, and similar enjoyments were awaiting me." One of the "influential personages" happened to be a friend with whom Sassoon had played cricket before the war. The friend

John Singer Sargent, *Gassed*, 1919

Gas! GAS! Quick, boys!—An ecstasy of fumbling
Fitting the clumsy helmets just in time,
But someone still was yelling out and stumbling
And flound'ring like a man in fire or lime.—
Dim through the misty panes and thick green light,
As under a green sea, I saw him drowning.

—Wilfred Owen, from "Dulce et Decorum Est"

Craiglockhart staff: seated in the front row are the commandant, Major William H. Bryce (center); to his right is Matron Margaret MacBean and Dr. William Halse Rivers; to his left are an unknown nurse and Dr. Arthur Brock.

Dr. Arthur Brock in his consulting room at Craiglockhart. An illustration hangs on the wall of the mythic wrestling match between Hercules and Antaeus. Brock wrote that each Craiglockhart patient "recognises that, in a way, he is himself an Antaeus who has been taken from mother earth and well nigh crushed to death by the war giant or military machine."

Dr. William Brown (left), who treated Wilfred Owen in France and later became commandant of Craiglockhart; Dr. William Halse Rivers (seated, center); and Dr. Grafton Elliot Smith (right), their colleague from the Moss Side Red Cross Military Hospital at Maghull near Liverpool.

Officers of the 5th (Reserve) Battalion, the Manchester Regiment, Milford Camp, Witley, July 1916. Wilfred Owen is second from the right, front row.

Wilfred Owen (left) in France in 1914 with Laurent Tailhade (right), whom he called "a great French Poet." French poetry would influence Owen's style as much as Keats and Shelley. When the bisexual Tailhade made a pass at him, Owen ignored rather than rebuffed it.

Siegfried Sassoon (left) and David Thomas, "little Tommy," whose death sent Sassoon into No Man's Land seeking revenge, earning him the nickname "Mad Jack."

SHELL SHOCK!

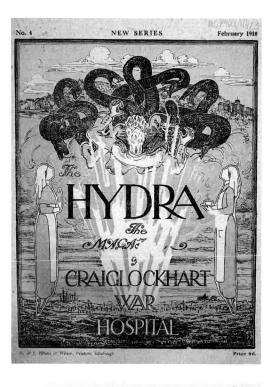

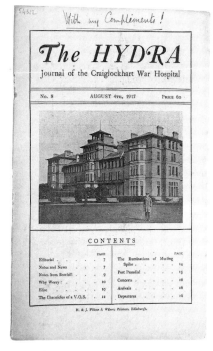

❀ ❀ ❀

"STARED AT."

Now if I walk in Princes Street,
Or smile at friends I chance to meet,
Or, perhaps a joke with laughter greet,
I'm stared at.

I've got a blue band on my arm,
But surely that's not any harm;
A small white tab may be the charm—
I'm stared at.

Suppose I dine out any night,
Drink Adam's wine, and don't get tight,
No wonder that my nerves ain't right,
I'm stared at.

Craiglockhart mem'ries will be sad,
Your name will never make us glad;
The self-respect we ever had
We've lost—all people think us mad.

If "Someone" knew who wrote this verse
My simple life would be much worse,
And on my tomb would be this curse,
"To be stared at."

                        "AN INMATE."

Wilfred Owen edited *The Hydra* in 1917.
Its name referred to the many-headed
Hydra of Greek mythology. Dr. Brock
wrote that dealing only with a patient's
symptoms was as futile as cutting off
one head of the Hydra to see another
emerge in its place. The journal
became a vehicle for some
of the war's finest poetry.

Lady Clementine Waring, "Clemmie,"
who welcomed Sassoon and other
overflow patients from Craiglockhart
to her Lennel House. Sassoon called
Lennel "a delightful house," where he
enjoyed "a series of excellent meals
presided over by Lady Clementine,
who managed her supposedly nerve-
shattered guests with undeviating
adroitness and good humour."

Wilfred Owen.

Miss MACBEAN,
Matron.

OUR COMMANDING
OFFICERS.

"The Hydra," November 1917.

MAJOR BRYCE,
Commanding Officer.

Matron MacBean and Commandant Bryce
in *The Hydra*, November 1917.

Lady Ottoline Morrell.

Owen's grave near the Sambre–Oise Canal, where he was killed by German fire five days before the Armistice that ended the war. For his bravery earlier in the campaign, he would be awarded the Military Cross.

gave Rivers a letter that all but assured a positive result from his Medical Board. Sassoon needed only to show up and look sane.

The board convening on the afternoon of October 23 had a large number of cases to review. While the three physicians interviewed Lieutenant E. J. Shater of the Royal Marines and several others, Sassoon waited in an anteroom. The lengthy delay made him "moody and irritable." His thoughts turned to the Astronomer Royal's invitation to show him the moon that evening through the lens of Scotland's largest telescope. Losing patience, Sassoon checked his watch and "said to myself the medical board could go to blazes, and then (I record it with regret) went off to have tea with the astronomer." He forgot about Rivers "and everything that I owed him." Then, riding the tram through Edinburgh, he realized he had done something "unthinkably foolish." Misfortune followed him to the Astronomer Royal's house, where the telescope was not working. "So even the moon was a washout."

The reckoning with his "father confessor" was not long in coming. Sheepishly, Sassoon proffered a "wretched explanation" that provoked Rivers, for the first time in their acquaintance, to intense annoyance. "The worst part was that he looked thoroughly miserable," Sassoon recalled. When he pointed out that his desertion of the board did not imply reneging on his "decision to give up being a pacifist," Rivers relaxed. Their eyes met. Sassoon, relieved, admitted he had been stupid to miss going back to the army merely for tea with an astronomer. Rivers "threw his head back and laughed in that delightful way of his" and agreed to arrange another Medical Board. A second board required the approval of a new commandant, who might be less sympathetic than Bryce.

Bryce left a void not only at the top but in the patients' lives. The Camera Club, of which he had been president, "expressed its appreciation of the genial courtesy of the retiring President, Major Bryce, R.A.M.C., on the occasion of his departure from the Hospital." No longer would he play cricket and golf with the men, and the Saturday concerts would miss his lilting Scottish ballads. His replacement had much to live up to.

To succeed Bryce, the War Office turned to the fifty-seven-year-old president of Scotland's Recruiting Medical Board, Lieutenant Colonel Robert Balfour Graham. His record as a military physician was impeccable. Son of a clergyman, he was born in Roxburghshire in southeast Scotland on August 25, 1859. After leaving the respected Kelso Grammar School, he studied art for a year before enrolling at Edinburgh University's Medical School and earning his degree in 1884. There followed a period of public service: in 1887, volunteering as a surgeon in the Medical Staff Corps of the 1st Fifeshire Artillery Corps; in 1890, working for the Saint John Ambulance Association; and, in 1911, becoming public health examiner for Edinburgh's Royal College of Surgeons. His army career saw him promoted to captain in 1889 and lieutenant colonel in 1908. At the onset of war in 1914, he became senior medical officer at the Western Command Depot and county director of the Scottish Territorial Red Cross Brigade. With no expertise in psychiatry, Balfour Graham was not an obvious choice to oversee Craiglockhart. The War Office must have seen the able surgeon and public health specialist as a solid administrator who could put the hospital into proper, military shape.

Dr. Arthur Hiler Ruggles, as an American subject to his own chain of command, could not resign in protest at Major Bryce's departure. He assumed Bryce's responsibilities with the Camera Club, which he hosted every Sunday evening in his room. Ruggles went on treating neurasthenic officers and "saw many fine Scottish lads who had broken down dramatically at the front in those terrifying days of the war . . . Among them were cases of acute dementia praecox [schizophrenia] and other disorders, all incorrectly lumped together as 'shell shock.'" The men's families visited them at Craiglockhart, telling Ruggles they wanted to take their sons and fathers home to the Highlands and care for them there. Ruggles opposed removing them from the hospital. "Nevertheless," he noted, "many of the patients were taken out against advice and returned to the simple and familiar environment of the hills upon which they had been raised."

The outcome surprised the psychiatrists. "I was in Scotland long enough," wrote Ruggles, "to see many of these men return to the hospital for a follow-up visit, sufficiently recovered to have taken their place at home and to carry on actively and successfully their simple vocations." He concluded that, despite their once debilitating symptoms, "they could recover when early removed from the stress and strain of danger, of frustration, and of battle complications." As Rivers maintained, they were normal human beings reacting to the abnormal circumstances of war. Removed from them, they regained their health. It was an important lesson for Ruggles, but his mission in France would be to send American boys back into battle rather than to the nurturing environment of home.

ON OCTOBER 28, Brock informed Owen that his impending Medical Board would probably discharge him from the hospital. That did not necessarily mean a return to France, only that his agreeable existence at Craiglockhart would end. "I am rather upset about it," Owen wrote to his mother. "Especially as I am so happy with Sassoon." He spent the day with Sassoon—"Breakfast, Lunch, Tea & Dinner," as he boasted to Susan—most of it at the Scottish Conservative Club at 112 Princes Street, where Rivers had made Sassoon an honorary member. Before they parted, Sassoon gave him *A Human Voice* by Aylmer Strong, a poet who had visited him in September. Sassoon thought Strong's poems so ridiculous that he no doubt wanted to share the joke with Owen. In the book's favor, its introduction stated that all proceeds from sales would go to "the Recuperative Hostels (Hampstead and

Romford) established for the care of critical nerve-cases from the front."

Sassoon's letter that night to Lady Ottoline made no mention of Owen, dwelling instead on anxiety over his decision to "face the bare idea of going back to hell." Without telling her of his flight from the Medical Board five days earlier, he wrote that he expected soon to be declared "fit for General Service" abroad. Making a protest after that was futile, because "they will call it a 'recrudescence' or re-lapse and keep me shut up here or elsewhere. They will *never* court-martial me." He repeated to her his insistence on serving "*with my old Battalion in France*." If not, he would find an "alienist" to certify him as sane—the course he had rejected when Dr. Macamble pro-posed it—and force a court-martial. While Ottoline maintained their friendship, she did not accept his rationale for abandoning principles she held dear.

Having made his decision, Sassoon ceased debating the war with Rivers. Instead, he showed him his recent poems. Although Rivers had told his patient Max Plowman in April that he no longer read poetry, he examined Sassoon's work with interest and a critical eye. One poem struck him as "very dangerous." Sassoon's account of their conversation did not make clear whether the danger lay in his own unconscious or the War Office's possible reaction. Published in Ogden's *Cambridge Magazine* on October 27, "Fight to a Finish" attacked his favorite tar-gets: the jingoist press, the civilians who cheered soldiers to their deaths, and the politicians who sent them there. He sent it to Lady Ottoline with the caveat that it was "fairly effective in its way":

> The boys came back. Bands played and flags were flying,
> And Yellow-Pressmen thronged the sunlit street
> To cheer the soldiers who'd refrained from dying,
> And hear the music of returning feet.
> "Of all the thrills and ardours War has brought,
> This moment is the finest." (So they thought.)

Snapping their bayonets on to charge the mob,
Grim Fusiliers broke ranks with glint of steel,
At last the boys had found a cushy job.

. . .

I heard the Yellow-Pressmen grunt and squeal;
And with my trusty bombers turned and went
To clear those Junkers out of Parliament.

"Fight to a Finish" had not actually incited soldiers to attack Parliament, but it strayed as close to subversion as any poem published during the war. The War Office could ignore it or react by refusing to send him to France. The poem was a risky condemnation of those who advocated war without fighting it themselves. More like it were coming every day.

Another short poem attacked a different category of civilians for supporting a war they did not have to fight: women. "Glory of Women" began, "You love us when we're heroes home on leave, / Or wounded in a mentionable place." Another, "Their Frailty," portrayed women whose men had a "Blighty," a wound just serious enough to send them home without crippling them for life. Its caustic final verse showed no mercy:

Husbands and sons and lovers; everywhere
 They die; War bleeds us white.
Mothers and wives and sweethearts,—they don't care
 So long as He's all right.

His most scathing poem at this time, "Suicide in the Trenches," assaulted both women and men on the home front. Its final stanza would become one of the most quoted of the war:

You smug-face crowds with kindling eye
Who cheer when soldier lads march by,

Sneak home and pray you'll never know
The hell where youth and laughter go.

Guilt at his noncombatant status was eating away at him. "I can't see any way out of it except in France," he explained to Ottoline. "Nothing definite has been heard from the War Office. They are very fed up with me, as I was supposed to attend a Board last Tuesday, and didn't go." He wanted to discuss it with her, but he hesitated over inviting her to Craiglockhart: "It would be jolly to see you; but it seems a terrible long way for you to come, especially if you are rather broke, as I gather you and Philip generally are!"

Owen prepared his manuscript for Sassoon to send to William Heinemann. Some of the poems resembled Sassoon's. One that he had finished a few weeks earlier, "The Chances," in particular qualified as what Graves called "Sassoonish." It employed, as Sassoon often did, the working-class voice of the regular soldier:

"Ah well," says Jimmy,—an' 'e's seen some scrappin'—
"There ain't more nor five this as can 'appen;
Ye get knocked out; else wounded—bad or cushy;
Scuppered; or nowt except yer feeling mushy."

. . .

But poor young Jim 'e's livin' an' 'e's not;
'E reckoned 'e'd five chances, an' 'e's 'ad;
'E's wounded, killed, and pris'ner, all the lot—
The ruddy lot all rolled in one. Jim's mad.

While the style mimicked Sassoon's, Owen's "pity of war" differed from his mentor's. Sassoon raged *against* those who collaborated in the destruction of soldiers like Jim, but Owen pleaded *for* Jim and his comrades. To both poets, the war was damnable. Sassoon blamed the country's rulers and its complacent citizenry, while in Owen's poetry the war appeared as a natural catastrophe beyond human control. It drove men, himself as much as Jim, mad. Nothing, including Sassoon's protests, was changing that.

OWEN'S VISITS TO friends and students accelerated in the days before his probable departure. On October 28, it was his turn to see the moon through the Astronomer Royal's telescope. Luckily, the telescope was working. The next evening, he delighted in writing to his mother, "Today, since 3 o'clock High Jinks reigned at Mrs. Fullerton's Apartments; we gave the boys Tea & Supper; Mrs. F. says she never enjoyed so much any party in her 23 years experience. I can say almost as much." The festivities ended at nine o'clock, when Owen returned to Craiglockart to tell Susan about it. All his recent days and nights were so enjoyable that he admitted, "Strange, if you like, but I am seriously beginning to have aching sensations at being rooted up from this pleasant Region." While he was writing the letter, Sassoon appeared in his room. Owen told him about Brock's certainty that the Medical Board would send him away. Sassoon was "deeply annoyed about this news, and is going to siege his Dr. Rivers about me!"

Rivers, if Sassoon sieged him at all, would not interfere with one of Brock's patients. Scrupulous practitioners like Rivers and Brock could not keep Owen at Craiglockhart merely as company for Sassoon. Nothing came of Sassoon's intended intercession, as Owen learned on Tuesday, October 30, when the Medical Board discharged him from the hospital and required him to vacate his room immediately. Although he had been under Dr. Brock's care for 126 days, he was still "Unfit G.S. [General Service] permanently." He would have three weeks' leave and then report to the Manchester Regiment's garrison near Scarborough to assume light duty "of a clerical nature."

Owen was in no hurry to depart, writing to his mother, "Some time ago the Grays made me promise to stay 2 or 3 days with them before leaving Edinburgh." He took his luggage to 21 Saint Bernard's Crescent, where Maria Steinthal continued work on his portrait. Maidie played hostess without "gushing" over him, her passion but not her affection having abated. He returned books he had borrowed and prepared to make "a graceful exit from these scenes."

Among Owen's many farewells, the one with his German tutor, librarian Frank Nicholson, drew the most poignant recollection. After their last lesson, they retired to a tea shop. "It was really the only occasion on which he had an opportunity of speaking freely to me," recalled Nicholson, "and it was then that I got a hint of the effect that the horrors he had seen and heard of at the Front had made upon him. He did not enlarge upon them, but they were obviously always in his thoughts, and he wished that an obtuse world should be made sensible of them." Owen had saved photographs of battlefield "mutilations, wounds, surgical operations, and the like" that he was going to show Nicholson. He reached into his pocket and suddenly stopped. Nicholson assumed he was sparing him the shock of images that the War Office kept from the public.

The conversation turned to literature: "His interest in it was unmistakable: the problem of literary form was an absorbing one for him, and he felt that he had found, or was finding, an adequate medium in which to express himself." Nicholson confessed he did not understand Owen's "idea of substituting a play of vowels for pure rhyme," but he admired his "engaging assurance and perhaps a touch of wilfulness, like that of a child insisting, half humorously and half defiantly, that he is in the right . . . He was one of those to whom the miseries of the world are misery and will not let them rest, and he went back to spend his life in doing what he could to palliate them." It was with profound regret that Nicholson said goodbye to his pupil for the last time.

CHAPTER FIFTEEN

Love Drove Me to Rebel

During Wilfred Owen's final days at Saint Bernard's Crescent, the One O'Clock Gun went on firing from Edinburgh Castle. As always, the sudden detonations sent Craiglockhart patients on Princes Street into paroxysms of terror. Some shuddered, others dived for cover. Civilians gazed on them without understanding. Officers with hospital blue bands were already self-conscious in Edinburgh, as one would write in *The Hydra*:

> Now if I walk in Princes Street
> Or smile at friends I chance to meet,
> O, perhaps, a joke with laughter greet
> I am stared at.

The Scotsman published a letter from "Citizen" calling "on the authorities to relieve the peaceful inhabitants of the city from the diurnal shock of the one o'clock Castle gun." The writer's overriding concern was for the soldiers: "Two of those from Craiglockhart, suffering from shell shock, had to be carried home from Princes Street the other day after the shot was fired." A reader signing himself "F. H. S." backed "Citizen" a week later: "There is so much ignorance in regard to neurasthenia, shell shock & c., that it isn't at all surprising to hear that it has taken the collapse of two of these poor victims of the war to call forth these letters."

Craiglockhart Commandant Robert Balfour Graham demanded an end to the practice. "The firing of the gun," he informed Edinburgh's Town Council, "is detrimental to the well-being of soldiers or officers suffering from shell shock or nerve affections, and this is the opinion of my medical officers here." The council referred the matter to a subcommittee of its Lord Provost's Committee, delaying a decision for months. In the meantime, the explosion evoked, if only for a few seconds, "the hell where youth and laughter go" that the men had left in France and to which some would return.

On a more jocular note, *The Hydra* wrote, "We consider it our duty to deny, once and for all, the absurd rumour that an officer from this hospital was seen walking with a girl in Princes Street." The November *Hydra* was the first under Owen's former deputy editor, James Bell Salmond. Salmond published articles and poems that exposed its contributors' growing anger about official mistreatment of soldiers and their families. One poem, "Any Private to Any Private," reacted to a newspaper report calling war widows "a great burden on the state." "S.," as the author signed himself, wrote in Scots dialect:

> I canna mak' it oot. It fair beats a',
> That Wullie has tae dee for God kens what.
> An' Wullie's wife'll get a bob or twa,
> Aifter they interfere wi' what she's got.
> They'll pester her, and crack a dagoned lot;
> An Heaven kens, they'll lave her awfu' ticht.
> "A burden to the state." Her Wullie's shot.
> I kenna, hoo I canna lauch the nicht.

The Hydra's New Series replaced the black-and-white cover photograph of the hospital's main building with a color illustration symbolizing its readers' mental turmoil: below, a denuded battlefield of barren trees and craters; above, the lush Pentland Hills and Craiglockhart. Between the two, an explosion mushrooming skyward was blowing a soldier into the grasp of a many-headed Hydra. The frightful image was offset by the presence of two serene nurses in white cowls and aprons, one on each side framing the scene in a reassuring manner. Brock's influence on the symbolism was obvious, a man wrenched like Antaeus from the earth, the mighty Hydra of Greek myth capturing him, Craiglockhart's staff poised to connect him to the safer land above.

The cover design was the work of one of Brock's patients, Lieutenant Adrian Berrington of the Royal Engineers. It stemmed from his own experience of being blasted into the air by a shell in Flanders on July 14, 1917. Thirty-year-old Berrington, suffering severe symptoms, including amnesia, had entered Craiglockhart on August 16, 1917. It was no accident that Brock assumed his care. Both doctor and patient were disciples of sociologist Patrick Geddes. Berrington had worked with Geddes before the war as architect and painter. Brock's ergotherapy, as it had Owen, inspired him to explore the countryside, sketch the Pentlands, meet Scottish artists, and work on *The Hydra*—in his case, creating cartoon images to head the various sections.

Another *Hydra* stalwart, Owen's friend Charles Mayes, left Craiglockhart on November 2. Owen's correspondence did not indicate whether they met before Mayes returned to duty with the Royal Garrison Artillery. Owen spent that night with the Grays and Maria Steinthal at Saint Bernard's Crescent. The next evening, his last in Scotland, was reserved for Sassoon.

The two soldier-poets met at the Scottish Conservative Club in Princes Street and luxuriated in what Sassoon called a "good dinner and a bottle of noble Burgundy." Fortified with the wine, they moved from the oak-paneled dining area to the staid confines of the smoking room. Seated in leather chairs before imposing oriel windows, they had the space to themselves apart from one aged clubman reading *The Scotsman*. The venue's usual hush gave way to their laughter, as Sassoon read passages from "a volume of portentously over-elaborated verse," Aylmer Strong's *A Human Voice*, which he had given to Owen:

> Oh is it true I have become
> This gourd, this gothic vacuum.
>
> What cassock'd misanthrope
> Hawking peace-canticles for glory-gain,
> Hymns from his rostrum'd height th' epopt of Hate?

At the word "epopt," apparently Strong's rendering of "epopée" for "epic song," the two subalterns became hysterical. Sassoon read on, "O is it true I have become / This gourd, this gothic vacuum?" That drew more laughter. Noticing the old gentleman peering from behind his *Scotsman*, they laughed all the more. The hour was growing late. Sassoon had to return to Craiglockhart before curfew, and Owen's overnight train to London departed at midnight. They walked down to the Princes Street exit. Sassoon recalled, "When saying good-bye I gave him a letter of introduction to Robbie Ross," knowing his kind-hearted old friend would introduce Owen to literary London. Sassoon left, and Owen went up the staircase to open the envelope under a stained-glass window of Benjamin Disraeli. Imagining that Sassoon was "entrusting me with some holy secret," he was disappointed to find ten pounds and a note from Sassoon saying, "Why <u>shouldn't</u> you enjoy your leave? Don't mention this again or I'll be very angry. S." The present of ten pounds seemed belittling, and Owen went upstairs to compose a letter to Sassoon that he later described, alluding to Aylmer Strong, as "a gourd, a Gothic vacuum of a letter." Deciding not to send it, he left the club and walked to the station.

Wilfred Owen had arrived at Craiglockhart 130 days before. His experiences there had transformed him, the boy becoming a man, the hesitant versifier a fine poet, the self-conscious provincial accepted into the Edinburgh art world, and the trembling, shell-shocked subaltern a self-confident officer capable of leading men in battle. The trenches, however, had to wait. A Medical Board would review his progress reintegrating into his regiment in England before determining that his cure was complete.

Sassoon woke the next morning to his first day deprived of his only friend among the patients at "Dottyville" and, worse, without Rivers, who was on sick leave at his brother's house in Kent. Anyway, Rivers's time at Craiglockhart was ending. The RAMC had accepted his resignation and was transferring him to London and the Royal Air Flying Corps, whose pilots were succumbing as much as infantrymen to nervous collapse.

A letter came to him almost immediately from Owen, who had returned to his family in Shrewsbury. Its frank intimacy was unexpected:

> Know that since mid-September, when you still regarded me as a tiresome little knocker on your door, I held you as Keats + Christ + Elijah + my Colonel + my father-confessor + Amenophis IV in profile.
>   What's that mathematically?
>   In effect it is this: that I love you, dispassionately, so much, so very much, dear Fellow, that the blasting little smile you wear on reading this can't hurt me in the least.
>   If you consider what the above names have severally done for me, you will know what you are doing. And you have fixed my Life—however short. You did not light me: I was always a mad comet; but you have fixed me. I spun round you a satellite for a month, but I shall swing out soon, a dark star in the orbit where you will blaze.

Owen added that "Robt. Ross" had written to him, suggesting they meet in London. On November 9, Ross took him to lunch at the Reform

Club in Pall Mall and introduced him to H. G. Wells and other famous writers. While Owen was entering a world that seemed impermeable to him before he knew Sassoon, Sassoon was dealing with a visitor whose arrival in Scotland was not entirely welcome.

Lady Ottoline Morrell had been longing to see Sassoon since he told her of his intention to fight again. She took an all-night train that arrived in Edinburgh on the morning of November 9. "When I arrived I looked everywhere for Siegfried but he was not at the station to meet me," she wrote, "he had been playing golf and was late, but I took a cab to the hotel where he had engaged rooms for me." Sassoon came to her in time for dinner in the hotel's dining room. The conversation was less the younger man seeking matronly counsel than the stubborn soldier determined to rejoin his regiment. After dinner, they went on talking in the sitting room of her suite. She recalled that "he told me how haunted he was by the thought of the men at the front. Their spirits seemed to come and rap on the window calling him to go out to them." Their discussion was going nowhere, and they agreed to continue in the morning.

Sassoon was late again, arriving at lunchtime. Afterward, they visited a chapel and strolled through "a wooded valley; golden leaves still on the trees, and a golden carpet underneath." Ottoline felt too shy to speak, but Sassoon was friendly and open. "He had been engaged to a girl at the beginning of the War," she said he told her, "'felt he ought to be [engaged] as all his brother officers had a girl,' but he soon found it impossible, as he really only liked men, and women were antipathetic to him." When his youthful homosexuality tormented him, he "would roam the country all night in despair." The redemptive moment came when he revealed himself to his brother Hamo, "who laughed at him and said he was the same himself." Ottoline and Sassoon meandered to the beach. As the tide subsided, Sassoon walked away. "He always had an odd way of going off without a word and without attempting to say good-night or good-bye."

The next morning, Sassoon played golf without coming to say fare-well. Ottoline cried in the train on her way home, "but in spite of the many things he has done to hurt and annoy me, I always remain fond of him." Her journal entry about her Scottish sojourn ended with Sassoon's recent poem "Banishment." Its final lines expressed better than he had in their conversations why he had to fight again:

> Love drove me to rebel.
> Love drives me back to grope with them through hell;
> And in their tortured eyes I stand forgiven.

ON NOVEMBER 21, Sassoon wrote to Ottoline, "Rivers has gone to town to his new hospital job, but will do his best for me, I know." Craiglockhart without Rivers and Owen offered Sassoon no solace as he awaited what would be his decisive Medical Board on November 26. He took two days' leave in London to see "an intermediary," who might influence the board in his favor. He dined with Robbie Ross and met the poet Robert Nichols before returning to Scotland.

Despite Sassoon's unsatisfactory reception of Lady Ottoline in Edinburgh, he persisted in his attempts to convince her that his decision did not mean he had abandoned his ideals. His letter of November 21 played on their mutual animosity toward the country's leaders: "Reading about 'The New British Triumph' in the evening paper. Those things always bring black despair. I can visualise the horror too clearly, and the result is not triumphant. O God the yellings of politicians seem to get worse and worse. But the poets will get the upper hand of them—some day (when bound in half-calf, suitable for wedding presents)."

He wrote the same day to Graves, telling him to "forget about that d. . . . d money" he had lent him. Sassoon was making every effort to get to his unit at the front. He had conspired with Rivers to return to the 1st Battalion in France, but the battalion was on its way to the "side show" in Syria. By November 28, it was heading to Naples, "Nero's native city," en route to the Middle East. "I wish to God I were with them—the prospect of being messed about and finally sent out to the 19th Battalion haunts me badly." Fate was keeping him away from the trenches where he longed to prove himself. In answer to Graves's proposal that they travel together after the war, he wrote, "It is all very jolly, but I can't see beyond the war, and I don't care if I'm dead or alive." He added that Owen "will be a very good poet some day, and he is a very loveable creature."

At last, on November 26, Sassoon's Medical Board convened. Rivers came up to Craiglockhart to conduct the board with Lieutenant Colonel Balfour Graham. Sassoon did not run away this time. "The Board asked if I had changed my views on the war," he wrote, "and I said I hadn't, which seemed to cause surprise." The officers on the board concluded:

> Since his last Board he has continued to improve & is now fit for General Service. He has been instructed to return to his Reserve Bat[talion]: has been furnished with a warrant for that purpose.

Sassoon left Craiglockhart that day, determined never to return.

CHAPTER SIXTEEN

Things Might Be Worse

Craiglockhart was changing as 1917 drew to a close. Its affable and effective first commandant, Major Bryce, and Captain Rivers, its most illustrious clinician, were gone. Owen and Sassoon had returned to their regiments. *The Hydra*'s new editor, J. B. Salmond, left soon after publishing his first issue. The American doctor, Major Ruggles, was awaiting orders to join U.S. troops in France. From the hospital's original staff, Captain Brock, Matron MacBean, head gardener Henry Carmichael, and the VAD nurses carried on.

Scotland in late December enjoyed barely seven hours of daylight, leaving Craiglockhart to slumber into darkness around four each afternoon. Long nights, storms, and high winds did little to relieve depression or prevent nocturnal howling. The hospital received its 496th patient, Lieutenant L. Brook of the Royal Fusiliers, on Christmas Eve. *The Hydra* published "A Christmas Message": "No need to pretend we are not homesick, for we are. We did not like being shelled, but we did not run away. And at Christmas here there is much that we can do to pass the time right merrily along." The suggestion that the Officers' Club substituted for family may not have impressed many, but the magazine assured its readers "that Things might be Worse. For we are going to have a Happy Christmas—doctors, sisters, nurses, patients, orderlies, and all."

A full-page cartoon in *The Hydra* furnished a counterpoint to the Christmas bonhomie: a bedridden patient is jolted upright and transfixed by an artillery shell flying straight at him. His hair stands on end. His mouth and eyes are agape with fright. Four spectral figures, somewhere between ghosts and spacemen, taunt him. The vision, not unfamiliar to the journal's readers, bore the simple caption, "Shell Shock!"

Plum pudding, turkey, and carols compensated in some measure for the bleak ambience; but officers about to be pronounced "fit for General Service" expected to face again a war that showed no sign of ending. The battle front was frozen, following a recent German counterattack that annulled British tank-led advances at Cambrai. Bolshevik Russia's December 15 armistice with the Central Powers released vast German military resources for the Western Front. Soon to challenge Germany's increased strength were the American divisions crossing the Atlantic. Patients at Craiglockhart could ask, as Sassoon had Graves in October, "O Robert, what ever will happen to end the war?"

The Hydra's new editor, Lieutenant George Henry Bonner, encouraged goodwill for Christmas without ignoring his readers' mental torments in his selection of articles and poems. He was, after all, as shattered as they were. Born in May 1895, Bonner was four when his Baptist minister father died. His mother, Margaret Elizabeth Johnson, raised him and his younger brother, Augustine, on her own in Birmingham. The boys attended King Edward's School, where George edited the school magazine, *The Chronicle*, and was captain of his house swimming and soccer teams. Among his older schoolmates was J. R. R. Tolkien, future author of *The Lord of the Rings*, whose passion for Celtic myth he shared. His brother, Augustine, although only seventeen, volunteered for military service as soon as Britain declared war. George instead began Classics study at Magdalen College, Oxford, in the autumn of 1914; but he left in November to follow his brother into the army. By November 1915, both brothers were in France as second lieutenants—George in the Royal Field Artillery's 25th Anti-Aircraft Battery and Augustine, or Austin as his family called him, in the South Staffordshire Regiment. Austin was wounded on the Somme in April 1916, recovered in England, and returned to France in September as a Royal Flying Corps aerial observation officer in balloons over the German lines. In November, after a year at the front, George was diagnosed with shell shock. His War Office file did not stipulate a cause.

RAMC physicians sent George to England for treatment on January 6, 1917, beginning his odyssey through a succession of mental hospitals. Monthly Medical Boards found him "unfit," until, on November 30, 1917, his thirteenth board at the Western General Hospital transferred him to Craiglockhart. Within a few days, the five-foot-eight, 148-pound subaltern with rimless glasses and dark hair neatly parted on the right became editor of *The Hydra*. Surviving hospital records did not indicate which psychiatrist took his case, but a poem he wrote left little doubt:

> When I came to Craiglockhart I saw my MO
> My MO said to me what were you till the war
>   I said nothing and very nice too
> So he said now that you're here you must do something more
> Some of the things you should do
>   Just take a cold swim every morning at six
> Then a walk <u>say</u> to the Pentlands and back
>   After breakfast go down to the farm and drop sticks
> Or by ploughing you'll soon get the knack
>   After lunch make some rugs or read Homer a bit
> You may think you'll get tired but you won't
>   If you do what I've said we shall soon have you fit.

Bonner afforded space to Craiglockhart alumni in *The Hydra*'s pages. Salmond contributed an amusing short story about golfers, "A

Pair of Trousers." Owen supplied an essay, "Antaeus, Or Back to the Land," that he signed "Arcturus," the Bear Star. In what amounted to a manifesto of Brockian philosophy for the benefit of new patients, Arcturus briefly told the familiar tale of Hercules upending Antaeus and explained its relevance: "Now surely every officer who comes to Craiglockhart recognises that, in a way, he is himself an Antaeus who has been taken from Mother Earth and well-nigh crushed to death by the war giant or military machine."

Arcturus noted that two of Hercules's seven labors were his struggles with Antaeus and the Hydra, two prime figures in the Brock canon. "We are all," he continued, "to a large extent, creatures of our environment—that is, we are all offspring of earth." To restore health, the men needed to return "to natural conditions, and also to have relation to our surroundings . . . It is when our heads are in the clouds of unpracticality, our feet clean off the earth, that the Hercules of war will overcome us. *Labor omnia vincit.*"

Sassoon, spending Christmas at the Royal Welch Fusiliers' Litherland base, sent *The Hydra* two poems under his full name rather than, as before, "S." The first, "Break of Day," began in a trench:

> Legs wrapped in sand-bags—lumps of chalk and clay
> Spattering his face. Dry-mouthed, he thought, "To-day
> We start the damned attack; and, Lord knows why,
> Zero's at nine; how bloody if I'm done in
> Under the freedom of that morning sky!"

The scene shifted abruptly to the consolatory setting of a hunting field: "In joyous welcome from the untroubled past; / While the war drifts away, forgotten at last." For Sassoon, despite exhilarating days chasing foxes over fence and field near Litherland, the war was anything but forgotten. His preoccupation with it emerged in the second poem. "Base Details" harked back to a familiar "Sassoonish" trope: mockery of indifferent staff officers who dispatched men to their doom.

If I were fierce and bald, and short of breath,
I'd live with scarlet Majors at the Base
And speed glum heroes up the line to death.

. . .

"Poor young chap,"
I'd say—"I used to know his father well.
Yes, we've lost heavily in this last scrap."
And when the war is done, and youth stone dead,
I'd toddle safely home and die—in bed.

In mid-January 1918, a Mr. S. Sullivan of 192 Washwood Heath Road, Saltley, Birmingham, found a document on the Birmingham to Preston train. He mailed it to the Minister of War, Lord Derby. The paper circulated within the War Office, whose officials jotted comments in its margins. One civil servant noted, "The document, dated July 1917, purports to be a 'statement made by 2nd Lieutenant Siegfried Sassoon, 3rd Battalion Royal Welsh [*sic*] Fusiliers regarding what he terms the deliberate prolongation of the War by those having power to end it." He forwarded it to another civil servant, who wrote before passing it farther along the chain, "I think you wd like to see this. Lt. Sassoon was undoubtedly the author but when it was written he was a lunatic." No action was taken. Sassoon proceeded with his battalion to Ireland, not yet the Western Front proving ground he was demanding.

CRAIGLOCKHART'S PATIENTS IN early 1918 were painting distressing pictures of their lives. One, Philip Mercer-Wright, wrote, "Well, there are moments that are absolutely desperate. They culminate in the Panic in the Night." Hallucination and reality, as with Sassoon's vision of the late Lieutenant Orme, were hard to distinguish.

Many patients, in addition to morbid fear of explosives, were haunted by their friends' horrifying deaths. One wrote about "J. M. S. P.," "because he was my friend, and I loved him." J. M. S. P. had seen a German soldier interrupt his charge across No Man's Land to blow out the brains of a wounded and defenseless young British subaltern. This so outraged him that he jumped over the parapet and charged the German. "He was killed at the same instant as his bayonet wrought vengeance on the monster Teuton." Others could not forget the sight and sound of comrades vaporized by high explosives, frothing from poison gas, and burned alive by flamethrowers. The resulting "survivors' guilt" complicated their treatment. Many believed, against medical advice, that repressing such memories was safer than reliving them.

AT THE END of 1917 and in early 1918, Medical Boards reaffirmed the noncombatant status of Max Plowman due to a dilated heart, breathlessness, and insomnia. Plowman, whose pamphlet, "The Right to Live," had focused his mind on Christ's and William Blake's admonitions against killing, had resolved never to kill again. Though this was a bold decision for a serving soldier in wartime, commanders would not require him to kill anyone while he remained a mild neurasthenic case restricted to Home Service. Plowman transferred to the Durham Light Infantry in Stockton-on-Tees, becoming its mess officer.

Despite his noncombat status, Plowman wrote to the Adjutant, 52nd Battalion, Durham Light Infantry, on January 14, 1918:

> For some time past it has been becoming increasingly apparent to me that for reasons of conscientious objection I was unfitted to hold my commission in His Majesty's army & I am now absolutely convinced that I have no alternative but to proffer my resignation.

The letter quoted the prime minister's statement that war was "a relic of barbarism," adding his own belief that "organised warfare of any kind is always organised murder." Christ's Incarnation meant that

God lived in every human being and "killing men is always killing God." Resigning before the army ordered him to active service showed his determination to play no part, including as mess officer, in the military machine. He asked the adjutant to forward his letter to the commanding officer so that he could leave the army at once. Neither the adjutant nor the commanding officer replied, undoubtedly as reluctant to prosecute him as Sassoon's commanders had been to court-martial him.

On February 2, 1918, his situation changed when a Medical Board deemed him healthy enough to rejoin the West Yorkshire Regiment for service abroad. Plowman responded the next day that he had "tendered resignation of commission more than five weeks ago." The army, claiming it had no record of his letter, ordered him again to report for duty.

Plowman did not know Sassoon, but he admired his poetry and his protest. Trusting in the fact that both had been patients of Rivers, Plowman wrote to Sassoon about his predicament. Sassoon forwarded the letter to Rivers, who wrote, "I'd quite forgotten Plowman. His story is very different [from] yours. He has an idea that in killing men, you are also killing God, and this highly abstract proposition seems to him sufficiently definite to take action . . . but I'm still hoping that I may be able to help." Rivers initiated a correspondence that Plowman described to his friend Hugh de Selincourt:

> I wrote & explained things to him & he has written again very nicely asking me to let him know at once whenever, or if ever, I think he can be of any use which is extraordinarily decent of him, don't you think? If I were to have any trouble with the Medical people he might be an excellent Court of Appeal.

Rivers's regard for Plowman did not extend to accepting his pacifism any more than he had agreed with Sassoon's. He wrote to Plowman that Sassoon, then with the Royal Welch Fusiliers in Ireland, had returned to duty and was happy with his decision. This appeared to be a hint for Plowman to do the same. His and Sassoon's reasons for refusing to serve, however, differed. In Plowman's view, Sassoon had protested only against "British war aims," while his own objection was to war itself. Viewing Plowman's stance as more dangerous, the military ordered him on January 19 to return to the regiment or face the court-martial that Sassoon's friends had avoided for him. Plowman chose court-martial. Lieutenant Colonel H. H. S. Alexander, commanding officer of the 52nd Battalion, Durham Light Infantry, went to Plowman that day to tell him his resignation was not accepted. Plowman persisted, leaving Alexander no choice but to arrest him or put him on the sick list. In the event, he opted for the sick list pending a Medical Board. When the board confirmed Plowman's sanity, Alexander had him arrested.

On February 27, Plowman received the "Summary of Evidence" against him, "but whether for a Court Martial or just to fully explain the case to those anxious to accept the resignation I don't know." The army offered him, as a Conscientious Objector (C.O.), the option of noncombat service—something many C.O.s, including those laboring on the Morrells' farm at Garsington, had accepted. Plowman refused. "Civil conscription for purposes of war seems to me if possible more abhorrent than military conscription," he insisted. "To decline one & to accept the other during war seems to me the meanest way of assisting in the carrying on of the war . . . The soldier in the trenches understands the position of the C.O. in prison. He doesn't understand the position of the C.O. who helps provide the means for keeping the soldier in the trenches while he (the C.O.) is out of range."

AMERICAN MAJOR RUGGLES was active at Craiglockhart in early January, attending Field Club lectures and earning plaudits from the Debating Society for his rhetorical skills: "With great pleasure we welcome Major Ruggles, whose contributions to the debates have been most valuable—so much so that, like Oliver Twist, we ask for more." The weekly concerts continued throughout February. On the ninth, May Mackay, whom Major Bryce had caught receiving a kiss from Lieutenant James Butlin the previous June, returned to sing opera arias in her "sweet soprano" voice. The concerts and plays, including Wilde's *An Ideal Husband*, relieved the tedium of Saturday nights. Sunday mornings were reserved for church services.

Lieutenant Bonner worked hard editing *The Hydra*, but, like Owen before him, needed more copy. Shortage of material forced him, as it had Owen, to write much of it himself. The seven poems that he contributed to the magazine's pages from January to March 1918, signed with various initials, showed a playful young officer enjoying himself with language. They also exposed his torment. In January, he published three poems of his own, alongside offerings from other patients, Sassoon, and some of the hospital's women supporters. His first poem, called "Triolet" for its traditional eight-line stanza form, was a jocular lament to a woman who "blew me a kiss / From the tips of her fingers—/ The mischievous miss." The kiss fell short of his desire: "That to blow such a kiss / Is to cast an aspersion— / My thought is this / She should give it in person."

The second, "The Passing of the Turk," romanticized a medieval contest of chivalry as if warfare had been consigned to the distant past: "Sing me a song of the day that is gone / Song of an age that is fled." It was the kind of war—"Our sabres flashed, our spearsmen dashed"— that boys like Bonner imagined they would fight in 1914. His last poem in the January edition, "A Song of Ordnance," was a comic yarn about "a coal-black horse of pride" whose nose froze in its feed bag. The Master-Gunner and the Sergeant of the Guard tried to prise the bag off. Bashing it with a pick and pulling with a rope were of no avail, "Till the horse, becoming bored with life, incontinently died." The report of the horse's death reached the General:

> But this is why we are supplied, or so the story goes,
> With a Tool-Removing-Catch-Retaining-Bag-Horse Nose!

Bonner's respect for Dr. Brock did not stop him publishing a satire of his therapist in a compendium of dubious rumors. "We Hear," the anonymous author wrote, "That a certain stoical M.O. has discovered an organism without environment." Bonner's January editorial, reprising Brock's Antaeus theme, declared, "Our late editor, Mr. Owen, has reduced the Antaeus saga to blank verse." This referred to Owen's "The Wrestlers," written for Brock in July 1917 and left incomplete. Bonner promised to reproduce Owen's epic in February, but he failed to do so without explaining the omission. His own poem under the signature "G. A." in February similarly harked back to ancient Greece, no doubt with Brock's approval, and made a clear connection to his readers' predicaments. A choral voice, in classical tradition, sang his "Invocation":

> Mother of gods and men receive us now:
> Foredone with fear we stagger through the night
> Where shapes of doom pursue us, ghostly arms
> Reach out to grasp our spent and shivering souls.

The chorus, representing Craiglockhart's emotionally ravaged cohort, pleaded with the "Mother of gods" that they "May drink of quietude and fear no more." Leaving behind "the twilight haunts of fear," they sought rehabilitation through nature as Brock recommended:

> By plough and pasturage, by wood and moor,
> Leading us up from hell's dim shadowlands
> To the far sunrise where on the edge of day
> I see the Gold City of our Dreams.

Bonner became chairman of a new Literary Society. Its Tuesday evening lectures included discourses on Thomas Hardy, H. G. Wells,

Alfred Lord Tennyson, Samuel Butler, and "Poetry—Its Place in Modern Life." He added, "Everyone interested in literature and modern thought is invited."

The departure in late January of Major Ruggles and another visiting American physician prompted the hospital to express its gratitude: "Major Ruggles and Captain Hall, of the United States Army, have left us, having been called away at very short notice for service in France. We thank them for all their kindness towards us, and wish them luck in their new work." The major's posting was to the U.S. Army 2nd Division as its chief psychiatrist in France. He applied skills honed on British soldiers at Craiglockhart to American shell-shock victims. His heroism treating them on the front lines would earn him France's Croix de Guerre with bronze star.

GEORGE BONNER, as evidenced by his poetry, fluctuated between hope and profound pessimism in the freezing winter of 1918. Where Brock counseled patients like him to confront their demons, Bonner sought distraction. Editing the hospital journal took his mind off his problems. Seeking female company became an alternative to introspection. He inscribed a triolet in Nurse Florence Mellor's autograph book that hinted at infatuation:

> I must think of a verse
> For the book of Nurse Florence—
> Something witty and terse
> I must think of a verse
> But my thoughts all disperse
> And my tears fall in torrents.
> I must think of a verse
> For the book of Nurse Florence.

His preoccupation with Miss Mellor became clearer in a revised, pseudonymous triolet that he called "A Valentine":

I meant it for Nurse
But I gave it to Sister,
Which made it much worse
(As I meant it for Nurse);
'Twas an excellent verse
Rhyming "Mr" with "kissed her";
I meant it for Nurse,
But I gave it to Sister.

Bonner was not the only patient to take an interest in the nurses, despite Matron Margaret MacBean's disapproval. Captain Harold Stevens fell for Nurse Mary McGregor after his arrival at the hospital in late 1917. Fighting with the Royal Scots, Britain's oldest regiment, he had been wounded at the Battle of Loos in 1915 and again on the first day of the Somme in July 1916. Like Sassoon, he had earned the Military Cross. The death of his best friend, blown to pieces beside him, produced the symptoms that sent him to Craiglockhart. His daughter, Betty Stein, would later recall, "The greatcoat that my father was wearing at the time was bespattered with this poor man's remains and he refused to have it cleaned in any way." Despite the trauma, Stevens recovered, married Mary McGregor, and resumed service in France.

George Bonner penned another poem, titled simply "Sonnet," positing a woman's love as the force that broke "the spell" of the "grinning host of fears." Brock had identified such longing in any patient as a "substitute for this feeling of *bienêtre* which is lost to him. And this he finds in some form of what may broadly be called a *drug* . . . attempts to compromise with life—to gain its solaces without facing its tasks; they are indications that the patient is endeavouring to shirk his *milieu*." A hint of shirking appeared in Bonner's "At Dusk." He is lying half awake, when a thought comes to him in the form of "A bright green moth / Flitting silently / Through the grey air." He is too lethar-

gic to capture the moth/thought, and "It danced away / Into the shadows." The poem hinted at Bonner's preference for avoiding unbearable
memories.

The hidden reason for letting the moth flit away emerged in a
poem he wrote in November, before he came to Craiglockhart. The
varied stanza lengths and short lines of "Let Us Taste the Glory of
Battle" read as if the poet were out of breath:

> In a shell-hole,
> He crouches,
> This officer,
> Unable to go forward.
> He is afraid.
>
> His men
> Are either dead
> Or have gone forward.
>
> Except one
> Who,
> A few yards away.
> Shattered and screaming,
> Prays to be shot.

Artillery shells explode in front of him, but he cannot get up and
lead the men against the opposing trenches:

> He has reached that point
> Where the mind
> No longer controls the body.

He remembers how at war's outset he longed to prove himself brave,
but now he finds himself immobilized and wonders how friends would
judge him.

Now they will despise him, his friends,
And speak of him in whispers
As one who failed.
Pity will be his at their hands.
Pity not unmixed with contempt.

. . .

"Once I was a brave man
And she loved me;
Now I am a coward
Will she love me still?"
An aeroplane overhead
Hums "Coward, coward!"

Hearing the accusation of cowardice from the sky alluded to Bonner's role as anti-aircraft gunner. His brother, Austin, was an aerial observation officer and a daily target for Germans doing the same work Bonner had. In the poem, the soldier breaks down, believing that fear is stronger than both love and death:

He cries like a child.

"Coward, coward!"

The sound of a heavy shell
Grinding through the zenith.
The end of misery.
Death.

Rivers classified such fear, not as cowardice, but as the mind's retreat from the impossible choice between duty and life. Even as this soldier, undoubtedly Bonner himself, longs for death, he cannot move. Paralysis prevents him from running away or into the fray. He is paralyzed between fight and flight. Bonner, unable to expose his shame, never published the poem.

He was putting his third and final *Hydra* to bed, when on March 5, 1918, the hospital's Medical Board discharged him as unfit for further duty. The next editor praised him for increasing the circulation: "It is impossible to estimate the work done by him, but it is sufficient to say that, by dint of great persuasive power and much 'midnight oil,' the Magazine always appeared to date." A week after Bonner's departure, the military ordered him to relinquish his commission. He resisted, perhaps hoping to vindicate himself. "I would therefore much prefer," he wrote to the War Office on April 1, "if it is possible, to remain on Anti-Aircraft work." It was not possible.

At the end of the month, Austin, was killed by anti-aircraft fire in a balloon over German lines. His commanding officer commended him as "one of our best observers." George, hard on the stigma of dismissal from the Royal Field Artillery and the loss of his nineteen-year-old brother, met a young woman named Eleanor Mary Ford. They married and had a son. However, the love he had longed for in his "Sonnet" did not break the "spell" of war trauma. Brock had warned that love was no substitute for the labor of self-healing. At the age of thirty-three, after trying to build a career as a writer and poet, Bonner committed suicide.

CHAPTER SEVENTEEN

A Second Chance

The first post-Bonner *Hydra* lampooned hospital staff and patients alike in an imaginary listing of "Favourite Books of Famous People." The author, calling himself "CYNIC," wrote:

Capt. BROCK had some difficulty in choosing his favourite book. He decided at length in favour of "Actions and Reactions." He said to me: "I have never read the book, but the title is suggestive. I should imagine that the writer deals with the 'Art of Doing.' Action, action and again action is what we want, as he no doubt points out. To act well is to be well. In the Bolsheviks we have an example . . ." and so on.

Boarding school whimsy prevailed. "Don't argue in the corridors!" declared a poster on the noticeboard. "Come to the Debating Society and argue there!" Drama critic "LOLLIUS" described a Saturday concert skit by two junior officers, Marshall and Dundas, as "a string of chestnuts, bad puns, and weak jokes." Lieutenants Robinson's and Hughes's comic song-and-joke act "can only be described as a 'regrettable incident.'"

Hilarity disguised the strains of mental struggle, but evocations of past suffering were unavoidable. A simple walk along Princes Street continued to induce terror when the One O'Clock Gun fired from Edinburgh Castle. It was to remove that danger that the commandant, Lieutenant Colonel Balfour Graham, had petitioned for its suspension. The onset of spring, he reminded Edinburgh's Town Council, would draw patients outdoors to the city's parks and avenues: "I am of opinion that anything that interferes with the comfort, well being, health, or happiness in any shape or form of our officers and soldiers at the present time should be done away with for the period of the war at least, and the time gun is one of these." The Lord Provost's Committee, after considering the commandant's plea, "agreed to recommend the discontinuance meantime of the firing of the gun." The gun, for the first time since its inauguration in 1861, ceased reverberating throughout Scotland's capital.

Engine misfires from buses and cars, however, could not be stopped. One patient wrote about "vainly trying to dodge motor buses which invariably seemed to back fire at the sight of my blue band." Another, C. Wakelin Scott, recorded the same, unavoidable experience in Princes Street. "The motor-bus, as it passed me, backfired—as buses always do when anywhere near me—causing me to start in the way that sets a hallmark on the denizens of Craiglockhart."

Edinburgh, as the closest city to Craiglockhart, was vital to the rehabilitation of Brock's patients. It was there that they met civilians and took advantage of cultural attractions: museums, art galleries, libraries, book shops, and cinemas. The new *Hydra* editor asked Brock to explain how "Craiglockhart's temporary residents" should utilize Edinburgh in their therapy. "Well," Brock answered, "this is a big order, but I'll have a shot." He said the city was not merely a place to "kill the time" but "an integral part of the Craiglockhart 'cure.'" Men blown up in war, "more dead than alive," would find in Edinburgh ideal conditions for their restoration. The place was "a sort of microcosm" of Western Europe. Human beings first settled there for the safety of its easily defended Castle Rock. Around it, they found abundant water and fertile ground that eventually produced fine paper—"hence, doubtless, contributing to Edinburgh's historical reputation as a literary and educational centre"—and excellent beer. Brock's civic history covered North Sea trade with the Baltic, Roman roads, Renaissance art, and modern imperialism, all of which marked the cityscape. He urged readers to visit the Wall of Antoninus, where the ancient Rome they had read about in school would become real.

Edinburgh, he added, "is not something stationary; it is rather something which grows; it is, in fact, rather a 'process' than a 'thing,' and if we wish to understand it, it must, like any vital process, imperatively be considered in its time-relations." Mental and moral health required the men to embrace the civic environment and find their place in it: "Each of you can be 'a citizen of Edinburgh.'" Brock's ergotherapeutic emphasis on connection to community and locale, derived from the sociology of Patrick Geddes, was not common practice at other shell-shock hospitals. The Maghull Red Cross Military Hospital emphasized talking therapy without regard to the landscape outside its walls. One of the most famous psychiatrists treating neurasthenic soldiers, Canadian Dr. Lewis Yealland at the National Hospital for the Paralysed and Epileptic, employed electro-shock therapy ("faradism"), verbal abuse, and counter-suggestion to eradicate what he defined as cowardice rather than mental illness. Yealland and others of his persuasion saw no benefit in connecting patients to the London environment they could see from their windows in Queen's Square.

The Geddes-Brock "Place-Folk-Work" therapy succeeded with some, like Wilfred Owen, who worked hard at it. It failed others, including George Bonner, whose experiences did not let them meet the challenge. No therapy had a 100 percent success rate.

Brock's devotion to Scotland played out in studies of the local countryside, visits to Edinburgh's intellectual societies and the hospital's spring concerts. One Saturday evening in April, Lieutenant Maclean's bagpipes captivated his audience with traditional Celtic songs. One of those present recalled, "I saw at least two Scotch nurses break into a double from the dining-room to the concert hall, when they heard the strains of the pipes on the stage. What a bagpipe will do!!" When the same man heard the voice of Scottish soprano Maud Campbell, he enthused, "To *hear* her is to love her." The musical fare was especially touching to the Scottish nursing staff, headed by Matron Margaret MacBean, and the many Scottish officers who attended the concerts. On April 6, the entire evening was given over to a "Special Scottish Concert" with songs, dances, and dramas originating in Scotland.

Early spring snow did not deter officers from indulging in the country's indigenous sport, golf, at Baberton and other nearby greens. Several officers formed an Angling Club to pursue Scottish trout and salmon in the rivers and ponds around Craiglockhart. Bagpipe-playing Lieutenant Maclean lectured the Field Club on Scottish fishing, and a week later the club heard Brock discuss "Edinburgh in Evolution." Brock was turning his charges into honorary Scotsmen.

ON APRIL 5, a court-martial convened in Stockton-on-Tees charging Lieutenant Mark Plowman with "disobeying a lawful command given by his superior officer [to return to the 3rd Battalion, West Yorkshire Regiment]." Prosecuting lawyers had an easy time showing that Plowman had indeed disobeyed orders. Plowman, representing himself, declined to cross-examine the prosecution's witnesses. Nor did he testify in his defense. That, he admitted, had been a mistake: "I made quite a gratuitous & stupid howler in not giving evidence on my own account & of course there's no such thing as cross-examination in the proper & civil sense of the word at a Court Martial, & that rather badly handicapped me." The court permitted him to read out his three-page "Reasons for Resigning":

> I am resigning my commission because I now believe that "national responsibility" is an insufficient excuse for committing acts, in the name of the nation, which no sane person would be guilty of as an individual . . . If it is said that the middle of a war is no fit time to come to such a conclusion, I reply that every moment is opportune in which we cease to do evil and learn to do good . . . The designed and intentional killing of any person against whose personal character you can make no charge, is, I consider, murder of the worst possible kind . . . I am resigning my commission because I no longer believe that war can end war.

The court's fairness surprised him: "I fully expected to be most liberally insulted but I think they actually listened to my 'Reasons' & when it was over the Judge Advocate asked for a copy." However sympathetic the Judge Advocate may have been, the court found him guilty. The punishment, to be "dismissed from His Majesty's Service," was not harsh. The court delayed imposing even that sentence by instructing a Medical Board to examine him so that, in the words of one court officer, "we could then invalid him out of the Army for medical reasons which I think would not only demonstrate the humanity of the military machine but also the mentality of the majority of our conscientious objectors." A Medical Board under Dr. Charles Samuel Myers, one of Rivers's student companions on the Torres Strait expedition and subsequently an authority on neurasthenia, met at Stockton-on-Tees on May 1. It uncovered details of Plowman's family history that might have played a role in his mental collapse: "Father had a nervous breakdown when 45, necessitating a 6 months' holiday, a paternal uncle and aunt were under restraint for insanity, the latter suffering from religious mania." Yet Myers and his colleagues concluded that Plowman "shows no sign of insanity, has no loss of memory apart for [sic] events immediately following on his concussion." The court thus could not "invalid him out of the Army for medical reasons."

Plowman's resistance failed to achieve the exposure granted Sassoon, who had a privileged background, political connections, and the Military Cross. *The Times* gave Plowman's trial only three short sentences at the bottom of its "News in Brief" column on April 6. Five days later, the radical press picked up the story. *The Tribunal*, underground organ of the No-Conscription Fellowship, trumpeted Plowman's bravery on its front page alongside praise for "OVER 5,000 MEN" resisting military service: "These Anti-Militarists are actually serving their Country." The Independent Labour Party's *Labour Leader* reported the army's maltreatment of "Mark Plowman, author and journalist, a twice wounded soldier," and published in full his "Reasons for Resigning." While no member of Parliament rallied to his defense, the country's pacifists did. Three women he did not know offered financial assistance, a gesture he declined but appreciated "as a sign of the way in which women will redeem the world." Support from Britain's antiwar minority succored the beleaguered Plowman, but it did not alter the court's verdict.

THE WAR TOUCHED Craiglockhart's staff as well as its patients. April brought distressing communiqués from the front to George Bonner's putative inamorata, VAD nurse Florence Mellor, and head gardener Henry Carmichael. Miss Mellor's brother, nineteen-year-old Lance Corporal Haydn Mellor of the Gordon Highlanders, had been in the trenches for barely one hour when a shard of shrapnel struck and killed him. The Carmichael family received official notice that another of their boys, Henry's grandson, John "Jack" Carmichael, had been killed at the front. The army buried him at Ypres in Belgium. Soon afterward, James Stirling Carmichael, son of Henry's brother, came home alive. Having served with the Black Watch for more than a year on the front line, he suffered shell shock as severely as any officer at Craiglock-hart. Private Carmichael, however, was an enlisted man. Despite living on the Craiglockhart grounds, he could only watch while officers played cricket and tennis on the grass that his uncle and cousins mowed and watered. Sudden noises terrified him, as if they were exploding artillery rounds. He escaped into the woods for days at a time, sleeping on open ground. His family searched for him and brought him home, but he would disappear again. Henry Carmichael left no record to indicate how he viewed his nephew's treatment compared with that of the officers whose gardens he maintained.

Not everyone was oblivious to the military's disparate attitudes to shell-shocked officers and men. Lieutenant Colonel Arthur Osburn, a physician who had enlisted in 1911, noticed the difference during a heavy German artillery barrage near Montauban in 1918. Three soldiers dragged a shattered staff officer into the derelict shelter where Osburn was bandaging the wounded. "The Staff officer," Osburn wrote, "a biggish man, somewhere between twenty-five and thirty, lay moaning on the ground. We could find no wound." The shelling had unhinged him. "Driven mad with terror, slobbering and moaning, he clawed and scrabbled violently in the mud, his head under the chair," wrote Osburn, calling him "this pathetic, scrabbling incoherent animal that had once been a British staff officer." Orderlies forced him into an ambulance.

Osburn, who did not know whether the staff officer was lucky enough to receive therapy at Craiglockhart, reflected on his likely future:

Perhaps, recovered, he shoots partridges now in Norfolk, dines at Claridges, hunts with the North Cotswold, or keeps a chicken farm in Surrey. But when one thinks of how we treated this Staff officer, and how, on the other hand, some poor half-educated ploughboy, whose nerves had likewise given way, and who was not much more than half this Staff officer's age, was sent back to face the enemy or be shot for cowardice . . . But that is war. It must often be luck; it can never mean justice.

Private James Carmichael received no medical care for his neurasthenia, and he did not recover.

THE HYDRA CONTINUED Owen's, Salmond's, and Bonner's tradition of publishing patients' poems. Not all condemned the war as had Sassoon, Plowman, and Bonner. Captain E. A. E. Wilson, president of the Craiglockhart Officers' Club, wrote as if nothing had changed since 1914:

> Come to the Colours, a soldier lad calls,
> Whilst doing his bit he willingly falls
> Remember his blood has been spilt in the great cause
> For victory, for England, for you. Now, who will pause?

William Lambert-Patterson's short essay in the same issue, "The Drum of Fate: A Fantasy of Words and Philosophy," was a sharp counterpoint to the captain's jingoism. Born a colonel's son, Lambert-Patterson had followed his father's "drum whither it leads. And so I followed it, the drum that wakened the stillness of the world from its slumber of peace. To arms! To arms! And I fled to arms, and now rest in other arms."

THE WAR OFFICE, despite having replaced the convivial Major Bryce with traditionalist Balfour Graham, kept a sharp eye on Craiglockhart. The new commandant, as he demonstrated in silencing the One O'Clock Gun, was as devoted to his charges' welfare as Bryce had been. Yet Craiglockhart's relations with the War Office reached a crisis in the summer of 1918. The deputy director of Medical Services for

Scotland, Major General James Barnet Wilson, wrote to his superiors that Craiglockhart was "a source of more trouble and anxiety than any other in the Command." General Wilson's letter did not specify the source of "the troubles and anxieties," but a second team of inspectors visited the hospital in July.

Whether or not Balfour Graham declined, as Bryce had, to make special preparations, the result was new leadership. The War Office dismissed Balfour Graham and replaced him with Dr. William Brown, the physician Owen had met in France in May 1917 and called "a kind of wizard who mesmerises when he likes: a famous man." Since then, Captain Brown had distinguished himself in frontline psychiatric and neurological care and been promoted to major.

Craiglockhart's new commandant's interests, like those of Rivers and Brock, ranged well beyond the confines of psychology. Where Rivers had anthropology and Brock sociology, thirty-six-year-old Major William Brown was steeped in philosophy and mathematics. The schoolmaster's son from Horsham in West Sussex had attended Collyer's College, a local private school, where his scholastic achievements earned him a scholarship to Christ Church, Oxford, in 1909. The university awarded him a mathematics degree in 1902 and another in physiology in 1904. Two years later, he married a woman named May Leslie Rayment English with whom he soon fathered a son. They moved to Germany, where he studied "mental philosophy" as a John Locke scholar. On his return to England, King's College, London, appointed him lecturer in psychology. While teaching, he studied medicine at the college hospital and took the Bachelor of Medicine and Surgery (MBBCh) degree in 1914.

Brown enlisted in the RAMC and served as resident medical officer at Maghull Red Cross Military Hospital near Liverpool in 1915. After the death of his wife in 1916, he moved to London as neurologist to shell-shocked soldiers at the Maudsley Hospital. His next posting, in November 1916, was the Western Front, where he "was given charge of the treatment of all the nerve cases of the Fourth Army of the British Expeditionary Force" on the Somme front lines. In France, he met and married an English nurse, Dorothea Mary Stone. An average of twenty new cases a day, most shell-shocked but some with self-inflicted wounds, came to him for treatment. He detected a connection between extreme fear of high explosives and childhood terrors. Light hypnosis helped his patients to relive traumatizing experiences and thus release suppressed emotions. The process could be grueling. "They roll about," wrote Brown of his subjects, "gripping at the sides of the stretcher, or rolling on the floor, tearing at their hair with their hands, contorting themselves in every possible way, foaming at the mouth, becoming purple in the face, their eyes staring out of their heads, all their muscles tense."

For 70 percent of the men Brown treated in the field, "abreaction" or psychocatharsis proved successful within days of their breakdowns. He explained, "By the process of *abreaction* I remove the underlying cause of the patient's original dissociation, and in attacking this cause I cannot be accused of merely treating symptoms." The majority returned to their units without needing treatment across the Channel in Britain.

Brown transferred to Number 13 Casualty Clearing Station at Gailly on March 20, 1917, a few days after Wilfred Owen's first rest there. When Owen returned in May, Brown did his best for him before assigning him to Craiglockhart. Brown's frontline service ended in February 1918. Between November 1916 and his departure, he had dealt with more than three thousand shell-shock cases—more than any other British medical officer. At Craiglockhart, he would treat mentally troubled men as he had in France. He would also confront the daunting task of reforming the hospital as the War Office was demanding.

CHAPTER EIGHTEEN

Drastic Changes Were Necessary

Rivers had been living in bachelor's quarters near the Central Hospital in Hampstead, north London, since leaving Craiglockhart in December 1917. His patients, who were Royal Flying Corps pilots, took him up in their flimsy Sopwith Camels because he wanted to understand their fears. Many had crashed in aerial combat, leaving them concussed and neurasthenic. Their maladies, he told a War Office Committee of Enquiry into "Shell-Shock," were usually not severe: "All they wanted was to get rid of the repression and then to go off on holiday." In contrast, "the worst cases of psycho-neurosis that I think I have seen anywhere" were aerial observers, like George Bonner's brother, Austin. A pilot could maneuver his aircraft, but balloons were stationary targets. "This led me to the view that man's normal reaction to danger is manipulative activity," Rivers testified. "If he cannot have that, or if it is restricted in any way, you have a prominent condition for the occurrence of neurosis in one form or another."

While in London, Rivers maintained contact with officers he had treated in Scotland. He called on his former Bowhill patient Max Plowman in early July. Plowman was by this time a neighbor, living nearby in Hampstead High Street with his wife, Dorothy, and their son, Tim. Rivers wanted to help Plowman, who was in trouble with the army.

Plowman had received the final word on his conviction on June 8: "His Majesty the King was pleased to confirm the finding and sentence of the Court." The army "cashiered" him, equivalent to the American "dishonorable discharge." That should have begun his civilian life, but the army had other plans. A "Confidential Letter" from the War Office's director of organisation informed the Ministry of National Service that Plowman "would appear to be liable for service under the Military Service Acts." The War Office effectively ordered the ministry to draft him. The military bureaucracy that Plowman imagined he had escaped was dragging him back into its labyrinth.

On June 29, the Ministry of National Service delivered "Call Up" papers "telling me to present myself at Whitehall on Saturday, July 6, for re-enlistment, assuming that I was in the army Reserve." Not having access to his confidential War Office file, Plowman believed the draft notice was a mistake. He was appealing to one government office after another, when Rivers arrived.

Although Plowman had once dismissed Rivers as having "a mind which has become so divorced from nature that it cannot appreciate poetry," he welcomed the doctor's visit. Rivers promised to write to the authorities, but the two men argued. Plowman recalled, "Of course we disagreed heartily about the War. He thinks we must eat the German militarists up before we can have peace though he didn't say what you do with a thief who catches the thief." It was a measure of Rivers's compassion for his patients that he defended Plowman despite their differences.

Plowman discovered through the Board of Labour that "I *had* a right of appeal as I had never served under the Military Service Act but had enlisted as a volunteer." The ministry could draft a former conscript, but it had no legal right to draft someone who had volunteered and been discharged. Plowman had still to convince a tribunal. His wife, Dorothy, wrote,

> I forget how many times M. P. appeared before the Hampstead Tribunal, but it was several, and each time he was sent back to reconsider his decision (to do no approved work of national importance). Finally they pleaded that he surely could not object to reading to the blind of St. Dunstan's.

Plowman agreed that reading to the blind was worthwhile, but he would not do it under compulsion. He returned again and again to the tribunal until the end of the war, meanwhile writing poems and tracts against conscription and violence. Resolving the conflict between his deepest beliefs and his original, if reluctant, accommodation to the war restored his emotional health. Psychotherapy at Craiglockhart had succeeded in rehabilitating him but failed to make him fight again. He embarked on a productive career as a writer and political activist with his sanity restored and his conscience clear.

Major William Brown began his tenure at Craiglockhart in Scotland's high summer, when daylight at that northern latitude lingered for seventeen hours. The Gardening and Poultry Keeping Association was harvesting summer vegetables and collecting record numbers of eggs from the henhouses. The fields were alive with Scottish gorse, daylilies, and anemones. Henry Carmichael prepared the cricket pitches and laid out a third lawn court for tennis on rainless days for what the hospital called "American" tournaments, mixed doubles with nurses partnering patients.

Despite its idyllic grounds, Craiglockhart disappointed Brown. "When I took over the command of this hospital at the beginning of July," he wrote, "I found that drastic changes were necessary." Staff morale was low, housekeeping lax, and food unacceptable. Brown blamed the hospital's Scottish head nurse, Matron Margaret Mac-Bean. Having supervised the nursing staff, housekeepers, and kitchen from the beginning, Miss MacBean had resisted Balfour Graham's orders and resented Brown's intrusion into her spheres of responsibility. Brown accused her of mismanagement, including the fact that "the kitchen was in a disgraceful state and there had been innumerable complaints about the food and the cooking." He transferred control of the mess to a new chef and further lightened her duties by appointing a quartermistress to oversee housekeeping and supplies. The changes improved the quality of food and the state of the rooms. "Only in the matron's department," Brown lamented, "is the hospital going on in the same old hopelessly drifting and inefficient way." Although he had left Miss MacBean free to concentrate on nursing, Brown wrote "she only makes this a pretext for at last complaining that her authority with the staff is undermined." He decided to dismiss her, but that required the approval of the War Office and Queen Alexandra's Imperial Military Nursing Service, which oversaw military nurses.

Brown had an ally in the deputy director of Medical Services, Major General James Barnet Wilson. Wilson had complained to the War Office on June 6, before Brown's appointment, about "friction" between the matron, Margaret MacBean, and then-commandant Balfour Graham. It had been his intention to replace the matron rather than the commandant, but the decision was not his. "Miss MacBean," he wrote, "is not possessed of the personality or bearing, nor has she the requisite experience, necessary to render her suitable as Matron of an Officers' Hospital, and enable her to command respect as such." The War Office did not respond, apparently having mislaid the letter. Wilson wrote again when Brown assumed command, urging that "it is most necessary to supplement the efforts of the new Commandant, by giving him a suitable Matron to assist him in his most responsible duties."

Adding his voice to Wilson's on September 19, Major Brown composed what amounted to an indictment of Matron MacBean: "Her only plan of increasing the efficiency of her staff is to dismiss them. During the last few months, there have been large numbers of changes in her staff—apart from the few cases of nurses leaving for overseas." Since March 1918, she had discharged thirty-eight nurses and women workers. To Brown, this was less discipline than mismanagement.

He urged his superiors to replace her "at once by one who has a personality suitable for looking after the comfort of officer clients . . . The change should be made immediately." Without waiting for authorization, Brown sought a successor. On September 10, he sent a confidential letter to the assistant director of Medical Services to recommend a nurse with whom he had worked at the Maudsley Hospital in 1916: "I noticed she had really exceptional powers over neurological cases combined with marked administrative and organising ability. She knew how to make people under her work and this is one of the qualities especially required for a Hospital like Craiglockhart."

She was Mary Stuart MacInness, a young Scotswoman who had enrolled as a military nurse in October 1915. The Maudsley's matron wrote in her "Annual Confidential Report" of January 1918: "She is a woman of high intellect, marked ability, wide experience and definite knowledge and skill in the treatment of neurological diseases . . . and her work with the acute cases of shell-shock has been conspicuously successful." Miss MacInnes accepted Brown's offer, provided the position became available.

Brown sent Matron MacBean a handwritten letter of dismissal on September 22: "Acting on instructions received from D. D. M. S. [deputy director of Medical Services] Scottish Command, you are hereby informed that your appointment as Matron in this Hospital will terminate on or about October 23rd 1918, & that you will proceed on leave forthwith, during which period you will be entitled to full pay and allowances."

The summary discharge hurt and outraged Miss MacBean, who believed she had given good service for two grueling years. She protested to the director of Medical Services and the War Office. When neither proved sympathetic, she appealed to Dame Ethel Hope Becher, matron in chief of Queen Alexandra's Imperial Military Nursing Service. "The more I reflect on the treatment I received at Craiglockhart the more I feel the injustice of it . . . Indeed I think it ought not to be possible that any Matron should have to submit to all the worry & opposition I have had to endure." Dame Ethel, however, sided with Major Brown.

Miss MacBean demanded a Court of Enquiry. Major General Wilson replied that such courts met only "if a question of character or conduct arose. But no question affecting Miss MacBean's character or conduct has arisen in any sort or kind of way whatsoever." Her reputation at stake, Miss MacBean feared the dismissal would damage her "future prospects." She wrote in frustration to the secretary of state for war, Viscount Milner. His response was negative.

Sister Mary Stuart MacInnes took Miss MacBean's place as matron of Craiglockhart on October 23.

CHANGE OF LEADERSHIP at Craiglockhart did not augur a change of regimen. Major Brown's former medical school students had described him as "a tall, distinguished looking intellectual with a natural reserve and reticence that gave him an air of aloofness." The aloofness was more apparent than real in a psychiatrist who premised therapy on earning his patients' trust. Brown utilized the same Freudian psychoanalysis that Major Bryce had introduced when the hospital opened.

Several of Brown's patients had been under his care in France, including one twenty-five-year-old subaltern. The young man had been wounded during an assault on German trenches. He lay bleeding for hours in No Man's Land, shells tearing at the earth around him. When his wounds healed, he returned to duty. For the next few months, fear of artillery fire sent him shuddering to the nearest dugout. By December 1916, he was in the Casualty Clearing Station where Brown first encountered him, listless and staring blankly at a heating stove and repeatedly counting the decorative squares on its edges.

Since childhood, the patient recounted, he had suffered from poor memory and fearfulness. His mother had told him he nearly drowned at the age of three, but he had no recollection of it. When Brown hypnotized him, he gasped "with terror as he again, in memory, fell into the water. He described the whole event with such a wealth of detail that it was difficult not to believe that he had been taken straight back to this early period in his life and was living again through the terrifying experience." In subsequent sessions, he recalled other harrowing moments. One, when he was eighteen, was seeing the coffin of his baby brother lowered into the grave and "feeling the desperation of grief as a present emotion."

Brown deduced that the man's memory was not impaired so much as blocked. The solution involved more hypnosis, during which Brown enabled his "abreaction . . . i. e., the working off of their [the recollections'] emotional accompaniments." The man's memory improved, as did his mental state. He left the CCS for the front lines. A year later, however, he broke down again. On seeing him at Craiglockhart, Brown observed a resumption of his neurasthenic symptoms. Hypnosis and abreaction combined to effect a cure.

Another of his patients from the war zone was a regular army captain, who had served at the front from August 1914. On his second day in France, intense shellfire demolished the farmhouse where he was billeted. Subsequent shelling gave him a concussion. His left eye went foggy, and his head ached. His health deteriorated, bringing blindness and numbness on his left side "similar to that when one's fingers become bloodless on a very cold day." That led to hemiplegia, paralysis of one side of his body, by the time Brown saw him in France. Therapy in the field produced no results, and Brown sent him to hospitals in

Britain. He was able to walk five months later, but the headaches worsened. He performed light duty in England until May 1917, when he was well enough to return to France. Then, in November, a light wound to his finger triggered the old symptoms. By the summer of 1918, he was at Craiglockhart, semiparalyzed and nearly blind. Brown treated him again, this time producing a recovery.

A twenty-four-year-old lieutenant, whom Brown called "Case G," had also been his patient in France. While at the front, he had watched a German 200-pound mortar arcing through the air toward him. He was judging which way to jump, when the sun blurred his vision. Suddenly, his ribs were crushed and his eyes burned. He felt a crack in the head and did not wake up for five hours. After ten days of more fighting, doctors ordered him to a field hospital. He went blind and lost movement on his entire right side. The right half of his head ached and throbbed with incessant noise. He had also become impotent. Brown learned from him that, before his frontline service, he had been in three accidents, two on a motorcycle and one on his horse. The horse kicked him in the head, and he blacked out. Brown made a connection between the horse injuring his head on the right and the subsequent paralysis of the right half of his body. His infirmity defied treatment in France, and he was sent to England. After two years of home leave, he was sent to Craiglockhart and again to Brown's care.

Under analysis, the lieutenant began to recover. Tinnitus, headaches, and pain around his right eye recurred only at longer intervals, although exhaustion and impotence persisted. Gradually, the symptoms lessened, and his potency returned. Brown concluded that "commotion rather than emotion seems to have originated the symptoms." The horse's kick and the mortar's blast had injured him physically, but his paralysis had become psychosomatic. Brown produced a catharsis, as he had with the two others he saw in France and Scotland, by making him relive his most frightening moments. He wrote of the three, "They all made good recoveries, although they were chronic cases of many months' standing, and every other conceivable method had been used with them in vain."

THE HYDRA CEASED publication with the July issue, leaving a void in the hospital's record of sports, clubs, concerts, and societies. Its demise deprived budding poets and journalists of an outlet for their writing, but the editors had all along pleaded for copy and been exhausted by filling the pages themselves. It may have been that no one was willing to work as hard as Whitehead, Owen, Salmond, and Bonner had.

Over the summer, devout officers constructed Craiglockhart's first purpose-built Anglican chapel, complete with stone altar and hand-crafted wooden pews, in the villa's basement. Reports from France that American, British, Commonwealth, and French forces were pushing the Germans back from the River Marne gave them hope that their prayers might be answered.

CHAPTER NINETEEN

Mad Jack Returns

On August 17, 1918, nine months after leaving Craiglock-hart, trusting he would never see it again, Siegfried Sassoon was back. The institution appeared as gloomy as it was when he lived there, but there were changes. Major Bryce and Matron MacBean were gone, as were the patients he remembered. No new copies of *The Hydra* were stacked in the foyer, and another patient occupied his old garret. Sassoon had come for a Medical Board arranged by Rivers, who had also traveled north to take part in it. The three-doctor panel examined Sassoon and observed no external symptoms of shell shock—no paralysis, shaking, blindness, or mutism. Yet he was clearly shattered. Their prescription was not psychotherapy, but rest. Three days after his arrival, Sassoon transferred to Craiglockhart's Lennel Auxiliary Hospital fifty miles away at Coldstream on the Scottish Borders.

Lennel House was not as imposing as Craiglockhart's other adjunct, the Duke of Buccleuch's Bowhill; but it offered amenities to soothe Sassoon's troubled mind: a room of his own, a substantial library, views of the Cheviot Hills, fishing on the River Tweed, golf, an excellent kitchen, and a charming hostess in the person of its vivacious chatelaine, thirty-nine-year-old Lady Clementine Waring. "Clemmie" and her husband, Liberal member of Parliament Major Walter Waring, had bought the late-Georgian manor in 1904 and commissioned one of Craiglockhart's architects, John Dick Peddie, to renovate it. When Sassoon checked in, the atmosphere was less hospital than family house. No doctors lived on the premises, and only fifteen other officers were in residence. The Waring children had the run of the place, and the patients lavished particular affection on the youngest, four-year-old Kitty.

Clemmie, regarding the men as guests, supervised the household while her husband was serving with the army in Morocco. Sassoon called Lennel "a delightful house," where he enjoyed "a series of excellent meals presided over by Lady Clementine, who managed her supposedly nerve-shattered guests with undeviating adroitness and good humour." Sassoon's companions were more than "supposedly" nerve-shattered. Visiting psychiatrists from Craiglockhart observed of some: "Has vivid dreams of war episodes—feels as if sinking down in bed"; "Sleeping well but walks in sleep: has never done this before: dreams of France"; "Patient fears gunfire, death and the dark . . . In periods of wakefulness he visualizes mutilations he has seen, and feels the terror of heavy fire."

Sassoon wandered through woods and bicycled up hills, taking his usual interest in landscape, flowers, and wildlife. His other pleasure was reading in Major Waring's library. The untroubled days and nights at Lennel afforded him leisure to recall the period between his departure from Craiglockhart and his return to care in Scotland.

When he left Craiglockhart the previous November, the Royal Welch Fusiliers welcomed him without recrimination. His first posting was Ireland, then in a tense but peaceful hiatus between the Easter Rising of 1916 and the April 1918 insurrection against Britain's imposition of military conscription on the Irish. For Sassoon, it was a glorious respite of hunts on wild Irish chargers with characters out of the Somerville and Ross *Irish R. M.* novels he had read in his youth. On January 21, two weeks after his arrival, he discovered he might be sent to Egypt. This put him in two minds, noting points in favor and against. In favor: "New country—conditions not so trying (probably Palestine)— less chance of being killed." Against: "I want to go back to the regular battalions. The other place is only a sideshow, and I'd be with an inferior battalion . . . Can't make up my mind."

His inclination was against, as indicated by his urgent cable to the 2nd Battalion in France: "To Major Kearsley, 2nd Royal Welch Fusiliers. Am ordered to Egypt can you do something to get me back to France. Signed, Sassoon." He appealed as well to Rivers, who replied that he could not alter War Office orders, and anyway, a spell in the Levant would not harm him. Sassoon left Ireland on February 9, pausing in London for a late-night reunion with Rivers. Next came a ship to Cherbourg, a train to Italy, and another ship to Alexandria, which he reached on February 28.

To his chagrin, the Royal Welch Fusiliers assigned him to a territorial battalion, the 25th, in his eyes a demotion from the older 1st and 2nd. By the time he joined them in Palestine, the fighting had moved north. His duties consisted in supervising C Company road repairs near Ramallah until the Royal Welch Fusiliers appointed him second-in-command of A Company. On April 4, a rumor circulated that the battalion was going to France. "Probably untrue," he wrote, but the rumor proved accurate. On May 1, he left the Middle East aboard the SS *Malwa*, unimpressed by his fellow 25th Battalion officers: "Perhaps there's a Bernard Adams or a Robert Graves among them; if so, he's very well camouflaged!"

The ship docked in Marseille a week later. As he waited to travel north to the war he had protested against the year before, he recorded in his diary, "I must never forget Rivers. He is the only man who can save me if I break down again." "Again" was a rare admission that he had broken down at all, and a hint at the fragility of his nerves. The battalion soon left by train and foot for Abbeville on the Somme. The familiar, devastated landscape set him brooding again on the war's absurdity. A poem, "Testament," that he mailed to Ottoline Morrell on May 9 included the couplet "For the last time I say—war is not glorious, / Though lads march out superb and fall victorious." A few days later, he listened for the second time to Major Ronald Campbell's fiery "Spirit of the Bayonet": "His lecture is much the same as when I heard it at Fourth Army School two years ago and only disgusted me this time. It was the spirit of Militarism incarnate." Disgust with militarism vied with his lust for battle.

A passage he quoted in his diary from French military surgeon Georges Duhamel's *Vie des Martyrs*, a war book he rated as highly as Barbusse's *Under Fire*, hinted at a solution to his mental turmoil: "To make up one's mind to die is to take a certain resolution, in the hope of becoming quieter, calmer, and less unhappy." His mood changed three days later. "Getting nearer the line is working me up to a climax. Same feeling of confidence and freedom from worry." Then, in a letter to Graves, he wondered whether he wanted to die. His conclusion: "I don't know yet."

He trained A Company in the intricacies of the Western Front's static conditions, a marked contrast to the mobile warfare it had waged across Sinai, Beersheba, and the Judaean hills. While the 25th Battalion troops had much to learn about trenches, noted a regimental history, "their previous experience made them adepts at patrolling, and the 'top,' the open country in face of the enemy, held no terrors for them." Their aptitude for raiding suited Sassoon, the fox-hunting man, for whom storming German dugouts was war's greatest excitement. Yet May was all drill, drill, drill.

The delay frustrated Sassoon, especially with the battalion stuck in reserve during one of the war's heaviest battles. It began on May 27, when German general Erich Ludendorff's artillery battered a forty-three-mile front between Soissons and Reims with more than two million rounds. German infantry followed the barrage, piercing Anglo-French lines and bypassing demoralized Tommies and *poilus*. They crossed the River Aisne on bridges the French had neglected to demolish and reached the banks of the River Marne, less than fifty miles from Paris. Panic led to a mass civilian exodus from Paris and fears in London that the war was lost.

The speed of the Germans' advance—twenty miles in three days—left their divisions overstretched and exposed. French and American forces stopped them at the Marne, leaving the Germans nowhere to go but back. The battle was raging on June 9, when Sassoon was promoted "temporary captain." He longed to lead his men, of whom he was increasingly proud and fond, into action. The 25th Battalion's relegation to the rear made him so furious that he blurted to the Company Mess on June 14, "Damn it, I'm fed up with all this training!" Rising from his chair, he declared to the assembled subalterns, "I want to go up to the Line and *fight*!" When one of them seconded his motion, he walked outside into the warm night and regretted the "moment of folly."

Sassoon's opportunity came at the end of June, when the 25th Battalion was ordered to relieve the East Lancashire Regiment's 1st Battalion at the front near Saint-Venant. Sassoon rode out a day before to reconnoiter the position. Scanning a flat horizon of cornstalks and not much else, he saw a death trap. There were few trenches in the marshy ground and only a scattering of barbed-wire defenses. The sentry posts were mud mounds no higher than a man's chest. The Germans were dug in a mere two hundred yards away. Sassoon left this sorry redoubt after a few hours, returning the next day with his company. He and his second-in-command, Lieutenant Vivian da Sola Pinto, spread their four platoons along A Company's stretch of the line and waited.

It was not long before Sassoon took the initiative. Determined to assert British dominance in No Man's Land, he led patrols over exposed ground in keeping with his "Mad Jack" reputation. The forays, more than demonstrating his bravado, allowed him to map German gun emplacements and probe weak points. Huddling underground, in any case, was no safer, as he observed when an artillery shell crashed into his dugout. Miraculously, it did not go off.

Declining to wait for the fresh company that was relieving him the next day, Sassoon organized a raid for the evening of July 12. The adventure "was at any rate an antidote to my suppressed weariness of the entire bloody business." His objective was a machine gun at the edge of a German parapet. The darkness of night and a sunken road gave cover to him and a corporal he described as "a trained scout, young, small and active," as they approached the German line. "Just when I least expected it," he wrote, "the German machine-gun fired a few rounds, for no apparent reason except to allow us to locate it." Sassoon and the corporal crawled toward the gun and showered it with Mills bombs. Without pausing to see what their grenades hit, they ran back, with Sassoon feeling "exuberantly excited."

The sun was rising when he relaxed, removed his helmet, and stood to look at the German trenches. "A second later I was down again, half stunned by a terrific blow to the head," he recalled. Blood gushed from his forehead, convincing him he was "as good as dead." Lieutenant Pinto hurried to him, also fearing the worst. The corporal, carrying Sassoon's helmet, and Pinto managed to get Sassoon back to their trench. They soon learned that the shot that hit Sassoon had been fired by a British soldier, who mistook his platoon commander for a German. Sassoon wrote, "Thus ended my last week at the War." He left the war, but it was not leaving him.

THE "HALF-HEALED HOLE" in Sassoon's head was serious enough for doctors to send him first to Boulogne, where someone stole his lucky fire opal, and over the Channel on July 20 to American Red Cross Hospital Number 22 at Lancaster Gate in London. The high windows in his ward overlooked Hyde Park, whose chestnut trees and expansive lawns were somehow reassuring. Robbie Ross, his most faithful friend and benefactor, brought him reviews of *Counter-Attack*, the poetry volume Heinemann had published in July. Twenty of its poems had been composed at Craiglockhart. An unexpectedly hostile critique in *The Nation* by a writer who had supported his protest, John Middleton Murry, hurt. Most of the others were favorable, notably one by fellow soldier-protester Max Plowman in the *Labour Leader*: "He has delivered the finest counter-attack in the war by making a breach in the sinister ranks of official reticence and unofficial ignorance and self-complacency." Initial sales were good, enhancing his reputation as one of the leading poets of war.

More visitors, including Winston Churchill's mother and two members of the royal family, poured in to offer tribute and sympathy to the wounded soldier-poet. The hospital, for the sake of Sassoon's health, banned further visits. When he found sleep impossible, staff moved him to a double room whose second bed was empty. Alone at last, he tormented himself with the futility of his life.

He returned to poetry, writing "Dug-Out," about a young soldier lying at the front with his arm over his face and his legs tucked under him: "You are too young to fall asleep for ever; / And when you sleep you remind me of the dead." The dead populating his thoughts and dreams were receding into the past. It was the future that frightened him.

"How could I begin my life all over again," the now thirty-one-year-old veteran asked himself, "when I had no conviction about anything except that the War was a dirty trick which has been played on me and my generation?" The perpetual conflict between the warrior and the pacifist raged within him. He wondered, "What the hell was wrong with me?" Combat had taught him "that if we continue to accept war as a social institution we must also recognize that the Prussian system is the best, and Prussian militarism must be taught in the schools." While his head healed, his mind was in anguish. He felt that only Rivers could help him.

"And then, unexpected and unannounced, Rivers came in and closed the door behind him," he recalled. "Quiet and alert, purposeful and unhesitating, he seemed to empty the room of everything that needed exorcising." Rivers as a physician was exempt from the no-visitors rule. Sassoon, looking fondly on his "father confessor," realized how lonely he had been and looked to Rivers for salvation. Rivers sat beside the bed. Sassoon blurted, "Oh, Rivers, I've had such a funny time since I saw you last!"

Sassoon wrote to Graves the next day, July 24, Graves's twenty-third birthday,

> . . . O Rivers please take me. And make me
> Go back to the War till it break me.
> Some day my brain will go BANG,
> And they'll say what lovely faces were
> The soldier-lads he sang . . .
>
> Does this break your heart? . . . What do I care?

Rivers decided to send his former patient back to Scotland. The rural peace would grant him what he needed: rest far from the war, far from cities, far from visitors, and nearer himself.

LADY CLEMENTINE EMPLOYED a version of Brock's ergotherapy, whether or not she intended it, at Lennel. One activity she assigned her guests was painting their families' coats of arms. Those without heraldic crests were invited to design their own. Clemmie hung the finished shields on cornices above mounted stags' heads in her sitting room. Sassoon, as at Craiglockhart the year before, went his own way. Leaving the other officers to Clemmie's tasks, he became, in his words, "a liberated and irresponsible person," bicycling for miles in daytime and writing poems at night. Evenings found him reading in Major Waring's library.

It was in the library that he met "a fellow convalescent who also wrote poetry . . . He was a remarkable character, delightful when in a cheerful frame of mind, though liable to be moody and aloof." Not unlike Sassoon himself. Lieutenant Francis "Frank" Prewett, nicknamed "Toronto" for his Canadian birthplace, had abandoned study at the University of Toronto in February 1915 to enlist. The British Army commissioned him in the Royal Field Artillery a year later and deployed him to France in time for the Battle of the Somme. He served in artillery batteries and trench mortars until early 1918, when a high-explosive shell shattered his spine and buried him alive on the Ypres Salient.

His spine healed, but the shock lingered. A Medical Board diagnosed neurasthenia and sent him to Craiglockhart. A week later, Lady Clementine welcomed him to Lennel. Frank Prewett succeeded Owen as Sassoon's disciple-protégé. Sassoon's growing attachment to his new friend moved him to write, "He was quite young, and the verses he was writing were blurred and embryonic, but there was a quality in them that interested me and raised expectations."

Sassoon, as with Owen, tutored Prewett in poetry. One poem that Prewett wrote in France so impressed him that he copied it by hand:

> Comrade, why do you weep?
> Is it sorry for a friend
> Who fell, rifle in hand,
> His proud stand at an end?
>
> . . .
>
> The sweet lark sings on high
> For the peace of those who sleep
> In the quiet embrace of earth . . .
> Comrade, why do you weep?

Lady Clementine organized a costume party one evening, attended by the usually reticent Sassoon. Prewett appeared in North American Indian buckskins with feather headdress. His dark eyes and tawny skin reinforced his claim of Iroquois ancestry that, true or not, increased Sassoon's interest in the seemingly exotic figure from the Canadian prairies. Sassoon needed male companionship. He had found it at Craiglockhart with Owen and Rivers. At Lennel, it was Prewett. The two grew closer while discussing poetry and exploring the Cheviot Hills on bicycle, despite Prewett's indifference to Sassoon's erotic interest in him.

Soon after meeting Prewett, Sassoon received an invitation from publisher William Heinemann to visit him at Lindisfarne Castle on eastern Scotland's Holy Island. Heinemann was visiting *Country Life* magazine proprietor Edward Hudson. Seeking to introduce Prewett, as he had Owen, to literary society, Sassoon took him along. The two officers cycled about twenty miles to discover Heinemann and Hudson had just left for London. One guest, famed cellist Guilhermina Suggia, remained. The thirty-three-year-old musician, whom Sassoon called "the loveliest and most romantic of modern executants," played a Bach suite for them. Sassoon, always moved by beautiful music, suddenly found peace: "For it was the first time I had felt completely remote and absolved from the deadly constraints of the war." On August 8, he turned thirty-two.

Clemmie drove Sassoon to Craiglockhart on September 19 for another Medical Board. It judged him too unwell for service abroad or at home and gave him another four weeks at Lennel. He took a short break on September 30 to see friends in London—among them Ottoline Morrell, Robbie Ross, Eddie Marsh, and Arnold Bennett—usually over lavish lunches or dinners. He also met the economist John Maynard Keynes, who took him to see Léonide Massine in the ballet *Cleopatra*; and "a young actor called Noel Coward," whom he did not like. Eddie Marsh arranged a meeting with his chief at the Ministry of Munitions, Winston Churchill. Marsh assured Sassoon, "Winston knows several of the *Counter-attack* poems by heart." Churchill's informality and courtesy surprised him, and his self-assurance made Sassoon feel "that I should like to have him as my company commander—in the front line." Churchill, smoking a large cigar, offered him work in his ministry, which supervised the manufacture and distribution of the military's lethal weapons. Sassoon did not accept, believing it "would be inconsistent with my previous outburst against the prolongation of the War and the views I had expressed in my poems." Churchill told him to consider it anyway before lecturing him in what became a "monologue" on war, "the finest activity on earth." While clinging to their opposed views of warfare, the two parted on good terms.

On the morning of October 4, William Heinemann received him at his office in Covent Garden to tell him that *Counter-Attack* had sold more than three thousand copies and was going into its third printing. Sassoon then had a brief rendezvous with Rivers before lunch with Ottoline in Soho. That evening saw him dining with his Lennel friends, Prewett and Clemmie, at the Carlton Club in Pall Mall. They went on, no doubt a nod to Toronto Prewett, to the three-act comedy *The Man from Toronto* in the West End. The next morning, after his hectic four days in London, Sassoon returned "very exhausted" to Lennel.

A telegram came the next morning. Robbie Ross, for years a close friend and defender, was dead. Ross had been suffering from accusations by jingoist member of Parliament Noel Pemberton Billing, who claimed to possess a "black book" of forty-seven thousand homosexuals and lesbians whom the Germans had blackmailed into committing treason. One of those whom Pemberton Billing defamed, actress Maud Allen, sued him for criminal libel. Allen had starred in *Salomé* by Oscar Wilde, whose literary estate Ross managed. Wilde's aggrieved and petulant former lover, Lord Alfred "Bosie" Douglas, testified for Pemberton Billing and slandered Ross as a pervert. When Allen lost the case in June, Britain's "yellow press" railed against homosexuals. Ross and many of his associates feared disgrace and worse. The shock,

Ross's friends believed, killed him. Sassoon felt the loss of this kindest of men as deeply as he had that of friends, like David Thomas, killed in the war.

At Lennel, Toronto Prewett offered what solace he could. While he substituted for Owen as Sassoon's youthful poet-soldier-acolyte, he did not displace him. Sassoon and Owen maintained a steady correspondence with exchanges of poems from the time they left Craiglockhart. With encouragement from Sassoon, *The Nation* published three of Owen's poems, "Miners" in January and "Hospital Barge" and "Futility" in June.

Owen was at last, like Sassoon and Graves, a poet whose work had been printed in the national press. He was stationed with the Manchester Regiment in Ripon, awaiting a Medical Board to declare him fit for frontline service. Returning to the front did not appeal to him as it had to Sassoon. Charles Scott Moncrieff, his and Sassoon's mutual acquaintance at the War Office, lobbied on his behalf for a safe posting in Britain. His superiors, however, rebuffed him.

Two days before Sassoon had reported to Craiglockhart, on August 15, Owen learned that he was at the American Hospital and went to London to see him. "We met at the house of Osbert Sitwell, to whom we had both been introduced by Robbie [Ross]," Sassoon remembered. Sitwell, who had served in the Grenadier Guards in France and wrote poetry, lived in Swan Walk beside the Thames in Chelsea. He took Sassoon and Owen to a harpsichord concert at a friend's house, after which they wandered through the herbs and plants in Chelsea's four-acre Physic Garden. Sassoon and Owen left to meet Roderick Meiklejohn for dinner at the Reform Club. "My only opportunity for intimate talk with Wilfred was while he saw me back to the hospital," Sassoon wrote. "I parted from him in deluded ignorance that he was on final leave before returning to the Front." Sassoon warned him not to go back, threatening to stab him in the leg if he tried.

Owen wrote to Sassoon at the end of August, "Goodbye,—dear

Siegfried, I have been incoherent since I tried to say good-bye on the steps of Lancaster Gate." To Sassoon's astonishment, the letter had come from France. Owen went on, "But everything is clear now, and I'm in hasty retreat towards the Front. Battle is easier here; and therefore you will stay and endure old men and women to the End, and wage the bitterer war and more hopeless . . . What more is there to say that you will not better understand unsaid. Your W." Owen wrote again the next day, explaining why he had not told Sassoon where he was going: "If you had said In the heart or brain you might have stabbed me, but you said only in the leg; so I was afraid." Apparently cured by Brock of shell shock, "little Wilfred" set out in France to emulate Sassoon as a devoted leader of men, righteous poet, and, perhaps, winner of a Military Cross.

CHAPTER TWENTY

The Loathsome Ending

In June 1917, when Wilfred Owen stopped in London on his way to begin treatment at Craiglockhart, a chance encounter humiliated him. Walking along fashionable New Bond Street on that warm afternoon, he "ran into the last person on earth or under the earth that I wished to meet: Major, now Colonel, Dempster, of the 2nd Battalion." Forty-one-year-old Colonel James Finlay Dempster was "the horrid old major" he mentioned in a letter to his mother a month earlier. The veteran soldier had served in the Manchester Regiment long before the war, left to work as a wine merchant, and reenlisted in 1914. Owen first came across him in the wake of his harrowing experience beside Lieutenant Gaukroger's dismembered corpse. Dempster, then in temporary command of the 2nd Battalion, noticed Owen's uncontrollable shaking and sent him to a Casualty Clearing Station. Owen sensed that Dempster questioned his courage.

Seeing Dempster in London revived the old suspicion. "We stopped, of course," Owen wrote to Susan, "and he pretended to be very affable and cordial. Yet I know a more thorough-going Snob does not exist—even in the imagination of Thackeray. To meet him in my first hour in town. Alas!" Owen, going on to King's Cross Station for the night train to Edinburgh, could not shake what he took to be Dempster's disdain. Among those who detected Owen's sensitivity to charges of cowardice were Maidie Gray and Robert Graves. Maidie wrote that he set himself high standards "and in moments of despondency grieved deeply over what he regarded, quite unjustifiably, as his failure to live up to them." Graves went further, writing in a passage to which Sassoon objected that "it preyed on his mind that he had been accused of cowardice by his commanding officer."

After his Craiglockhart therapy and his return to the war at the end of August 1918, Owen gave every impression of striving to prove Dempster, or what he imagined of Dempster, wrong. On arrival in France, he requested a transfer to a frontline Welsh regiment, in deference to his part-Welsh ancestry and knowing that his soldier-poet mentors, Sassoon and Graves, were Royal Welch Fusiliers. Commanders turned him down, returning him to the Manchester Regiment's 2nd Battalion. On September 15, he and another subaltern, Second Lieutenant John Foulkes, assumed command of two thirty-five man platoons in D Company. Luckily, Dempster had gone and no one seemed to remember Owen's breakdown.

One private who recognized and greeted him affably put Owen in "a confident mood" as he began organizing his platoon behind the lines near Amiens. Owen emulated Sassoon in taking care of the men, who reciprocated with praise for him in letters home that he, as their censor, was gratified to read. The battalion moved forward on Friday, September 13, to La Neuville for an intense period of weapons training, physical exercise, and sports. Their next destination was a bivouac near Tertry in the "forward area" to await the coming battle.

On the night of September 26, British cannons announced an all-out offensive to breach the Hindenburg Line with the firing of sixteen hundred high-explosive shells. The 2nd Manchesters, as part of the 96th Infantry Brigade, leapfrogged other units of Britain's Fourth Army in the advance eastward. When one brigade conquered territory, it consolidated its position to allow another to go forward. The Germans pulled back, but they fought strong rearguard actions to cover their withdrawal from lands they had occupied since 1914.

On September 28, the Manchesters passed through the 46th Division near Manguy-la-Fosse. Owen positioned his platoon in an abandoned German support trench. Germans overlooked them from a ridge just ahead. At 4:00 p.m. the next day, C and D companies attacked on the Beaurevoir–Fonsemes Line. Ferocious defensive fire disabled three of the four British tanks leading the assault and inflicted casualties on both companies. Owen's young batman, Private Jones, took a bullet near his temple. Under relentless German fire, Owen cradled Jones's bleeding head on his shoulder. "Can you photograph the crimson-hot iron as it cools from the smelting?" Owen would write to Sassoon. "That is what Jones's blood looked like. My senses are charred." Owen and Jones lay side by side for forty minutes, until the German barrage let up and stretcher-bearers evacuated the wounded.

Owen, his uniform drenched in blood, charged up the hill into the enemy guns. "I lost all my earthly faculties," he wrote to his mother, "and fought like an angel." The avenging angel recounted to her that he pointed his revolver at one German and shot him dead. He failed to elaborate, lest he shock her; but an official account of his action that day noted: "He personally manipulated a captured enemy M.G. [Machine Gun] from an isolated position and inflicted considerable losses on the enemy." He had killed not one German as he led his mother to believe, but many.

A poem he had been writing through many drafts in early 1918 bared feelings about killing Germans that went beyond sparing his mother's feelings. In "Strange Meeting," a soldier escaped the battle through a "profound dull tunnel" to the deeper tunnel where the dead dwell. Another soldier "sprang up, and stared / with piteous recognition in fixed eyes . . .

And by his smile, I knew that sullen hall,
By his dead smile I knew that we stood in Hell.

. . .

"Strange friend," I said, "here is no cause to mourn."
"None," said the other, "save the undone years,
The hopelessness. Whatever hope is yours,
Was my life also; I went hunting wild
After the wildest beauty in the world . . ."

The dead enemy spoke of "the truth untold, / The pity of war, the pity war distilled." With no bitterness over the fate that brought them face-to-face, the now former enemy concluded,

"I am the enemy you killed, my friend.
I knew you in this dark; for so you frowned
Yesterday through me as you jabbed and killed.
I parried; but my hands were loath and cold.
Let us sleep now . . ."

Sassoon would call "Strange Meeting" Owen's "passport to immortality." It revealed a poetic genius, but also guilt at killing even as he engaged it. The poem's soldiers had not been carried through the gates of Paradise, as in *Avatar*, John Lintott's painting of angels bearing a slain warrior heavenward that he had admired at Saint Bernard's Crescent. Owen's fighters were doomed to lie side by side in hell.

As more Germans fell or surrendered on the day Owen took many lives, D Company captured their gun positions. More hard fighting loomed. The Manchesters seized their next objective, a nearby farm the British called "Swiss Cottage." They were consolidating their position when a massive German counterattack pushed them out. Bloody hand-to-hand combat saw the farm change hands again and again. When C Company troops launched another attack on the farm, Owen grabbed a captured German machine gun to cover their exposed flank. Within sight of the enemy, he went on firing until C Company drove the Germans back. Owen's fearless action saved the important Joncourt Ridge for the British and earned him a recommendation for the coveted Military Cross. His commander, Captain Taylor, wrote in words that make clear Owen had no lingering effects of shell shock: "This officer shewed great coolness throughout the operation and the enemys attempts to drive us out and his energetic devotion to duty is worthy of the highest praise."

Owen established a forward command post in an abandoned German pillbox. Explosive shells churned the earth, while poison gas crept over the British positions. Owen, to his relief, kept his composure while a career officer beside him quaked in fear. Morning brought a renewed German assault from three sides that trapped the British where they lay. Attempts to rescue the wounded in No Man's Land brought casualties to the rescuers, including three stretcher-bearers. "I had to order one to show himself after that," wrote Owen, "and remembering my own duty, and remembering also my forefathers the agile Welshmen of the Mountains, I scrambled out myself & felt an exhilaration in baffling the Machine Guns by quick bounds from cover to cover." He was experiencing "Sassoonish" excitement.

At nightfall, Owen lay alongside the men deep in mud and braced against cold. Transport troops, at risk to their lives, brought up rations, ameliorating some of the misery. The situation was desperate: Germans all around and no prospect of regaining the initiative. Moreover, all D Company officers, except Owen and Second Lieutenant Foulkes, had been killed or wounded. The Manchesters endured frost and shelling until 5:00 a.m., when a unit of Lancashire Fusiliers arrived to relieve them. Recalling his childhood astronomy, Owen navigated by the stars to bring D Company to base.

"This is where I admired his work—in leading his remnants, in the middle of the night, back to safety," recalled Foulkes. "I remember feeling how glad I was that it was not my job to know how to get out. I was content to follow him with the utmost confidence in his leadership."

D Company settled into a dugout on the banks of the Saint-Quentin Canal. Owen wrote to assure his mother, "My nerves are in perfect order." He had risked his life, killed enemy soldiers, and taken others prisoner. Yet he confided a more important, Sassoon-like undertaking that the Christian in her would value: "I came out in order to help these boys—directly by leading them as well as an officer can; indirectly by watching their sufferings that I may speak of them as well as a pleader can." He was pleading in his poetry, which he went on writing between engagements.

By October 5, thanks to successes like that of the Manchesters at Swiss Cottage, the Hindenburg Line was no more. With British and imperial troops occupying German trenches and tunnels, Wilfred wrote to his mother, "The war is nearing an end." The Germans were retreating, but they had not given up.

Amid German reverses, the collapse of Austrian forces in Italy, and Turkey's defeats in Syria, rumors of an imminent peace circulated among the troops. Germany published a letter from its chancellor offering a qualified acceptance of peace terms President Wilson had offered in January. The Germans did not accede to Wilson's demand that a democratic government replace the monarchy, thus mooting its significance. Frontline soldiers nonetheless sensed an opening for peace. To avert a slackening of morale, Fourth Army commander General Sir Henry Rawlinson issued a Special Order of the Day on October 7: "All ranks are warned against the disturbing influence of dangerous peace talk . . . Peace talk in any form is to cease in the Fourth Army." The order infuriated Owen, who sent a copy to Sassoon and complained to his mother on October 10 about the harsh conditions the men were enduring: "Some of them look pretty scared already, poor victims. To-night I must stand before them & promulgate this General Order."

Sassoon received Owen's letters at Lennel, where he languished in comfort with no strong desire to get back to the war. In early October, he wrote to Owen that a golden-crested wren flew into his room and rested on his pillow. Owen replied on October 10, "While you were apparently given over to wrens, I have found brave companionship in a poppy, behind whose stalk I took cover from five machine guns and several howitzers." He added that he was up for the Military Cross, which would put him on an equal military footing with Sassoon; but he wanted it only "for the confidence it may give me at home."

The Germans reinforced their units along the River Selle, and Rawlinson's Fourth Army massed to cross the waterway and drive them from higher ground on the east bank. While the 2nd Manchester Battalion marched toward the new front on the morning of October 17, Rawlinson's forces pushed the Germans back. Owen's company "rested" in the small commune of Lehaucourt, where he wrote to his cousin Leslie Gunston that "'resting' does not mean lying in bed smoking." Artillery hit them from time to time, but the French civilians were welcoming. Two daughters of the mayor took a particular interest in Lieutenant Owen, showering gratitude on him for *La Délivrance*. His fellow subalterns became so jealous they put him on trial in a mock court-martial. "The dramatic irony was too killing, considering certain other things, not possible to tell in a letter," he confided. Gunston knew Owen was homosexual, but his fellow soldiers did not. It was something, like his poetry, he kept from them.

Over the following week, the Manchesters redeployed to a succession of villages. The Fourth Army was preparing to assault and cross the next natural obstacle in its path, the River Sambre, as October came to an end. Owen retrained D Company for the inevitable clash.

IN SCOTLAND, Lennel and its sister auxiliary hospital, Bowhill House, received notice to close in late October. The war was nearing a conclusion, as British, American, and French forces overran a German Army handicapped by mutinies and hunger. Rivers had long contended that mobile warfare in which soldiers were no longer powerless in trenches reduced their susceptibility to shell shock. The decline in neurasthenic cases was proving him right.

Another Medical Board saw Sassoon at Craiglockhart on October 17 and declared him fit, but only for service at home. He bade farewell to Lady Clementine, left Scotland, and began four weeks' leave. He visited his mother at Weirleigh before going to London to discuss what noncombat role he might play. On November 6, Winston Churchill received him again at the Ministry of Munitions, this time for only a few minutes. The minister was in triumphant mood, and everything he said convinced Sassoon that he had been right about the war being prolonged for Britain and France to acquire territory at their enemies' expense. His protest, he felt, had been vindicated. His diary entry that evening read: "They mean to skin Germany alive. 'A peace to end peace.'"

Sassoon was staying with Philip and Ottoline Morrell at Garsington Manor on the morning of November 11, when the Armistice that ended the Great War took effect. At 11:00 a.m., church bells pealed everywhere. The war that he considered wholly futile was over. He went to Oxford, where crowds waved flags, and took the train to London. There he found masses of humanity "making fools of themselves— an outburst of mob patriotism." After dinner with civilians who had no understanding of the war and what it had done to men he knew, he wrote in his diary, "It is a loathsome ending to the loathsome tragedy of the last four years."

Sassoon waited for a letter from Owen, whose postwar career beckoned. Heinemann was about to publish his poetry collection, which Sassoon, Graves, and other literati were waiting to promote. Days, then weeks, passed without word. Sassoon was not alone in wondering what had become of him. Owen's brother Harold, serving as a merchant marine officer near the West African coast, was too far from Europe to know the whereabouts of Wilfred and Colin, their youngest brother then serving in the Royal Flying Corps. When his ship anchored off the coast of Cameroon, which British and French troops had seized from Germany two years earlier, he went to his cabin to rest from the long voyage. "I drew aside my curtain and stepped inside and to my amazement I saw Wilfred sitting in my chair," he wrote. "I felt shock run through me with appalling force and with it I could feel the blood run from my face." Harold's limbs went so stiff he could not sit down. All he could do was ask Wilfred how he got there. Wilfred did not answer, but "his whole face broke into his sweetest and most endearing dark smile." The vision did not alarm so much as puzzle him. "Wilfred dear," he said, "how can you be here, it's just not possible."

Wilfred went on smiling without speaking. Harold turned away for a moment. When he looked back at the chair, it was empty. The "strange meeting" wore him out, and he fell asleep. "When I woke up I knew with absolute certainty that Wilfred was dead," he wrote. A month later, at Christmastime, months' worth of mail reached him. He searched for a letter from Wilfred, but in vain. Among the many weekly missives from his mother was one postmarked just after Armistice Day. He opened it to read that she received a "dreaded telegram" at home in Owestry on November 11. The postman delivered it at noon, exactly one hour after the guns went silent on the Western Front, as the "church bells were ringing, the bands playing and the jubilant crowds surging together." Harold knew already what the telegram said.

The suspense over Owen's fate lasted longer for Sassoon. "Several months elapsed," he wrote, "before I was told about his death." He refused to accept it "philosophically" and felt a "blank miserable sense of deprivation." In the weeks that followed, details of Owen's last mission emerged.

ON THE EVENING of November 3, Owen sat snug with his company in the cellar of a forester's cottage. The modest building, two stories of brick with a slate roof, stood amid tall pines beside a small road in the Bois l'Évêque. Smoke was so thick that he could barely see. A candle lit the crowded space, where men on all sides poked and jostled him. He was writing a letter to his mother on paper she had sent him along with chocolate he shared with the enlisted man who acted as his servant.

The letter might have been from a camping holiday rather than a war zone. He described the scene. On his right, a soldier named Kellett "radiates joy & contentment from pink cheeks and baby eyes." Next to Kellett, a signaler was listening to the jokes of "a merry corporal . . . with a gleam of white teeth." An old soldier with a walrus moustache was preparing dinner, peeling potatoes and dropping them in the pot. A private named Keyes chopped wood for another soldier to feed into the cooking fire. In such good company, Owen was content. He assured her,

> It is a great life. I am more oblivious than alas! yourself, dear Mother, of the ghastly glimmering of the guns outside, & the hollow crashing of the shells.
>
> There is no danger down here, or if any, it will be over before you read these lines.

Owen neglected to add that 5:45 that morning was zero hour. The men rose well before then to march in darkness through a mile of thick forest along slushy ground to a position just west of a canal linking the rivers Sambre and Oise. The east bank of the forty-four-mile waterway had become the Germans' latest defensive fortification. To drive them back, the Manchesters and other British regiments needed to cross fifty feet of rushing water in full view of machine gunners and rifle-men on the other side. The operation began, as usual, with artillery bombarding the Germans. Shells exploded on the east bank for five minutes, then rolled back three hundred yards to German positions on higher ground. British engineers plunged into the canal, laying out pontoons from the west bank, fixing one plank to another like tracks in a child's electric train set, in a desperate effort to reach the other shore. The bridge was taking shape, but German machine guns, mortars, and gas slowed progress. Thirty of the forty-two engineers fell in the barrage.

Second Lieutenant James Kirk of the Manchesters' 10th Battalion leapt on a raft and paddled forward to fire his Lewis gun at short range. Kirk's brave maneuver enabled the engineers to resume work, until he was killed and a shell destroyed their bridge. Owen and Lieutenant Foulkes led D Company into the canal. With no bridge, they paddled forward on rafts. Men were dying all around, the kind of crisis that plunged some subalterns into the psychologists' "fight-or-flight" syndrome. Owen had no such hesitation. He urged the men on, patting their backs and saying to one after another, "Well done!" and "You are doing well, my boy!"

As Owen led them through the torrent, bullets from the opposite bank tore into his body.

Susan Owen, who heard the story from comrades who came to offer condolences, wrote that her son died as he was "*helping* his men to get across."

Owen, like his hero Keats, was twenty-six when he died. The regiment buried him in the cemetery at Ors village, where his white tombstone was inscribed with words from his poem "The End":

> Shall Life renew these bodies? Of a truth
> All death will he annul, all tears assuage

In the original, the second line ended with a question mark.

The army awarded him the Military Cross for his feat at Swiss Cottage the month before. Dr. Brock wrote that Owen had confronted his phantoms through his poetry and "had *all but* laid them to rest ere the last call came." Owen was a success for Craiglockhart and for ergotherapy, but for him the outcome was death.

Epilogue

Craiglockhart muddled through the first months of 1919 without the sense of mission war had supplied. Doctors who struggled to make men battle ready wondered what they were preparing them for. The War Office no longer needed vast numbers of junior officers to replace those fed into the Western Front. A parsimonious postwar government would not allocate resources to succor soon-to-be civilians. Debilitated officers, like damaged tanks and lame horses, were surplus baggage.

The Craiglockhart War Hospital for Officers gradually wound down, closing its doors in April 1919. Edinburgh's One O'Clock Gun resumed its daily salvo, providing the city with an element of prewar normality. Over Craiglockhart's thirty months of operation, it had returned 758 officers to combat. This was nearly half of the 1,801 it had treated since its inauguration in October 1916. The record compared favorably with that of the British military's oldest mental institution, Royal Victoria Hospital's D Block, which returned only 7.1 percent of the officers and men it treated to active duty. The majority of D Block patients, just over 60 percent, were discharged from the service. The Craiglockhart officers who did not return to the front were discharged, sent to light duties in Britain, or confined to lunatic asylums. Partly out of courtesy to those who sacrificed their sanity for their country, lunatic asylums were renamed mental hospitals. Moreover, public revulsion at the execution of three hundred shell-shocked men for desertion or cowardice forced the British government ten years later to abolish the death penalty for deserters.

While military psychiatrists stood accused of treating the mentally ill only to return them to the conditions that caused them to break down, the same could be said of physicians who extracted shrapnel, stitched wounds, and healed broken limbs. Their charges too would return to battle, where they might be shot, shelled, or gassed again. In civilian life, psychiatrists treating men and women unable to cope with peacetime trauma let them go back to the factories, offices, or troubled homes that laid them low. The physician's job was to heal, not to change the world to which the recovered patient returned.

Many of the "cured" officers from Craiglockhart suffered trauma for the rest of their lives. One, Captain John "Harry" Burns of the Cheshire Greys Regiment, trembled so much that he could barely hold a cup of tea. His daughter, Maureen Huws, told documentary filmmakers years later, "He had nightmares every night and my mother used to say, 'He has neurasthenia.' I thought neurasthenia meant that you couldn't sleep. I will always remember horrific shouting and screaming in the night and my mother trying to calm him down." Exacerbating his condition was the daily firing in his village of a one o'clock gun, resembling the one he had heard in Edinburgh. Its blast sent him running around the house calling for his wife and daughter. Whenever he saw an army cap or heard a car backfire, he hid under his bed and howled. Burns was not alone among Craiglockhart veterans whose war never ended.

Burns's wife and daughter were two of many British women who found their men changed by the war. Ford Madox Ford wrote in his postwar novel *Last Post*, the fourth in his *Parade's End* quartet, of a young woman, Valentine Wannop, who realizes that the man she loved,

Christopher Tietjens, has returned from the front physically unharmed but mentally damaged. "Ah," she thought, "the dreadful thing about the whole war was that it had been—the suffering had been—mental rather than physical. And they had not thought of it . . . He had suffered mental torture and now his pity was being worked on to make him abstain from the woman that could atone." Ford continued:

> Hitherto, she had thought of the War as physical suffering only. Now she saw it as mental torture. Immense miles and miles of anguish in darkened minds. That remained. Men might stand up on hills, but mental torture could not be expelled.

Ford understood shell shock, having succumbed to it during the Battle of the Somme in 1916.

CRAIGLOCKHART'S LAST COMMANDANT, Major Brown, his staff, and the remaining patients dispersed to other hospitals or went home. The War Office returned the Craiglockhart site to its owner, James Bell, who sold the property to the Roman Catholic Church for a teaching convent. Two shell-shocked soldiers remained on the premises. One was James Carmichael, head gardener Henry Carmichael's nephew, whose family continued to worry about his sudden disappearances and erratic behavior. The other was Henry's son Alexander, who had returned at war's end from a German prisoner-of-war camp. Like his cousin James, he had fought in the Black Watch and endured trench life and artillery fire. His experiences as a freezing and starved prisoner added to his woes. Traumatized and ill, he nonetheless labored beside his father and his brother Robert to keep Craiglockhart's gardens as lavish as on the day the War Hospital welcomed its first patients. Dr. Brock would have seen the healthy outdoor activity as useful therapy. It was the only therapy such enlisted men were likely to get.

Acknowledgments

It is impossible, at least for me, to write a book without help. Prime among the many who gave it is Catherine Walker, director of the War Poets Collection at Edinburgh Napier University in what was the Craiglockhart War Hospital. Mrs. Walker presided over the hospital's relics in Peddie and Kinnear's original building, which has survived many alterations and the intrusion of a spaceship structure beside it on Henry Carmichael's old garden. From the moment I contacted her about the project, she offered unstinting assistance. She arranged a bed-and-breakfast for me in Edinburgh, not far from the famed Princes Street that figures prominently in these pages. She drove me from there to Craiglockhart, opened her files and memorabilia collection, and answered my questions. As my research progressed in London and northern France, she responded to more queries and tracked down elusive documents. It is rare for a writer to have the benefit of such a kind and enthusiastic collaborator. Her death before I completed the book meant that, sadly, she could not read the result of our labors and know how grateful I am to her.

As with my first book, *Tribes with Flags*, and my last three volumes on aspects of the Second World War, I am indebted to my editor at Penguin Press, Ann Godoff. Her enthusiasm for the story gave me the confidence to begin and, after a longer than expected interval, complete it. She saw me through a near-fatal bout of COVID-19 and waited with admirable forbearance for a manuscript that her practiced eye made coherent and, I hope, readable. I am grateful as well to her colleagues at Penguin, especially Casey Denis, Victoria Lopez, Ryan Boyle, Alyson D'Amato, Gloria Arminio, Amanda Dewey, and Jessie Stratton.

Among fellow writers who generously gave of their time and knowledge, Jean Moorcroft Wilson deserves particular praise and gratitude. As the author of the assiduously researched biographies of Robert Graves and Siegfried Sassoon, she knew the war poets far better than I. Rather than regard me as an interloper on her territory, she invited me to her house in London with its impressive library and pointed me toward information I would otherwise have missed. She introduced me to Yvonne Morris of the Wilfred Owen Association, who provided invaluable assistance and sent me *The Wilfred Owen Association Journal*, which updated me on the latest research into Owen's life and works. Her colleagues Lucy Elder and Sam Gray also gave their time without hesitation to educate me about Owen. My thanks also to Professor Jacqueline Rose, author of *On Violence and on Violence Against Women*, for her enlightening insights into mental illness and violence.

Phil Tomaselli, the most conscientious researcher to set foot in Britain's National Archives and the Imperial War Museums, rendered yeoman service locating many of the documents that made this book possible. He provided useful advice when I sought out the documents in Britain early in my research. Later, when I was unable to travel to Britain from Italy during the pandemic, I relied on Mr. Tomaselli more than in the past. He never stinted, often coming up with files that I had not known existed. In the United States, Tess Weitzner found papers from Britain that had been deposited at the New York Public Library and Columbia University. I must also thank the staff of the London Library, especially Gosia Lawick. They found old military and medical journal articles that had yet to be digitized, copied them, and sent them to me without demur. At Southern Illinois University in Carbondale Aaron Lisec of the Morris Library's Special Collections Research Center and Gregory Budzban, dean of the College of Arts and Sciences, provided wartime and postwar correspondence of Robert Graves, Dr. William Halse Rivers, and others involved in the Craiglockhart story. The papers of Dr. Arthur Ruggles came through the kind offices of Peter Carini, college archivist, Dartmouth College.

Elizabeth L. Garver, research associate at the Harry Ransom Center, University of Texas at Austin, made available the center's collection of letters and works by the British war poets. Others who provided relevant documents and to whom I am grateful are: Robert McIntosh, curator, Museum of Military Medicine, Keogh Barracks, Mytchett, Surrey; Sally Kent, assistant archivist, Department of Archives and Modern Manuscripts, Cambridge University Library; and Jen Gallagher, reader services librarian, Bodleian Library, Oxford. Ian Stein, grandson of Craiglockhart patient Harold Stevens, kindly provided family memories of his grandfather's experiences.

That illustrious First World War aficionado Dan Snow introduced me to Mark Bannon of MGB Tours in northern France. Bannon gave me a weeklong tour of the battlefields where Siegfried Sassoon, Wilfred Owen, Robert Graves, Max Plowman, and other war poets fought. He also took me to the Sambre–Oise Canal, where Owen died, and to Owen's grave nearby. The landscape, more than a century after the war, with its scars and cemeteries recalls Canadian military physician John McCrae's homage:

> We are the Dead. Short days ago
> We lived, felt dawn, saw sunset glow,
>   Loved and were loved, and now we lie,
>   In Flanders fields.

I am grateful to my friends Alessandro de Renzis Sonnino and his bride, Caterina de Renzis Sonnino, who found me a house in Tuscany when I had wearied of life in France. My daily rendezvous with Alessandro, fortified with his excellent Sonnino wines, made my reintegration into Tuscan life not merely a pleasure, but a joy. His death from COVID-19 at the height of the pandemic was an inexpressible loss to his family, and to me. Also in Tuscany, I must thank Duccio and Clotilde Corsini and their daughters, Elena and Selvaggia, for their friendship and hospitality. I should add that my life while writing this book would have been a trial without the kind assistance of their staff, especially Fabiana and Alessandra Fedi, Daniele Marotta, Carina Scandolera, and Caterina Righi.

A final thank-you to the personnel at the cafés where I did much of my writing: Caffè Ricchi in Piazza Santo Spirito, Florence; Bar Alimentari in Ponterotto; Pasticceria Paolini in Montespertoli; and the Blu Bar, Caffè Vittorio, and Bar Centrale in San Casciano. Strong coffee, an ashtray, and a smile went a long way to getting me through.

CHARLES GLASS
San Casciano, Florence, Italy

Notes

Introduction

xiii All the armies: Charles S. Myers, "A Contribution to the Study of Shell Shock," *The Lancet* (February 13, 1915), 316–20.

xiii In December 1914, a mere five months: W. Johnson and R. G. Row, "Neurasthenia and War Neuroses," *History of the Great War Based on Official Documents; Disease of War*, vol. 2, 1–2 (London: His Majesty's Stationery Office, 1923), quoted in Ben Shephard, *A War of Nerves: Soldiers and Psychiatrists in the Twentieth Century* (Cambridge, MA: Harvard University Press, 2003), 20.

xiii An editorial that month: Quoted in Cathryn Corns and John Hughes Wilson, *Blindfold and Alone: British Military Executions in the Great War* (London: Cassell & Company, 2001), 73.

xiii A year later, the same publication: F. W. Burton-Fanning, "Neurasthenia in Home Forces," *The Lancet* (June 16, 1917), 907–11.

xiii Dr. Frederick Walker Mott: Frederick Walker Mott, "Lectures [to the Medical Society of London] on the Effects of High Explosives on the Central Nervous System," *The Lancet* (February 12, 1916), 331–38.

xiv Major E. T. F. Birrell of the Royal Army Medical Corps: British National Archives (BNA), War Office: Service Medal and Award Rolls Index, First World War, WO 372/24/5259.

xiv They suffered unexplained blindness: Dr. Octave Laurent, *La Guerre en Bulgarie et en Turquie* (Paris: A. Maoine, 1914), 24–25.

xiv Laurent referred to the soldiers' malady: Laurent, *La Guerre en Bulgarie et en Turquie*, 24–25.

xv Examining otherwise healthy men: Dr. William Aldren Turner, Temporary Colonel, RAMC, "Remarks on Cases of Nervous and Mental Shock Observed in the Base Hospitals in France," *British Medical Journal* (May 15, 1915): 833.

xvi That was the signal: Hugh Sebag-Montefiore, *Somme: Into the Breach* (New York: Penguin Books, 2017), 1.

xvi Novelist and official war propagandist John Buchan: John Buchan, *The Battle of the Somme* (New York: George H. Doran, 1917), 42.

xvii The Germans pitied the boys: William Manchester, *The Arms of Krupp, 1587–1968* (London: Michael Joseph, 1969), 335.

xvii Dr. Arthur Hurst: See www.youtube.com/watch?v=D1MixQbB-K0. Dr. Lewis Yealland, a Canadian RAMC physician in London who employed electro-shock therapy on traumatized soldiers, also filmed some of his patients before and after treatment. Yealland worked with Dr. William Aldren Turner. See Stefanie C. Linden, Edgar Jones, and Andrew J. Lees, "Shell Shock at Queen Square: Lewis Yealland 100 Years On," *Brain: A Journal of Neurology* 136, no. 6 (June 2013), 1976–1988. The authors write that no copies of Yealland's films by Pathé from July and August 1917 are known to have survived.

xvii **Although the British Army High Command:** My letter to Peter Jackson about the absence of shell-shocked soldiers in his film went unanswered.

Chapter One: The Hydro

1 **Historians surmise that Craiglockhart:** City of Edinburgh Council, "Edinburgh: Survey of Gardens and Designed Landscapes," 195 Craiglockhart Campus, Napier University, conducted by Peter McGowan Associates, 2007, 3.

2 **Expense was the least consideration:** City of Edinburgh Council, "Edinburgh: Survey of Gardens and Designed Landscapes," 4.

2 **A 50-by-20-foot swimming pool:** City of Edinburgh Council, "Edinburgh: Survey of Gardens and Designed Landscapes," 4.

3 **From there, they could wander:** "Thomas Duddingston Wilson," Obituary, *British Medical Journal* 17 (March 1906): 654.

3 **The owners sold it:** "James Bell," Basic Biographical Details, www.scottisharchitects.org .uk/architect_full.php?id=200486.

4 **His second wife, Mary Comrie:** Scottish Cultural Resource Access Network, "The War Poets at Craiglockhart: The Carmichael Family, Family Members," https://sites.scran.ac.uk /Warp/family_members.htm, and "The War Poets at Craiglockhart: The Carmichael Family, Family Members 2," https://sites.scran.ac.uk/Warp/family_members2.htm.

4 **Like the Carmichael family:** "The Craiglockhart Years," Scottish Croquet Association, www.scottishcroquet.org.uk/index.php/the-scottish-championship-1870-1914/the-scottish -championship/the-craiglockhart-years.

5 **In Scotland, volunteers were so numerous:** Adam Hochschild, *To End All Wars* (London: Pan Publishing, 2012), 100.

5 **Two of Henry Carmichael's sons:** British National Archive (BNA), War Office: Service Medal and Award Rolls Index, First World War, WO 372/4/18288, "Archibald Carmichael," and WO 372/4/18241, "Alexander Carmichael."

5 **Soon afterward, Henry's youngest son:** BNA, WO 372/4/18615 and WO 372/4/18288.

5 **Lieutenant Bernard Law Montgomery:** Peter Vansittart, *Voices from the Great War* (London: Jonathan Cape, 1981), 30.

5 **The poet Rupert Brooke:** Rupert Brooke, *The Complete Poems* (London: Sidgwick & Jackson, 1942), 146.

6 **Patriotic disapproval of such frivolity:** The Scottish Croquet Championships did not resume until 1968. See "The Craiglockhart Years," Scottish Croquet Association; and D. C. M. Prichard, *The History of Croquet* (London: Cassell & Company, 1981).

6 **Britain had launched an amphibious invasion:** National Records of Scotland, First World War, "Gallipoli 28 June 2015," www.nrscotland.gov.uk/research/learning/first-world-war /gallipoli-28-june-1915.

7 **Although Edinburgh lacked air defenses:** David MacLean, "Lost Edinburgh: Zeppelin Air Raid of 1916," *The Scotsman*, April 14, 2014, www.scotsman.com/lifestyle-2-15039/lost -edinburgh-zeppelin-air-raid-of-1916-1-3375536. See also National Records of Scotland, First World War, "Zeppelin Air Raid on Edinburgh 1916," https://www.nrscotland.gov.uk /research/learning/first-world-war/zeppelin-air-raid-on-edinburgh-1916.

8 **Seventeen German incendiaries:** National Records of Scotland, "Zeppelin Air Raid on Edinburgh 1916," HH31/21/8, folders 23–26.

Chapter Two: The War Hospital

9 **"At the outbreak of the late European War":** C. Stanford Read, *Military Psychiatry in Peace and War* (London: H. K. Lewis and Company, 1920), 40.

9 **Dr. Read ran the army's only mental asylum:** Edgar Jones, "Shell Shock at Maghull and Maudsley: Models of Psychological Medicine in the UK," *Journal of the History of Medicine and Allied Sciences* 65, no. 3 (2010): 369.

9 Maghull filled to capacity: Peter Leese, *Shell Shock: Traumatic Neurosis and the British Soldiers of the First World War* (Houndmills: Palgrave Macmillan, 2014), 53.

9 "hospitals," not "asylums": Read, *Military Psychiatry in Peace and War*, 42.

10 Craiglockhart War Hospital opened: Major Thomas W. Salmon, *The Care and Treatment of Mental Diseases and War Neuroses ("Shell Shock") in the British Army* (New York: War Work Committee of the National Committee for Mental Hygiene, Inc., 1917), 96.

10 Craiglockhart's O. C., officer commanding: British National Archives (BNA), War Office: Service Medal and Award Rolls Index, First World War, WO 374/10387.

10 It was his belief: W. H. Bryce, "The Management of the Neurotic-Institutional," in *Functional Nerve Disease: An Epitome of War Experience for the Practitioner*, ed. H. Crichton Miller (London: Henry Frowde/Hodder & Stoughton, 1920), 163.

10 Subordinates were not required: Imperial War Museum (IWM), Siegfried Sassoon Papers, Documents 9059, "Notes on the Staff of Craiglockhart War Hospital." In contrast, Dr. (Major) Frederick Mott at the Maudsley Hospital in south London required patients to stand to attention and salute all officers who entered their wards. Mott, a distinguished psychiatrist himself, maintained that discipline was an important element in the cure of neurosis. See Frederick Mott, *War Neuroses and Shell Shock* (London: Henry Frowde, 1919), 277.

11 It seemed they understood: C. L. R. James, *Beyond A Boundary* (London: Yellow Jersey Press/Penguin Books, 2005), 308. James's famous question echoed that of Rudyard Kipling in his poem "The English Flag": "And what should they know of England who only England know?"

11 The principal medical officers: Rivers's full name was William Halse Rivers Rivers. His biographer wrote, "It has been suggested that the use of Rivers as a given name was merely a clerical error in the baptismal record." Richard Slobodin, *W. H. R. Rivers: Pioneer Anthropologist, Psychiatrist of "The Ghost Road"* (Stroud, Gloucestershire, UK: Sutton Publishing, 1997), 6.

11 Aged thirty-eight in 1916: David Cantor, "Between Galen, Geddes, and the Gael: Arthur Brock, Modernity, and Medical Humanism in Early-Twentieth-Century Scotland," *Journal of the History of Medicine and Allied Sciences* 60, no 1 (January 2005): 4.

12 A meeting with Patrick Geddes: "Sir Patrick Geddes, Scottish Biologist and Sociologist," *Encyclopaedia Britannica*, www.britannica.com/biography/Patrick-Geddes.

12 The admiration between the two men: Professor Patrick Geddes, introduction to Arthur J. Brock, *Health and Conduct* (London and Edinburgh: Williams and Norgate, 1923), vii.

12 Brock spent months: Letter from Arthur J. Brock to Patrick Geddes, May 6, 1902, National Library of Scotland, MS 10533, folder 70.

12 His study of tuberculosis: A. M. Crossman, "The *Hydra*, Captain AJ Brock and the Treatment of Shell-Shock in Edinburgh," *Journal of the Royal College of Physicians of Edinburgh* 33, no. 2 (2003): 120.

12 He noted that at Woodburn: Brock, *Health and Conduct*.

12 His first posts: Cantor, "Between Galen, Geddes, and the Gael," 12.

12 While there in 1916: Galen, *On the Natural Faculties*, trans. A. J. Brock (London: Heinemann, 1916).

13 The shell-shock hospital: Arthur J. Brock, "The Re-Education of the Adult," *Sociological Review* A10, no 1, (March 1918): 25.

13 He stammered when: W. H. R. Rivers, *Conflict and Dream* (London: Kegan, Paul Trench, Trubner & Co., 1923), 7: "In October 1916 I was transferred to a hospital for officers . . ."

13 "I have been able": W. H. R. Rivers, *Psychology and Ethnology* (New York: Harcourt, Brace and Company, 1926), 53.

14 Two ancestors, a father: "Rivers, William Halse Rivers," *Oxford Dictionary of National Biography*, May 28, 2015, https://doi.org/10.1093/ref:odnb/37898.

14 Family legend had it: Charles S. Myers, "The Influence of the Late W. H. R. Rivers on the Development of Psychology in Great Britain," Presidential Address to the Psychology Section of the British Association, *Nature* 110, no. 2762 (October 7, 1922): 485.

14 A friend and colleague: Slobodin, *W. H. R. Rivers: Pioneer Anthropologist, Psychiatrist of "The Ghost Road,"* 82.

15 With the German experience: Slobodin, *W. H. R. Rivers: Pioneer Anthropologist, Psychiatrist of "The Ghost Road,"* 13.

15 One recalled that: F. C. B., "W. H. R. Rivers," *The Eagle*, Saint John's College, Cambridge, vol. 43, 1923, 11. (F. C. B. was Frederic C. Bartlett, Rivers's student at Saint John's, later a prominent psychologist and author.)

16 It was a discipline: Rivers, *Conflict and Dream*, 11.

16 His books on the Todas: W. H. R. Rivers, *The Todas* (London: Macmillan, 1906); W. H. R. Rivers, *The History of Melanesian Society*, Percy Sladen Trust Expedition to Melanesia, 2 vols. (Cambridge: Cambridge University Press, 1914).

16 Dr. Grafton Elliot Smith: Edgar Jones, "Shell Shock at Maghull and the Maudsley: Models of Psychological Medicine in the UK," *Journal of the History of Medicine and Allied Sciences* 6, no. 3 (2010): 373.

17 The challenge had awaited him: Imperial War Museum (IWM), Siegfried Sassoon Papers, Documents 9059, "Notes on the Staff of Craiglockhart War Hospital."

17 The Red Cross supplied: Mary McGregor later married Captain Stewart Kaye. Grace Barnet's sister worked at the Edinburgh War Hospital and Bangor Village Hospital. Craiglockhart War Poets Collection, Edinburgh Napier University.

17 and the housekeepers worked: BNA, WO 399/5084, "Matron Margaret MacBean," display at Craiglockhart War Poets Collection, Edinburgh Napier University.

17 A letter of reference: BNA, WO 399/5084.

18 Craiglockhart's initial intake: BNA, MH 106.

18 Second Lieutenant Sandison came: BNA, WO 339/57792.

19 Brock's therapy revolved: Robert Graves, *The Greek Myths*, vol. 2 (London: Folio Society, 1996), 464–65.

19 Brock felt that each officer: Dr. Arthur J. Brock, "Antaeus, Or Back to the Land," *The Hydra, the Magazine of Craiglockhart War Hospital*, no. 3, New Series, January 1918, 5; and Brock, *Health and Conduct*, 137.

19 The key for Brock: IWM, Siegfried Sassoon Papers, Documents 9059.

19 While Craiglockhart offered: Brock, *Health and Conduct*, 31.

20 War hospitals utilizing: Brock, "The Re-Education of the Adult: The Neurasthenic in War and Peace," 30.

20 Brock had encountered: Brock, *Health and Conduct*, 137.

20 Second Lieutenant George Walpole Lightfoot: BNA, WO 339/50861. Lightfoot served in the Royal Welch Fusiliers' 1st Battalion until his injury.

21 Thirty-two-year-old Edward Curwen: BNA, WO 339/4246. Brock wrote that treating symptoms rather than causes was as useless as cutting one of the heads of the mythological Hydra. When one head went, another took its place. *Health and Conduct*, 29. Therapeutic conversations were "the stage between analysis and re-synthesis," *Health and Conduct*, 31.

21 The same Medical Board: BNA, WO 339/62493.

21 Another casualty from Eaucourt l'Abbaye: BNA, WO 374/54031.

22 Two days after Pickering arrived: BNA, WO 339/26540.

22 The first eight officers: Bryce, "The Management of the Neurotic-Institutional," 162.

22 While the nightmares distressed their victims: Rivers, *Conflict and Dream*, 5.

23 Nightmares of those: Rivers, *Conflict and Dream*, 68.

23 Officers in Rivers's consulting room: Rivers, *Conflict and Dream*, 35. Rivers shared this outlook with Carl Jung, who wrote, "Relationships must be fostered as far as possible and maintained, and thus a morbid transference can be avoided." Carl Jung, Cornwall Seminar, July 1923, unauthorized notes by M. Esther Harding, 5, https://collections.library.yale.edu /catalog/10076043.

23 Rivers's patients sat in chairs: Rivers, *Conflict and Dream*, 35.

23 **One of the men he treated:** "W. H. R. Rivers: A Miscellany, Rivers in WW1—Sassoon and Yealland," https://whrrivers.com/rivers-in-ww1-sassoon-and-yealland.

23 **Rivers followed Major Bryce's lead:** IWM, Siegfried Sassoon Papers, Documents 9059.

24 **One Craiglockhart patient observed:** Siegfried Sassoon, *The Complete Memoirs of George Sherston* (London: Faber and Faber, 1937), 651.

24 **Rivers shared Brock's rejection:** W. H. R. Rivers, "An Address on the Repression of War Experience," *Lancet* (February 2, 1918), 174.

24 **The men needed:** Rivers, "An Address on the Repression of War Experience," 176.

24 **In the second half of 1916:** Leese, *Shell Shock: Traumatic Neurosis and the British Soldiers of the First World War*, 104.

Chapter Three: Interpreting Dreams

25 **Among those examined:** British National Archives (BNA), War Office: Service Medal and Award Rolls Index, First World War, WO 374/54031.

25 **By the first of March:** *Report of the War Office Committee of Enquiry into "Shell-Shock,"* Presented to Parliament by Command of His Majesty (London: His Majesty's Stationery Office, 1922), 57.

26 **as E. M. Forster wrote:** E. M. Forster, *Howards End* (1910; New York: Alfred A. Knopf, 1991), 195.

27 **Four years later:** John Middleton Murry, *Katherine Mansfield and Other Literary Portraits* (London: Peter Neville Limited, 1949), 133.

27 **Plowman's compromise between fighting:** Max Plowman, *Bridge into the Future: Letters of Max Plowman*, ed. Dorothy L. Plowman (London: Andrew Dakers Limited, 1944), 28.

27 **The RAMC inducted him:** BNA, WO 339/50680.

27 **He drilled with the 4th:** Simon Heffer, *Vaughan Williams* (London: Weidenfeld and Nicholson, 2000), 46.

27 **His equivocal role:** M. Plowman, *Bridge into the Future*, 34.

27 **"Who am I":** M. Plowman, *Bridge into the Future*, 37.

27 **Having enjoyed the benefits:** M. Plowman, *Bridge into the Future*, 37.

28 **The battalion had yet to recover:** Max Plowman, *The Right to Live* (London: Andrew Dakers Limited, 1945), 214.

28 **He confessed in letters:** M. Plowman, *Bridge into the Future*, 47.

28 **His first weeks:** Max Plowman (writing as Mark VII), *A Subaltern on the Somme* (New York: E. P. Dutton & Company, 1928), 49.

28 **Shrapnel and bullets:** M. Plowman, *A Subaltern on the Somme*, 52.

29 **Plowman's platoon struggled:** M. Plowman, *A Subaltern on the Somme*, 51.

29 **The war's caprice:** M. Plowman, *A Subaltern on the Somme*, 97.

29 **Nothing he witnessed:** M. Plowman, *Bridge into the Future*, 57.

30 **He wrote to his:** M. Plowman, *Bridge into the Future*, 58.

30 **October saw Plowman:** M. Plowman, *A Subaltern on the Somme*, 112.

30 **The officer was Major Ronald Campbell:** Philip Gibbs, *Now It Can Be Told* (New York: Harper and Brothers, 1920), 111.

30 **Campbell's bellicose performance:** M. Plowman, *A Subaltern on the Somme*, 112.

30 **Back on active duty:** M. Plowman, *A Subaltern on the Somme*, 127.

31 **One of the officers:** M. Plowman, *A Subaltern on the Somme*, 142.

31 **Taking advantage of a full moon:** Max Plowman, *The Faith Called Pacifism* (London: J. M. Dent and Sons, 1936), 97.

31 **In November, two four-day tours:** M. Plowman, *Bridge into the Future*, 59.

32 **Plowman's platoon brought the supplies:** M. Plowman, *A Subaltern on the Somme*, 148.

32 **On the first day:** M. Plowman, *A Subaltern on the Somme*, 161–62.

32 **Although conditions grew more desperate:** M. Plowman, *A Subaltern on the Somme*, 199.

32 **An outraged Second Lieutenant Plowman:** M. Plowman, *Bridge into the Future*, 60–61.

33 **January's snow froze:** M. Plowman, *A Subaltern on the Somme*, 223.

33 **His head burned:** BNA, WO 339/50680.

34 **Rivers treated him:** BNA, WO 339/50680.

34 **He finished the last chapter:** W. H. R. Rivers, *Conflict and Dream* (London: Kegan, Paul Trench, Trubner & Co., 1923), 121–22.

34 **Rivers woke early:** Rivers, *Conflict and Dream*, 121.

35 **had become premier:** "M. Ribot Premier," *The Times* (London), March 20, 1917, 6.

35 **Another publication Rivers read:** "Ogden, Charles Kay," *Oxford Dictionary of National Biography*, May 21, 2009, www.oxforddnb.com/view/10.1093/ref:odnb/9780198614128.001 .0001/odnb-9780198614128-e-35293.

35 **French pundits were writing:** Rivers, *Conflict and Dream*, 120.

36 **At the end of Rivers's workday:** Rivers, *Conflict and Dream*, 121.

36 **Upon waking, Rivers:** Rivers, *Conflict and Dream*, 120.

37 **Rivers recorded, "Sometimes":** Ernest E. Southard, *Shell-Shock and Other Neuropsychiatric Problems Presented in Five Hundred and Eighty-Nine Case Histories from the War Literature, 1914–1918* (Boston: W. M. Leonard, 1919), Case 507, 713.

37 **Rivers took on another patient:** Southard, *Shell-Shock and Other Neuropsychiatric Problems*, Case 506, 712.

38 **Another patient was having:** Southard, *Shell-Shock and Other Neuropsychiatric Problems*, Case 510, 716.

38 **An older officer:** Southard, *Shell-Shock and Other Neuropsychiatric Problems*, Case 509, 715.

39 **Nocturnal dreams carried Craiglockhart's inmates:** *The Hydra, the Journal of Craiglockhart War Hospital*, no. 1, April 28, 1917, 5, University of Oxford English Faculty Library, Wilfred Owen Collection. Page references are to the more accessible Edinburgh Napier University copies of *The Hydra* at www.napier.ac.uk/about-us/our-location/our-campuses/special-collec tions/war-poets-collection/the-hydra.

39 **Hens soon laid:** *The Hydra*, no. 1, 5.

39 **On April 11:** *The Hydra*, no. 1, 3.

40 **The new Debating Society:** *The Hydra*, no. 1, 3.

40 **Captain Archibald argued:** *The Hydra*, no. 1, 5.

40 **Billiards became a popular pastime:** *The Hydra*, no. 1, 6.

40 **Craiglockhart's musicians staged:** *The Hydra*, no. 1, 16.

41 **Women, usually wives:** *The Hydra*, no. 1, 16.

41 **Peas Blossom's review:** Arthur J. Brock, *Health and Conduct* (London and Edinburgh: Wil liams and Norgate, 1923), 29.

41 **"*The Hydra* must be made":** *The Hydra*, no. 1, 3.

41 **The Hydra's pages:** *The Hydra*, no. 1, 9.

42 **a poem entitled "Waiting":** *The Hydra*, no. 1, 10.

42 **Much of the journal's poetry:** *The Hydra*, no. 1, 9–10.

Chapter Four: A Complete and Glorious Loaf

44 **Dr. Rivers impressed Max Plowman:** Max Plowman, *Bridge into the Future: Letters of Max Plowman*, ed. Dorothy L. Plowman (London: Andrew Dakers Limited, 1944), 65.

44 **Plowman had no complaints:** M. Plowman, *Bridge into the Future*, 63.

45 **Concern for his wife:** British National Archives (BNA), War Office: Service Medal and Award Rolls Index, First World War, WO 339/50680.

45 **His support for the war:** M. Plowman, *Bridge into the Future*, 64.

45 **Among Rivers's other patients:** *London Gazette*, October 9, 1914, His Majesty's Stationery Office, 8050.

45 **By the time German troops:** Terry Norman, *The Hell They Called High Wood: The Somme 1916* (Barnsley, South Yorks, UK: Pen and Sword, 2009), 233.

46 **On October 29:** BNA, Ministry of Pensions: Selected First World War Pensions Award Files, PIN 26/22117.

46 A succession of military hospitals: BNA, PIN 26/22117.

46 Middlebrook was twenty-three: BNA, PIN 26/22117.

46 *The Hydra's* second issue: *The Hydra, the Magazine of Craiglockhart War Hospital*, no. 2, May 12, 1917, 2, University of Oxford English Faculty Library, Wilfred Owen Collection. Page references are to the more accessible Edinburgh Napier University copies of *The Hydra* at www .napier.ac.uk/about-us/our-location/our-campuses/special-collections/war-poets -collection/the-hydra.

46 All arriving patients: *The Hydra*, no. 2, 5.

47 one patient wrote a travelogue: *The Hydra*, no. 2, 11.

47 Calling the city: *The Hydra*, no. 2, 13.

47 Another writer criticized: *The Hydra*, no. 2, 16.

47 "Cockney" was Max Plowman: Max Plowman, *A Lap Full of Seed* (Oxford: B. H. Blackwell, 1917), 76.

48 On April 23, the Debating Society: *The Hydra*, no. 2, 4.

48 Votes for women: *The Hydra*, no. 2, 4.

48 Captain Bates conducted: *The Hydra*, no. 2, 19.

49 Military psychiatrists disagreed: Arthur J. Brock, *Health and Conduct* (London and Edinburgh: Williams and Norgate, 1923), 138.

49 On May 5, an officer: BNA, Ministry of Health, MH 106/2173. The remainder of the references to Snape's military and medical records are from this file and Craiglockhart's Admission and Discharge Book at BNA, 106/1887.

51 While Max Plowman marked time: M. Plowman, *Bridge into the Future*, 67.

52 Amid so many dead: M. Plowman, *Bridge into the Future*, 68.

52 Craiglockhart's eleven met: *The Hydra*, no 3, May 26, 1917, 5.

52 One spectator, Lieutenant James Haygate Butlin: Private Papers of James H. Butlin, Imperial War Museum, Documents 7915. All subsequent quotes from Butlin's letters are from this collection.

53 Butlin's next letter: The Imperial War Museum's description of the Butlin Papers states that "he seems to have been treated by W H R Rivers," although it provides no evidence for the assertion. See "Private Papers of Lieutenant J H Butlin," www.iwm.org.uk/collections /item/object/1030007787. The emphasis that Butlin's physician placed on outdoor activities, early morning swims, and work on *The Hydra*, all aspects of "ergotherapy," make it more likely that Brock treated him.

54 The young soldier, while: BNA, WO 372/3/21760.

55 In mid-May, Max Plowman: *The Hydra*, no. 4, June 9, 1917, 19.

56 The passage finished: *The Hydra*, no. 4, 20.

56 After submitting the baffling essay-poem: BNA, WO 339/50680.

58 When not busy: Max Plowman, *The Right to Live: Essays by Max Plowman* (London: Andrew Dakers Limited, 1945), 31.

58 Poor men who had slaved: Plowman, *The Right to Live*, 33.

59 The modern soldier: Plowman, *The Right to Live*, 37.

Chapter Five: Out of Place

61 on the morning of Wednesday: British National Archives (BNA), War Office: Service Medal and Award Rolls Index, First World War, WO 138/74. See also BNA, "Medicine on the Western Front, Part One: Wilfred Owen," www.nationalarchives.gov.uk/education/resources /medicine-on-the-western-front-part-one/wilfred-owen.

61 The eminent neurologist Captain William Brown: Edgar Jones, "Doctors and Trauma in the First World War: The Response of British Military Psychiatrists," in *The Memory of Catastrophe*, eds. Peter Grey and Kendrick Oliver (Manchester, UK: Manchester University Press, 2004), 96. See also William Brown, *Suggestion and Mental Analysis: An Outline of the Theory and Practice of Mind Cure* (London: University of London Press, 1922), 22.

62 That was all Brock had: Wilfred Owen, *The Poems of Wilfred Owen*, ed. Edmund Blunden (London: Chatto and Windus, 1933), 133.

62 His brother Harold: Harold Owen, *Journey from Obscurity: Wilfred Owen, 1893–1918*, vol. 1 (Oxford: Oxford University Press, 1963), 40.

63 Owen confessed in a letter: Wilfred Owen, *Wilfred Owen: Collected Letters*, eds. Harold Owen and John Bell (Oxford: Oxford University Press, 1967), Letter 172. Further references to the Owen correspondence are indicated as "Owen Collected Letters." Letter numbers are identical to those in *Wilfred Owen: Selected Letters*, ed. John Bell (Oxford: Oxford University Press, 1998).

64 When the war began: Owen Collected Letters, Letter 516.

64 A few days into the war: Owen Collected Letters, Letter 279.

64 Letters over the following weeks: Owen Collected Letters, Letter 283.

65 Owen wrote to his brother: Owen Collected Letters, Letter 288.

65 In early November: Owen Collected Letters, Letter 298.

65 But he could not banish: Owen Collected Letters, Letter 302.

65 His preoccupation with the war: Owen Collected Letters, Letter 357.

66 On his return to Bordeaux: Owen Collected Letters, Letter 357.

66 He swore an oath: Owen Collected Letters, Letter 383.

66 Drilled to exhaustion: Owen Collected Letters, Letter 388.

66 Two weeks later: Owen Collected Letters, Letter 426.

67 To his satisfaction: Owen, *The Poems of Wilfred Owen*, 12.

67 Owen soon moved: Owen Collected Letters, Letter 476.

67 The noise, if not the danger: Owen Collected Letters, Letter 477.

67 As the new commander: Dr. Stephen Bull, ed., *An Officer's Manual of the Western Front, 1914–1918* (Oxford: Osprey Publishing, 2015), 67.

68 Packed tight and trapped: Owen Collected Letters, Letter 480.

68 The one who relieved him: Owen Collected Letters, Letter 480.

69 He was next billeted: Owen Collected Letters, Letter 481.

69 On February 4: Owen Collected Letters, Letter 482.

69 Owen, although an able rider: Owen Collected Letters, Letter 484.

70 Between lessons, he wrote: Owen Collected Letters, Letter 484.

70 He thought about his first month: Owen Collected Letters, Letter 482.

70 The man who saved his life: Owen Collected Letters, Letter 491.

70 By this time, as Owen wrote: Owen Collected Letters, Letters 492 and 488.

71 It didn't last: Owen Collected Letters, Letter 494.

71 The reason was a concussion: Owen, *The Poems of Wilfred Owen*, 20.

72 His next letter: Owen Collected Letters, Letter 496.

72 The hiatus freed him: Owen Collected Letters, Letter 498.

72 "Constitutionally I am better able to do Service": Owen Collected Letters, Letter 500.

72 The CCS released Owen: Owen Collected Letters, Letter 502.

73 "In 24 hours": Owen Collected Letters, Letter 502.

73 As Owen traveled: Owen Collected Letters, Letter 502, note 5.

74 America's declaration of war: Martin Gilbert, *The First World War* (New York: HarperCollins, 1995), 325.

74 Haig's assault began: Douglas Haig, *The Private Papers of Douglas Haig, 1914–1919*, ed. Robert Blake (London: Eyre and Spottiswoode, 1952), 216.

74 Owen, who had been in reserve: Owen Collected Letters, Letter 505.

74 He described the encounter: Owen Collected Letters, Letter 510.

75 The 2nd Battalion commander: Owen Collected Letters, Letter 505.

76 War correspondent Philip Gibbs: Philip Gibbs, *The Struggle in Flanders: On the Western Front, 1917* (New York: George H. Doran and Company, 1918), 14.

76 The platoon settled: Owen Collected Letters, Letter 505.

77 Craiglockhart did not impress Owen: Owen Collected Letters, Letter 257 to Susan Owen, Wilfred's mother, on June 26, 1917.

77 **All he could do:** Wilfred Owen (unsigned), "Extracts from ye Chronicles of Sir Wilfred de Salope, Night," *The Hydra, the Magazine of Craiglockhart War Hospital*, no. 11, September 15, 1917, 11.

77 **Although Brock's case notes:** Owen, *The Poems of Wilfred Owen*, 29.

78 **To bring Owen back to earth:** Arthur J. Brock, "The Re-Education of the Adult," *Sociological Review* A10, no 1 (March 1918): 30.

78 **Brock's method often meant:** Arthur J. Brock, *Health and Conduct* (London and Edinburgh: Williams and Norgate, 1923), 34.

78 **Brock's choice to accompany Owen:** Dominic Hibberd, *Wilfred Owen: A New Biography* (London: Weidenfeld and Nicholson, 2003), 318. See also BNA, WO 372/13/187907.

79 **Lieutenant James Butlin:** Private Papers of James H. Butlin, Imperial War Museum, Documents 7915. All subsequent quotes from Butlin's letters are from this collection.

79 **On June 30, head gardener:** The letter is reproduced in full at https://sites.scran.ac.uk /Warp/Stay_home.htm.

80 **He wrote essays and poems:** *The Hydra*, no. 6, July 7, 1917, 2.

80 **The match lasted hours:** *The Hydra*, no. 6, 5.

80 **In July, Major Bryce:** *The Hydra*, no. 7, July 21, 1917, 11.

80 **Four days later:** *The Hydra*, no. 7, 5.

81 **He was forcibly retired:** Ben Shephard, *A War of Nerves: Soldiers and Psychiatrists in the Twentieth Century* (Cambridge, MA: Harvard University Press, 2003), 115.

81 **One of the founders:** Owen Collected Letters, Letter 534.

81 **A measure of his growing trust:** *The Hydra*, no. 7, July 21, 1917, 7.

81 **The club's function:** Brock, *Health and Conduct*, 33.

82 **Six months into Owen's stay:** Owen Collected Letters, Letter 537.

82 **As he had planned:** Charles Zueblin, "The World's First Sociological Laboratory," *American Journal of Sociology* 4, no. 5 (March 1899): 592. See also John Geddie, *The Official Guide to Edinburgh* (Edinburgh: Thomas Allan and Sons, 1920), 87–88.

82 **The seventeenth-century replica:** City of Edinburgh Council, City Development Department, "Pre-1750 Buildings in Edinburgh Old Town Conservation Area," n.d., 50.

82 **The tower contained:** Dominic Hibberd, "A Sociological Cure for Shellshock: Dr. Brock and Wilfred Owen," *Sociological Review* 25, no. 2 (May 1977): 378.

83 **Owen wrote to her:** Owen Collected Letters, Letter 533.

83 **He read his composition:** Dominic Hibberd, *Wilfred Owen: The Last Year* (London: Constable & Co., 1992), 25.

83 **Owen's debut *Hydra* included:** *The Hydra*, no. 7, 9–10.

83 **"I am glad you were eye-witness":** Owen Collected Letters, Letter 533.

83 **The impression Owen made:** Owen Collected Letters, appendix B, 594.

84 **Susan's presence was restoring:** Brock, *Health and Conduct*, 34.

Chapter Six: A Young Huntsman

85 **In the early afternoon:** Robert Nichols, introduction, in Siegfried Sassoon, *Counter-Attack and Other Poems* (New York: E. P. Dutton & Company, 1918), 1.

85 **Sassoon, in the words:** Margaret Mooers Marshall, "Poet Soldier Declares That Women Are Responsible for War and That Women Can End War," undated newspaper column, Imperial War Museum (IWM), Siegfried Sassoon Papers, Documents 9059.

85 **His Royal Welch:** British National Archives (BNA), War Office: Service Medal and Award Rolls Index, First World War, WO 339/51440.

85 **A neurologist on his Medical Board:** Siegfried Sassoon, *The Complete Memoirs of George Sherston* (London: Faber and Faber, 1937), 631.

86 **Sassoon allowed that:** Sassoon, *The Complete Memoirs of George Sherston*, 631.

86 **Yet the great man:** W. H. R. Rivers, "Medical Case Sheet," IWM, Siegfried Sassoon Papers, Documents 9059.

86 **On the Somme:** BNA, WO 339/51440.

86 Some men feigned neurasthenia: "Notes on the Staff of Craiglockhart War Hospital," IWM, Siegfried Sassoon Papers, Documents 9059.

86 Sassoon would recall: Sassoon, *The Complete Memoirs of George Sherston*, 631.

86 He would write: Letter from Siegfried Sassoon to Robbie Ross, July 26, 1917, IWM, Siegfried Sassoon Papers, Documents 9059.

87 His father, Alfred: "Sassoon," *Jewish Encyclopedia*, http://jewishencyclopedia.com/articles /13218-sassoon.

87 Called "the Rothschilds": Jean Moorcroft Wilson, *Siegfried Sassoon: The Making of a War Poet; A Biography (1886–1918)* (New York: Routledge, 2014), 26.

87 Both families were: "Events in 5676: June 1, 1915, to May 31, 1916," *American Jewish Year Book*, vol. 18 (New York: American Jewish Committee, 1916–1917), 220.

88 When Siegfried was nine: "Mr. Siegfried Sassoon: Poet, Fox-Hunter, Soldier and Pacifist," *The Times* (London), September 4, 1967, 10.

88 The Sassoon boys: Correspondence Relating to Dr. W. H. R. Rivers, Siegfried Sassoon Papers, IWM, Documents 9059.

88 The school Cadet Corps: BNA, WO 3391/51440. Government files record his time in the "Cadet Corps" at Marlborough, while Sassoon calls it the "Rifle Volunteer Corps" in *The Weald of Youth* (London: Faber and Faber, 1942), 275.

88 Aged fifteen, he succumbed: Medical Case Sheet, 2nd Lieut. Sassoon, Siegfried, IWM, Siegfried Sassoon Papers, Documents 9059. Dr. Rivers wrote, "He had an attack of double pneumonia when 8½ years old, and again at 15½. He was at Marlborough College, where he strained his heart at football."

88 His juvenile poetry: Siegfried Sassoon, *The Old Century and Seven More Years* (London: Faber and Faber, 1938), 288.

88 The school paper rejected: Wilson, *Siegfried Sassoon: The Making of a War Poet*, 113.

89 The friend was Edmund Gosse: Letter from Edmund Gosse to Siegfried Sassoon, February 13, 1913, Siegfried Sassoon Collection, Papers, 1952–1966, Special Collections and University Archives, Rutgers University Libraries.

90 Seeking to further Sassoon's writing career: Letter from Edmund Gosse to Siegfried Sassoon, February 13, 1913.

90 An atypical government functionary: C. K. Stead, *The New Poetic* (London: Hutchinson University Library, 1964), 88.

90 The first volume included: Stead, *The New Poetic*, 166.

90 Brooke, probably the best-known poet: *Rupert Brooke: The Collected Poems, with a Memoir by Edward Marsh* (London: Sidgwick & Jackson, 1943), lxxvi.

91 Sassoon wrote, "When bidding": Sassoon, *The Weald of Youth*, 232.

91 Ross befriended Sassoon: Siegfried Sassoon, *Siegfried's Journey* (London: Faber and Faber, 1945), 11.

91 Sassoon became a regular visitor: Sassoon, *Siegfried's Journey*, 6.

92 In late July, he cycled: Sassoon, *Siegfried's Journey*, 273.

92 On August 4, 1914: BNA, WO 339/51440.

92 The training was not onerous: Sassoon, *Siegfried's Journey*, 17.

93 Through family connections: BNA, WO 339/51440. Sassoon joined the 3rd Battalion.

93 The regimental motto: BNA, WO 339/51440.

93 Drill instructors taught him: Sassoon, *Siegfried's Journey*, 37.

93 A friend who survived: Max Egremont, *Siegfried Sassoon: A Biography* (London: Picador, 2013), 68.

93 The risks came home: Egremont, *Siegfried Sassoon: A Biography*, 72–73.

94 It was his first time: Siegfried Sassoon, *Siegfried Sassoon Diaries, 1915–1918*, ed. Rupert Hart-Davis (London: Faber and Faber, 1983), 19.

94 Two days later: Sassoon, *Siegfried Sassoon Diaries* 20.

94 Twenty-one-year-old: Sassoon, *Siegfried Sassoon Diaries*, 221.

94 They were otherwise: Sassoon, *Siegfried Sassoon Diaries*, 9.

95 An officer who knew him: Vivian de Sola Pinto, quoted in Edmund Charles Blunden, draft essay, Siegfried Sassoon Collection of Papers, MSS Sassoon, Berg Collection, New York Public Library.

95 Yet their devotion: Wilson, *Siegfried Sassoon: The Making of a War Poet*, 214. See also Edward Carpenter, *The Intermediate Sex: A Study of Some Transitional Types of Men and Women* (London: George Allen and Unwin, 1908).

95 They had friends and mentors: BNA, WO 339/51440. Sassoon joined C Company on November 28, 1915.

95 In the days that followed: Robert Graves, *Goodbye to All That: An Autobiography* (London: Jonathan Cape, 1929), 222.

96 Sassoon wrote in his diary: Sassoon, *Siegfried Sassoon Diaries*, 21.

96 Afterward, no doubt: Siegfried Sassoon, *The Old Huntsman and Other Poems* (London: William Heinemann, 1917), 22.

97 His batman, Private Molyneux: Sassoon, *Siegfried Sassoon Diaries*, 79.

97 Bandsmen paraded through: Sassoon, *The Complete Memoirs of George Sherston*, 311.

98 On Christmas Day: Sassoon, *Siegfried Sassoon Diaries*, 27–28.

98 There was no Yuletide turkey: Major C. H. Dudley Ward, DSO, MC, *Regimental Records of the Royal Welch Fusiliers (Late the 23rd Foot)*, vol. 3, *1914–1918, France and Flanders*, eds. A. D. L. Cary and Stouppe McCance (Uckfield, East Sussex, UK: Naval and Military Press Limited, 2005), 161.

98 The somber anniversary: Sassoon, *Siegfried Sassoon Diaries*, 28.

98 Sassoon harbored no doubts: Sassoon, *The Complete Memoirs of George Sherston*, 314.

99 Sassoon was back in France: Siegfried Sassoon, *Collected Poems, 1908–1956* (London: Faber and Faber, 1951), 17–18.

100 The 1st Battalion's new commander: Jonathon Riley, "Everyman's Land: The Second Christmas Truce, 1915," Generalship.org, http://generalship.org/royal-welch-fusiliers-articles/2nd-christmas-truce-1915.html.

100 The Germans gave: Frank Richards, *Old Soldiers Never Die* (Cardigan, Wales: Parthian Books, 2016), 46. Private Richards recalled that the impetus for a truce came from the enlisted men, who painted a board with the words "A Merry Christmas" at the German line. The Germans responded, and men from both sides came out to meet.

100 At noon the next day: Sassoon, *The Complete Memoirs of George Sherston*, 333.

101 That evening, he rode: Sassoon, *The Complete Memoirs of George Sherston*, 334.

101 Robert Graves, standing beside: Graves, *Goodbye to All That*, 249.

101 On the night of March 26: Sassoon, *Siegfried Sassoon Diaries*, 52–53.

101 He would prove: Sassoon, *Siegfried Sassoon Diaries*, 54.

101 He boasted to Eddie Marsh: Letter, April 3, 1916, Sir Edward Howard Marsh Collection, Henry W. and Albert A. Berg Collection of English and American Literature, New York Public Library.

101 Three weeks later: Letter to Eddie Marsh, April 19, 1916, Marsh Collection, Berg Collection of English and American Literature.

102 Sassoon wrote of the major: Sassoon, *The Complete Memoirs of George Sherston*, 352.

102 Campbell urged his listeners: Sassoon, *The Complete Memoirs of George Sherston*, 353.

102 The erotic implications: Sassoon, *The Old Huntsman and Other Poems*, 21.

103 They plodded over: Sassoon, *Siegfried Sassoon Diaries*, 65.

104 After twenty minutes: Sassoon, *The Complete Memoirs of George Sherston*, 371. See also Dudley Ward, *Regimental Records of the Royal Welch Fusiliers*, 186. The raiders had run into "masses of wire and got hung up." The report noted that Lieutenant N. Stansfield led twenty-five men, of whom eleven were wounded and one killed.

104 Two men carried him: Sassoon, *Siegfried Sassoon Diaries*, 66.

104 The death of a soldier: Sassoon, *Siegfried Sassoon Diaries*, 68.

105 The only result: Ward, *Regimental Records of the Royal Welch Fusiliers*, 185.

105 Sassoon learned the MC: Sassoon, *The Complete Memoirs of George Sherston*, 402.

105 **Sassoon watched the Battle:** Sassoon, *Siegfried Sassoon Diaries*, 82–83.

106 **Sassoon woke to a clear sky:** Sassoon, *Siegfried Sassoon Diaries*, 87.

107 **The Welch Fusiliers:** Ward, *Regimental Records of the Royal Welch Fusiliers*, 205.

107 **The young man's death:** Sassoon, *The Complete Memoirs of George Sherston*, 419.

107 **Bellowing the old hunting cry:** Sassoon, *Siegfried Sassoon Diaries*, 89.

107 **When Colonel Stockwell learned:** Sassoon, *Siegfried Sassoon Diaries*, 90.

108 **July 21 brought:** Sassoon, *Siegfried Sassoon Diaries*, 98.

108 **Medical treatment and convalescence:** Sassoon, *The Complete Memoirs of George Sherston*, 486. Although Sassoon wrote that the men were executed for cowardice, War Office files cited in Cathryn Corns and John Hughes-Wilson, *Blindfold and Alone: British Military Executions in the Great War* (London: Cassell & Company, 2001), appendix 2, 484–503, named five private soldiers shot by firing squad between the end of January and the date Sassoon read the names in the mess. All had been convicted, not of cowardice, but of desertion.

109 **Death was the punishment:** Corns and Hughes-Wilson, *Blindfold and Alone*, 461.

109 **The regular soldiers:** Richards, *Old Soldiers Never Die*, 169.

109 **Six more days of marching:** Sassoon, *The Complete Memoirs of George Sherston*, 514–15.

110 **The British-occupied trenches:** Sassoon, *Siegfried Sassoon Diaries*, 154–55.

110 **Sassoon went ahead:** Captain J. C. Dunn, *The War the Infantry Knew: 1914–1919: A Chronicle of Service in France and Belgium* (1938; London: Abacus, 1988), 316.

111 **Captain Kirkby told Sassoon:** Ward, *Regimental Records of the Royal Welch Fusiliers*, 281.

111 **He spent the next day:** Richards, *Old Soldiers Never Die*, 172.

112 **Sassoon took the first:** Richards, *Old Soldiers Never Die*, 320.

112 **Angry about the wounded:** Ward, *Regimental Records of the Royal Welch Fusiliers*, 283–84.

113 **One of Sassoon's twenty-five raiders:** Richards, *Old Soldiers Never Die*, 172–73.

113 **Second Lieutenant W. G.:** Ward, *Regimental Records of the Royal Welch Fusiliers*, 111.

Chapter Seven: The Protest

114 **Doctors moved him:** Siegfried Sassoon, *Siegfried's Journey* (London: Faber and Faber, 1945), 48.

114 **Robbie Ross visited him:** Ottoline Morrell, *Ottoline at Garsington: Memoirs of Lady Ottoline Morrell*, ed. Robert Gathorne-Hardy (London: Faber and Faber, 1974), 90–91.

115 **On December 12, 1916:** "A Historic Address by the Chancellor, with Text of Notes Transmitted Through Neutral Powers," *Current History: A Monthly Magazine of the New York Times* 5, no. 4, January 1917, 587.

115 **Philip Morrell's insights:** Sassoon, *Siegfried's Journey*, 21–22.

115 **Sassoon confided his doubts:** Sassoon, *Siegfried's Journey*, 51.

116 **The manor was a refuge:** "Conscientious Objectors in Their Own Words," Imperial War Museum (IWM), www.iwm.org.uk/history/conscientious-objectors-in-their-own-words.

116 **Sassoon finished a draft:** Sassoon, *Siegfried's Journey*, 52.

116 **The protest dismayed most of his mentors:** Sassoon, *Siegfried's Journey*, 181.

116 **Robbie Ross was:** Letter from Robbie Ross to Siegfried Sassoon, July 8, 1917, in Siegfried Sassoon, *Siegfried Sassoon Diaries, 1915–1918*, ed. Rupert Hart-Davis (London: Faber and Faber, 1983), 179.

116 **Eddie Marsh, who had moved:** Letter from Eddie Marsh to Siegfried Sassoon, July 10, 1917, in Sassoon, *Siegfried Sassoon Diaries*, 179.

117 **He wrote in his diary:** Sassoon, *Siegfried Sassoon Diaries*, 175.

117 **His diary called:** Sassoon, *Siegfried Sassoon Diaries*, 175.

117 **Sassoon was in full revolt:** Sassoon, *Siegfried Sassoon Diaries*, 177.

118 **The noise inspired him:** Siegfried Sassoon, *The War Poems* (London: Faber and Faber, 1983), 76. The poem, when completed, would take the title "Repression of War Experience," from an article in *The Lancet* of February 1918 by William Halse Rivers, "The Repression of War Experience."

118 Sassoon's medical furlough: Sassoon, *Siegfried Sassoon Diaries*, 175. Also Morrell, *Ottoline at Garsington*, 177. In Siegfried Sassoon, *The Complete Memoirs of George Sherston* (London: Faber and Faber, 1937), 605, Sassoon wrote that the telegram said "Report how situated."

118 He enclosed a single-page: British National Archives (BNA), War Office: Service Medal and Award Rolls Index, First World War, WO 339/51440. See appendix A for the full text.

119 Among the many recipients: Letter from Siegfried Sassoon to Charles Kay Ogden, undated (July 1917), Siegfried Sassoon Collection of Papers, Henry W. and Albert A. Berg Collection of English and American Literature, New York Public Library. Sassoon wrote by hand at the top of the *Cambridge Magazine*'s typed copy, "I have sent this to my commanding officer with a letter saying I refuse to perform any military duties. S.S."

119 Hansard, the official record: Sassoon, *Siegfried's Journey*, 52.

119 Sassoon wrote the next day: Letter from Siegfried Sassoon to Charles Kay Ogden, July 7, 1917, Southern Illinois University, Carbondale, Archives, MS 64-28-7.

119 Lady Ottoline encouraged: Sassoon, *Siegfried Sassoon Diaries*, 178.

119 In her journal: Morrell, *Ottoline at Garsington*, 183.

120 His fellow poet: Robert Graves, *Goodbye to All That: An Autobiography* (London: Jonathan Cape, 1929), 322. In Graves's account, written twelve years after the events, the chronology is inaccurate. He recalls receiving a letter with a cutting from the *Bradford Pioneer* of July 27, 1917, that contained Sassoon's statement. He writes that he then contacted Evan Morgan and others to save Sassoon through a Medical Board, but the board convened on July 20, a week before the *Pioneer* published Sassoon's statement. See also BNA, WO 372/8/103867.

120 Graves approached Welsh poet: Graves, *Goodbye to All That*, 322–23.

120 Ross wrote to Gosse: Sassoon, *Siegfried Sassoon Diaries*, 182.

120 Sassoon reported on July 12: Sassoon, *The Complete Memoirs of George Sherston*, 615.

120 The major pleaded: Sassoon, *The Complete Memoirs of George Sherston*, 616.

121 He wrote that night: Sassoon, *Siegfried Sassoon Diaries*, 181.

121 While he was studying: Sassoon, *The Complete Memoirs of George Sherston*, 618–20.

121 The walk south: Sassoon, *The Complete Memoirs of George Sherston*, 621.

121 The next morning: Sassoon, *The Complete Memoirs of George Sherston*, 623.

121 He had assumed wrongly: Graves, *Goodbye to All That*, 325.

122 Graves accompanied his friend: Graves, *Goodbye to All That*, 326.

122 Twenty-one-year-old Graves: Graves, *Goodbye to All That*, 326.

123 Sassoon moved into a double room: Email from Catherine Walker, curator, Edinburgh Napier University's Craiglockhart War Poets Collection, to the author, August 5, 2019.

123 His roommate was: Sassoon, *The Complete Memoirs of George Sherston*, 633.

123 At night, he discovered: Sassoon, *The Complete Memoirs of George Sherston*, 680.

123 Rivers's orders were to cure: Sassoon, *The Complete Memoirs of George Sherston*, 632.

124 Sassoon appreciated his psychiatrist's informality: Sassoon, *The Complete Memoirs of George Sherston*, 632.

124 The rapport between psychiatrist: Graves, *Goodbye to All That*, 342.

124 Sassoon and Graves left: Sassoon, *Siegfried Sassoon Diaries*, 183.

124 After Graves's departure: Siegfried Sassoon, "Soldier Learns the Truth," *Workers' Dreadnought* 4, no. 18, July 28, 1917, 1.

125 The seizures, however: *Hansard*, vol. 95, col. 1797 (London: His Majesty's Stationery Office, July 30, 1917).

126 Sassoon feared he had been forgotten: Sassoon, *The Complete Memoirs of George Sherston*, 632.

126 On July 31: "An Officer and Nerve Shock," *The Times* (London), July 31, 1917, 8.

126 Sassoon had failed: Sassoon, *The Complete Memoirs of George Sherston*, 634.

127 Watching his tee shots: Sassoon, *The Complete Memoirs of George Sherston*, 635.

Chapter Eight: Poet by Day, Sick by Night

128 At the end of his first week: Siegfried Sassoon, *Siegfried Sassoon Diaries, 1915–1918,* ed. Rupert Hart-Davis (London: Faber and Faber, 1983), 183.

128 He used the evening: Siegfried Sassoon, *The Complete Memoirs of George Sherston* (London: Faber and Faber, 1937), 636.

129 The May 1916 Sykes–Picot: The Sykes–Picot Agreement would remain secret until November 23, 1917, when the Bolsheviks published it in *Izvestia* and *Pravda.*

129 Rivers accused Sassoon: Sassoon, *The Complete Memoirs of George Sherston,* 637.

129 Rivers diagnosed Sassoon's anxiety: W. H. R. Rivers, "Medical Case Sheet," Imperial War Museum (IWM), Siegfried Sassoon Papers, Documents 9059.

130 What struck Sassoon: Sassoon, *The Complete Memoirs of George Sherston,* 637.

130 Literary creativity fascinated him: W. H. R. Rivers, *Conflict and Dream* (London: Kegan, Paul Trench, Trubner & Co., 1923), 148.

130 No less a critic: Virginia Woolf, "Mr. Sassoon's Poems," *Times Literary Supplement,* May 31, 1917, 259.

131 took a Berlitz course in German: Owen Collected Letters, Letter 539.

131 He called it: Owen Collected Letters, Letter 539.

131 Brock suggested he visit: Owen Collected Letters, Letter 533.

132 Owen made his stage debut: Second Lieutenant J. W. G. Pockett served in the Liverpool Regiment. See *London Gazette,* Supplement, May 31, 1917, His Majesty's Stationery Office, 5355. See also British National Archives (BNA), War Office: Service Medal and Award Rolls Index, First World War, WO 372/16/29094. Born in Cork, Ireland, in 1881, Pockett remained an actor and producer until his death in 1950.

133 Owen wrote to his mother: Owen Collected Letters, Letter 536.

133 *Hydra* critic Peas Blossom: *The Hydra, the Magazine of Craiglockhart War Hospital,* no. 8, August 4, 1917, 21.

133 Owen wrote to his cousin: Owen Collected Letters, Letter 535.

133 His novel theory: Quoted in Jon Stallworthy, *Wilfred Owen* (London: Pimlico, 2003), 199.

133 The question-and-answer session: Owen Collected Letters, Letter 536.

134 Its monthly General Meeting: *The Hydra,* no. 8, 5.

134 After the meeting: Owen Collected Letters, Letter 537.

134 At breakfast on Saturday: *The Hydra,* no. 8, 2.

134 That weakness did not prevent: *The Hydra,* no. 8, 5.

134 A poem of equal banality: *The Hydra,* no. 8, 9. The poem began "Make for yourself a good strong box / Fashion each part with great care . . ." and ended "Lock all your heartaches within it, / Then sit on the lid, friend, and laugh." See also Owen Collected Letters, Letter 537.

135 That evening's musical program: *The Hydra,* no. 9, August 18, 1917, 14.

135 Salmond accepted Owen's offer: Owen Collected Letters, Letter 538.

135 The two officers: Owen Collected Letters, Letter 538.

135 After the film: Wilson Barrett Papers, Harry Ransom Center, University of Texas at Austin, https://norman.hrc.utexas.edu/fasearch/findingAid.cfm?eadid=01178.

135 Owen had only four: Owen Collected Letters, Letter 538.

136 Despite his excitement: Owen Collected Letters, Letter 538.

137 Owen began a poem: An image of the manuscript of "Lines to a Beauty Seen in Limehouse" is reproduced on Oxford University's First World War Poetry Digital Archive, http://ww1lit.nsms.ox.ac.uk/ww1lit/collections/document/5264/4862.

137 Owen's upbringing had excluded sex: Harold Owen, *Journey from Obscurity: Wilfred Owen, 1893–1918,* vol. 1 (Oxford: Oxford University Press, 1963), 40.

137 the symbols of manly love: Wilfred Owen, *The War Poems,* ed. John Stallworthy (New York: Vintage, 1994), 9.

138 He wrote that the first half: *The Hydra,* no. 9, 14.

138 The review praised all: Owen Collected Letters, Letter 540.

138 The biographer quoted a friend: Arthur Christopher Benson, *Alfred Tennyson* (New York: E. P. Dutton & Company, 1907), 79.

Chapter Nine: High Summer

140 Craiglockhart defeated the Merchants: *The Hydra, the Magazine of Craiglockhart War Hospital*, no. 8, August 4, 1917, 7, and no. 9, August 18, 1917, 3.

140 Team competitions bored Siegfried Sassoon: Letter from Sassoon to Robert Graves, October 1917, Southern Illinois University, Carbondale, Archives, MS 64-28-7, and Imperial War Museum (IWM), "Account of the Sinking of the HMT *Transylvania*, May 1917," www .iwm.org.uk/collections/item/object/1030008621.

140 Sassoon recalled, "His temper": Siegfried Sassoon, *The Complete Memoirs of George Sherston* (London: Faber and Faber, 1937), 640.

140 He remained convinced: Letter from Siegfried Sassoon to Roderick Meiklejohn, Harry Ransom Center, University of Texas at Austin, Manuscript Collection MS-3706.

141 With his statement suppressed: Sassoon, *The Complete Memoirs of George Sherston*, 640.

141 He was right: Captain J. C. Dunn, *The War the Infantry Knew: 1914–1919: A Chronicle of Service in France and Belgium* (1938; London: Abacus, 1988), 372.

141 On Monday morning: Letter from Siegfried Sassoon to Robert Graves, August 8, 1917, Southern Illinois University, Carbondale, Archives, MS 64-28-7.

141 That evening, he wrote: Letter from Sassoon to Graves, August 8, 1917.

141 An American surgeon: Harvey Cushing, *From a Surgeon's Journal, 1915–1918* (Boston: Little, Brown and Company, 1936), 176.

142 Pilckem Ridge fired: A. J. P. Taylor, *The First World War: An Illustrated History* (London: Hamish Hamilton, 1964), 194.

142 Sassoon felt a deserter's guilt: Sassoon, *The Complete Memoirs of George Sherston*, 635–36.

142 One Royal Welch Fusilier: *London Gazette*, Supplement 30272, September 4, 1917, His Majesty's Stationery Office, 9260.

142 Another Welshman lost: Translated by Alan Llwyd. See "Hedd Wyn (1887–1917)," Llenyddiaeth Cymru Literature Wales, www.literaturewales.org/our-projects/poetry-of-loss /hedd-wyn-1887-1917.

142 Edmund Gosse, despite: Edmund Charles Blunden, holograph draft of essay, Henry W. and Albert A. Berg Collection of English and American Literature, New York Public Library, Siegfried Sassoon collection of papers, MSS Sassoon, 8.

142 A junior officer: Vivian de Sola Pinto, "Memories of Siegfried Sassoon," handwritten manuscript, IWM, Siegfried Sassoon Papers, Documents 9059.

142 The poem was: Siegfried Sassoon, "To Victory," *Siegfried Sassoon, Collected Poems, 1908–1956* (London: Faber and Faber, 1986), 13.

143 When Pinto recovered: *Siegfried Sassoon, Collected Poems, 1908–1956*, 21. Pinto's manuscript quotes the passage in full. See also Siegfried Sassoon, *The Old Huntsman and Other Poems* (London: William Heinemann, 1917), 31.

143 Antiwar militant Bertram Lloyd: Lloyd's anthology was published after the war and included six poems by Sassoon. Bertram Lloyd, *The Paths of Glory: A Collection of Poems Written During the War, 1914–1919* (London: George Allen and Unwin, 1919).

144 Sassoon's life was improving: Letter from Siegfried Sassoon to Robert Graves, August 10, 1917, Southern Illinois University, Carbondale, Archives, MS 64-28-7.

144 An article in the August issue: 001, "War and Reconstruction: An International Magna Carta," *English Review*, no. 105 (August 1917): 149.

145 Reading *The English Review*: W. H. R. Rivers, *Conflict and Dream* (London: Kegan, Paul Trench, Trubner & Co., 1923), 168.

145 Sassoon said they often joked: Sassoon, *The Complete Memoirs of George Sherston*, 661.

145 The main blocks: Rivers, *Conflict and Dream*, 171–72.

146 **Owen boasted to Susan:** Owen Collected Letters, Letter 539.

146 **They ate a picnic lunch:** *The Hydra*, no. 9, August 18, 1917, 4. Owen's letter gives the date as August 13, but *The Hydra* stated the expedition was on August 10.

146 **He wanted Susan:** Owen Collected Letters, Letter 539.

146 **He asked her:** Owen Collected Letters, Letter 539.

146 **kept Owen busy:** Owen Collected Letters, Letter 540.

147 **"I have just been reading":** Owen Collected Letters, Letter 540.

148 **The meeting's purpose:** Olga Panczenko, "Some Notes on Mencken in the First World War," *Menckiana*, no. 215 (Fall 2016): 8. See also M. L. Sanders and Philip M. Taylor, *British Propaganda During the First World War* (London: Macmillan Press, 1982), 39.

148 **Robert Graves believed:** Phillip Knightley, *The First Casualty: From the Crimea to Vietnam; The War Correspondent as Hero, Propagandist, and Myth Maker* (London: Quartet Books, 1982), 88.

148 **Oxford classics scholar:** While the WPB focused on persuading neutral countries, notably the United States and Switzerland, to support Britain, its efforts extended to raising morale on the home front and encouraging enlistment. News from the front had to be positive, British defeats portrayed as setbacks or tactical retreats, and casualties as the price worth paying for victory over the barbarians. So strict was the control of information that only two photographers were allowed near the front, pictures of British corpses were banned, and unauthorized photography was punishable by firing squad. War correspondents' copy was strictly censored.

148 **The disinformation campaign:** Sassoon, *The Complete Memoirs of George Sherston*, 642.

149 **Thirty-nine-year-old Masefield:** John Masefield, *Poems by John Masefield* (New York: Macmillan, 1917), 310–11.

149 **Her *Daily Mail* contributions:** Jessie Pope, *Jessie Pope's War Poems* (London: Grant Richards Ltd., 1915), 11.

150 **Sassoon was more dismissive:** Siegfried Sassoon, *Siegfried Sassoon Diaries, 1915–1918*, ed. Rupert Hart-Davis (London: Faber and Faber, 1983), 247.

150 **Sassoon satirized and ridiculed:** Sassoon, *The Old Huntsman and Other Poems*, 35.

150 **Another, "The Death-Bed":** Sassoon, *The Old Huntsman and Other Poems*, 96.

151 **Shyness had so far:** Owen Collected Letters, Letter 540.

Chapter Ten: Mentors and Novices

152 **News from France began:** Huw Strachan, *The First World War* (New York: Penguin Books, 2004), 165.

152 **The Times declared:** *The Times* (London), August 18, 1917, 9.

153 **"The sun blazed into":** Owen Collected Letters, Letter 541.

153 **"Short, dark haired":** Siegfried Sassoon, *Siegfried's Journey* (London: Faber and Faber, 1945), 58.

153 **Owen was immediately in awe:** Owen Collected Letters, Letter 541.

154 **Sassoon thought at first:** Sassoon, *Siegfried's Journey*, 58.

154 **Owen's provincial, lower-middle-class:** Jean Moorcroft Wilson, *Siegfried Sassoon: The Making of a War Poet; A Biography (1886–1918)* (New York: Routledge, 2014), 400. Wilson quotes Sassoon telling poet Stephen Spender, "He was embarrassing. He had a Grammar School accent."

154 **"the velvety quality of":** Sassoon, *Siegfried's Journey*, 62.

154 **"Mustard Seed," replacing Peas Blossom:** *The Hydra, the Magazine of Craiglockhart War Hospital*, no. 10, September 1, 1917, 6.

154 **Having been at Craiglockhart:** Siegfried Sassoon, *Siegfried Sassoon Diaries, 1915–1918*, ed. Rupert Hart-Davis (London: Faber and Faber, 1983), 184.

155 **The quote was from his:** Siegfried Sassoon, *The Old Huntsman and Other Poems* (London: William Heinemann, 1917), 26.

155 **Wells wanted to visit Sassoon:** H. G. Wells, *God the Invisible King* (New York: Macmillan Company, 1917).

156 **Its Old Testament title:** Wilfred Owen, *The Poems of Wilfred Owen*, ed. Edmund Blunden (London: Chatto and Windus, 1933), 82.

156 **The near rhyming:** Eventually, the form would be called the "pararhyme." Some critics assert that Owen invented the pararhyme, but it occurs in, among others, Byron. In *The Bride of Abydos*, Byron half-rhymes "beheld" and "unnveiled": "Woe to the head whose eyes beheld / My child Zuleika's face unveiled!" In the same poem, there are other examples. See Lord Byron, *The Bride of Abydos: A Turkish Tale* (London: John Murray, 1813), Canto I, 3.

156 **Sassoon recommended Martin Secker:** Owen Collected Letters, Letter 541.

156 **He later admitted:** Sassoon, *Siegfried's Journey*, 59.

156 **That morning, *The Times*'s register:** *The Times* (London), August 15, 1917, 1.

157 **Virginia Woolf had praised:** Owen Collected Letters, Letter 543.

157 **Developments on the battlefield:** Owen Collected Letters, Letter 544.

157 **Writing to his sister, Mary:** "Editorial," *The Hydra*, no. 10, 2.

158 **The first was "Dreamers" by:** *The Hydra*, no. 10, 7. See also Siegfried Sassoon, *Collected Poems: 1908–1956* (London: Faber and Faber, 1986), 72.

158 **Sassoon had agreed to let:** Wilson, *Siegfried Sassoon: The Making of a War Poet*, 403.

158 **This was "Song of Songs":** Owen, *The Poems of Wilfred Owen*, 82.

158 **Sassoon sent *The Hydra*:** Dominic Hibberd, *Wilfred Owen: The Last Year* (London: Constable and Company, 1992), 43.

159 **The drawing room with its:** Owen Collected Letters, Letter 545.

160 **The Grays invited a sculptress:** John Kemplay, *The Two Companions: The Story of Two Scottish Artists, Eric Robertson and Cecil Walton* (Edinburgh: Ronald Crowhurst, 1991), 58.

160 **Such was Owen's excitement:** Owen Collected Letters, Letter 545.

160 **That world nonetheless welcomed:** Owen, *The Poems of Wilfred Owen*, 30.

162 **He reconsidered his opinion:** Owen Collected Letters, Letter 546.

164 **Owen recalled, "Tomaso":** Owen Collected Letters, Letter 548.

164 **She wrote, "The bond":** Owen, *The Poems of Wilfred Owen*, 29.

164 **Maidie saw Owen gravitate:** Owen, *The Poems of Wilfred Owen*, 30.

165 **"I thought he was mad":** Owen Collected Letters, Letter 548.

165 **It voted to extend Owen's:** *The Hydra*, no. 11, September 15, 1917, 14.

165 **Sassoon sent an apology:** Sassoon, *Siegfried Sassoon Diaries*, 184.

165 **He enclosed the poem:** Sassoon, *Siegfried Sassoon Diaries*, 186.

166 **Ruggles believed "the beginning of":** Arthur H. Ruggles, *The Place and Scope of Psychotherapy: Viewing Fifty Years in Psychiatry* (New York: Salmon Committee on Psychiatry and Mental Hygiene, 1952), 28.

166 **Ruggles joined the Sanitary Corps:** Colonel Charles Lynch, Lieutenant Colonel Fran W. Weed, and Loy McAfee, *The Medical Department of the United States Army in the World War*, vol. 1 (Washington, D.C.: Government Printing Office, 1923), 152.

167 **Ruggles wrote in words:** Lynch, Weed, and McAfee, *The Medical Department of the United States Army in the World War*, 54.

167 **An admirer called Ruggles:** Imperial War Museum (IWM), "Notes on the Staff of Craiglockhart War Hospital," Siegfried Sassoon Papers, Documents 9059.

167 **Craiglockhart's overworked physicians welcomed:** "Annual Report of the Butler Hospital Providence, R.I.," *Boston Medical and Surgical Journal* 178 (January–June 1918), April 4, 1918, 480.

167 **"While there," Ruggles wrote:** Ruggles, *The Place and Scope of Psychotherapy: Viewing Fifty Years in Psychiatry*, 9.

Chapter Eleven: Who Die as Cattle

168 **Rising at 5:30 each morning:** *The Hydra, the Magazine of Craiglockhart War Hospital*, no. 11, September 15, 1917, 1.

168 **The volunteers cut wheat:** *The Hydra*, no. 11, 2.

168 **While some officers were:** *The Hydra*, no. 11, 3.

169 "My discipleship was put": Owen Collected Letters, Letter 547.

169 Owen attended the performance: *The Hydra*, no. 11, 13.

170 The saga lauded: *The Hydra*, no. 11, 11.

170 More was on the way: Owen Collected Letters, Letter 548.

171 Sassoon's attachment to "proud isolation": Siegfried Sassoon, *The Complete Memoirs of George Sherston* (London: Faber and Faber, 1937), 639.

171 The letter he enclosed: Robert Graves, *In Broken Images: Selected Letters of Robert Graves, 1914–1946*, ed. Paul O'Prey (London: Hutchinson and Co., 1982), 83.

172 Sassoon wrote to Ross: Siegfried Sassoon, *Siegfried Sassoon Diaries, 1915–1918*, ed. Rupert Hart-Davis (London: Faber and Faber, 1983), 186.

172 The poem imagined the two: Robert Graves, *Fairies and Fusiliers* (London: William Heinemann, 1917), 30–32.

172 "I was rejoicing in getting": Sassoon, *Siegfried Sassoon Diaries*, 186.

173 Sassoon called the monocle-wearing officer: Sassoon, *The Complete Memoirs of George Sherston*, 642.

173 The poem savaged war correspondents: Siegfried Sassoon, *Counter-Attack and Other Poems* (New York: E. P. Dutton & Company, 1918), 30.

173 "Autumn was asserting itself": British National Archives (BNA), War Office: Service Medal and Award Rolls Index, First World War, WO 339/29482.

174 "Did you see anyone": Sassoon, *The Complete Memoirs of George Sherston*, 644.

174 Cecile Walton thought the occasion: John Kemplay, *The Two Companions: The Story of Two Scottish Artists, Eric Robertson and Cecile Walton* (Edinburgh: Ronald Crowhurst, 1991), 68.

175 With Leonard and Maria: Kemplay, *The Two Companions*, 69.

175 The two men had met: Wilfred Owen, *The Poems of Wilfred Owen*, ed. Edmund Blunden (London: Chatto and Windus, 1933), appendix (Frank Nicholson's reminiscences), 133.

175 At Maidie's birthday dinner: Owen Collected Letters, Letter 549.

176 An unsigned reminiscence: *The Hydra*, no. 11, 8.

176 In his book *Conflict and Dream*: W. H. R. Rivers, *Conflict and Dream* (London: Kegan, Paul Trench, Trubner & Co., 1923), 167.

177 Sassoon recalled that "it pained": Sassoon, *The Complete Memoirs of George Sherston*, 654.

177 The Medical Board that consigned: BNA, WO 138/74.

177 *The Hydra* commented that: *The Hydra*, New Series, no. 1, November 1917, 24.

177 While other officers taught: *The Hydra*, New Series, no. 1, 21.

178 "Last week has been": Owen Collected Letters, Letter 549.

179 He visited Lintott: Owen Collected Letters, Letter 550.

179 Owen's most assiduous biographer: Dominic Hibberd, *Wilfred Owen: The Last Year* (London: Constable and Company, 1992), 24.

179 Both poems drew: Owen, *The Poems of Wilfred Owen*, 81.

179 Sassoon thought the poem: Siegfried Sassoon, *Siegfried's Journey* (London: Faber and Faber, 1945), 59.

180 The sonnet became: Owen, *The Poems of Wilfred Owen*, 80.

181 Brock saw Owen's poetic achievements: Arthur J. Brock, *Health and Conduct* (London and Edinburgh: Williams and Norgate, 1923), 171.

181 Sassoon remembered Owen: Sassoon, *Siegfried's Journey*, 61.

181 When Owen at last: *The Hydra*, no. 12, September 29, 1917, 18.

181 Sassoon's morale, however: Sassoon, *The Complete Memoirs of George Sherston*, 639.

181 War was a forbidden topic: Sassoon, *The Complete Memoirs of George Sherston*, 639.

182 In common with Sassoon: Arthur J. Brock, "The Re-Education of the Adult: The Neurasthenic in War and Peace," *Sociological Review* 10, no. 1 (Summer 1918): 27.

182 Brock believed "a good grumble": Brock, "The Re-Education of the Adult," 27–28.

182 Sassoon stood firm: Siegfried Sassoon, "Stand-to: Good Friday Morning," *The Old Huntsman and Other Poems* (London: William Heinemann, 1917), 36.

183 "doesn't swear conversationally": Owen Collected Letters, Letter 548.

Chapter Twelve: The Celestial Surgeon

184 **The friend was Lieutenant Ralph Greaves:** Sassoon wrote of his alter ego George Sherston, "His experiences were mine . . ." See *Siegfried's Journey* (London: Faber and Faber, 1945), 69. The three volumes comprising *The Complete Memoirs of George Sherston* changed the characters' names, Dr. Rivers apart, and little else.

184 **"Wilmot," he wrote:** Siegfried Sassoon, *The Complete Memoirs of George Sherston* (London: Faber and Faber, 1937), 507.

185 **Greaves's loss inspired:** Siegfried Sassoon, *Counter-Attack and Other Poems* (New York: E. P. Dutton & Company, 1918), 28.

185 **On Thursday, September 27:** Siegfried Sassoon, *Siegfried Sassoon Diaries, 1915–1918*, ed. Rupert Hart-Davis (London: Faber and Faber, 1983), 187.

185 **Unfortunately, he wrote:** Owen Collected Letters, Letter 550.

185 **By the end of Craiglockhart's first year:** British National Archives (BNA), Ministry of Health, MH 106/1887.

185 **With as many as 170:** Arthur H. Ruggles, *The Place and Scope of Psychotherapy: Viewing Fifty Years in Psychiatry* (New York: Salmon Committee on Psychiatry and Mental Hygiene, 1952), 64.

185 **Treating each entailed:** W. H. R. Rivers, *Instinct and the Unconscious: A Contribution to a Biological Theory of the Psycho-Neuroses* (Cambridge: Cambridge University Press, 1920), 202.

186 **Relieved of what had become:** Rivers, *Instinct and the Unconscious*, 25.

186 **His latest text:** Henry Wadsworth Longfellow, *The Song of Hiawatha* (Mount Vernon, NY: Peter Pauper Press, 1942), 9.

187 **"While Rivers was away":** Sassoon, *The Complete Memoirs of George Sherston*, 645.

187 **"I only hope":** Sassoon, *The Complete Memoirs of George Sherston*, 648.

188 **Sassoon appreciated that:** Sassoon, *Siegfried's Journey*, 61.

188 **Owen's companionship, however:** Sassoon, *Siegfried Sassoon Diaries*, 188.

188 **When Sassoon told him:** Sassoon, *Siegfried Sassoon Diaries*, 189.

188 **Adams explained his title:** Bernard Pye Adams, *Nothing of Importance: A Record of Eight Months at the Front with a Welsh Battalion, October, 1915, to June, 1916* (London: Methuen and Co., 1917), xvi.

189 **Their conversations dwelled:** Siegfried Sassoon & Edmund Blunden, *Selected Letters of Siegfried Sassoon and Edmund Blunden*, vol. 1: *Letters 1919–1967*, ed. Carol Z. Rothkopf (London: Taylor and Francis, 2012), 302–3.

189 **It was only after:** Sassoon, *Siegfried's Journey*, 61.

189 **Only golf provided:** Sassoon, *Siegfried Sassoon Diaries*, 189.

190 **He wrote on Thursday:** Sassoon, *Siegfried Sassoon Diaries*, 189.

190 **During afternoon visiting hours:** Sassoon, *The Complete Memoirs of George Sherston*, 651.

190 **he saw Rivers at the door:** Rivers had spent his leave with family, first in Gravesend on the Thames Estuary at Mount House, where his brother, Charles, and Charles's wife, Bertha, lived. Charles had trained as a civil engineer, but chronic malaria contracted on a Torres Strait expedition with William ended that career. William recommended poultry farming, which provided healthy outdoor work if precarious finances. "Will always took the keenest interest in the farm," Bertha recalled of her brother-in-law, "and went through the accounts every time he came." Letter from Bertha Rivers to Siegfried Sassoon, October 12, 1936, Imperial War Museum, Siegfried Sassoon Papers, Documents 9059. The Rivers brothers worked the farm together for two weeks, depriving William of the rest he had earned during his year at Craiglockhart. From Gravesend, he visited his spinster sisters, Ethel and Katharine, in the seaside house they shared near Ramsgate in west Kent. Family obligations fulfilled, Rivers boarded the train to Edinburgh.

190 **He reached into his pocket:** Sassoon, *The Complete Memoirs of George Sherston*, 657–58.

191 **Sassoon's melancholy reminiscences:** Sassoon, *The Complete Memoirs of George Sherston*, 660.

191 **He needed to prove:** Sassoon, *The Complete Memoirs of George Sherston*, 660–61.

Chapter Thirteen: A Grand Gesture

192 No contemporary account: Siegfried Sassoon, *The Complete Memoirs of George Sherston* (London: Faber and Faber, 1937), 661.

192 What would happen: Sassoon, *The Complete Memoirs of George Sherston*, 661.

193 Sassoon wanted more: Sassoon, *The Complete Memoirs of George Sherston*, 662.

193 Rivers advised Sassoon: Siegfried Sassoon, *Siegfried Sassoon Diaries, 1915–1918*, ed. Rupert Hart-Davis (London: Faber and Faber, 1983), 190.

193 An overtly political piece: *The Hydra, the Magazine of Craiglockhart War Hospital*, New Series, no. 1, November 1917, 25.

193 The plot revolved: John Galsworthy, *The Silver Box: A Comedy in Three Acts* (New York: G. P. Putnam's Sons, 1909), 75.

194 The clear injustice: *The Hydra*, New Series, no. 1, 25.

194 Sassoon wrote to Robbie Ross: Sassoon, *Siegfried Sassoon Diaries*, 189.

194 "I shall sit": Sassoon, *The Complete Memoirs of George Sherston*, 655.

194 Rivers gave Sassoon: Sassoon, *Siegfried Sassoon Diaries*, 190.

195 One, "Death's Brotherhood": Siegfried Sassoon, *Counter-Attack and Other Poems* (New York: E. P. Dutton & Company, 1918), 43. For publication, Sassoon changed the title to "Sick Leave."

195 His new garret: Siegfried Sassoon, *Siegfried's Journey* (London: Faber and Faber, 1945), 63–64.

195 Sassoon invited Robert Graves: Letter from Siegfried Sassoon to Robert Graves, October 1917, Southern Illinois University, Carbondale, Archives, MS 64-28-7. The letter is dated only Saturday, but Sassoon probably wrote it on Saturday, October 6, one week before Graves arrived.

195 Graves had no idea: Robert Graves, *Goodbye to All That: An Autobiography* (London: Jonathan Cape, 1929), 327.

196 Having read Graves's poetry: Owen Collected Letters, Letter 551.

196 "It was a wet day": Siegfried Sassoon & Edmund Blunden, *Selected Letters of Siegfried Sassoon and Edmund Blunden*, vol. 1: *Letters 1919–1967*, ed. Carol Z. Rothkopf (London: Pickering and Chatto, 2012), 269.

196 Then Owen showed Graves: Wilfred Owen, *Poems*, introduction by Siegfried Sassoon (London: Chatto and Windus, 1921), 32.

196 He wrote to his mother: Owen Collected Letters, Letter 551.

197 Sassoon must have worried: Robert Graves, *In Broken Images: Selected Letters of Robert Graves, 1914–1946*, ed. Paul O'Prey (London: Hutchinson and Co., 1982), 85.

197 Graves wrote at first: "Wilfred Owen," Letter from Robert Graves to Wilfrid Owen, circa October 17, 1917, available at Introduction to WWI Poetry Seminar, Oxford University, markup Paul Groves, http://projects.oucs.ox.ac.uk/jtap/tutorials/intro/owen/graves.html.

198 At this time: Owen Collected Letters, Letter 551.

198 It revealed a poetic imagination: Owen, *Poems*, 15.

199 It was in praise: Owen, *Poems*, v.

199 Owen explained, "My subject": Owen Collected Letters, Letter 551.

200 Owen took his students: Owen Collected Letters, Letter 551.

200 While he believed: Owen Collected Letters, Letter 552.

200 He justified himself: Sassoon, *Siegfried Sassoon Diaries*, 190.

201 his poem "Glory of Women": Ottoline Morrell, *Ottoline at Garsington: Memoirs of Lady Ottoline Morrell*, ed. Robert Gathorne-Hardy (London: Faber and Faber, 1974), 177. In Sassoon, *The Complete Memoirs of George Sherston*, 229.

Chapter Fourteen: Fight to a Finish

202 Owen meanwhile was profiting: Siegfried Sassoon, *Siegfried's Journey* (London: Faber and Faber, 1945), 61.

202 As was his custom: Owen Collected Letters, Letter 551. Susan Owen destroyed Maria Steinthal's portrait of her son after the war.

203 its incomplete form pleased Owen: Dominic Hibberd, *Wilfred Owen: A New Biography* (London: Phoenix, 2002), 349.

203 He wrote to Graves: Siegfried Sassoon, *Siegfried Sassoon Diaries, 1915–1918,* ed. Rupert Hart-Davis (London: Faber and Faber, 1983), 191.

203 At last, he told Graves: Siegfried Sassoon, *The Complete Memoirs of George Sherston* (London: Faber and Faber, 1937), 670.

203 Major Bryce, who Sassoon: Sassoon, *The Complete Memoirs of George Sherston,* 672.

204 "the stupid thing": Sassoon, *The Complete Memoirs of George Sherston,* 672.

204 Rivers returned from the War Office: Sassoon, *The Complete Memoirs of George Sherston,* 668.

205 While the three physicians: Sassoon, *The Complete Memoirs of George Sherston,* 673.

205 Sheepishly, Sassoon proffered: Sassoon, *The Complete Memoirs of George Sherston,* 675.

205 The Camera Club: *The Hydra,* New Series, no. 2, December 1917, 31.

206 Son of a clergyman: Obituary, *British Medical Journal* (February 23, 1946): 298.

206 There followed a period: "Services," *Lancet* (September 21, 1889), 625.

206 in 1890, working for: Major W. H. Horrocks, ed., *Journal of the Royal Army Medical Corps,* vol. 11, *July–December, 1908* (London: John Bales, Sons and Danielsson, n.d.), 168.

206 as an American subject: "War Record of Dartmouth Men," File Name: Arthur Ruggles, 1902. Rauner Special Collections Library, Dartmouth College. Ruggles served at Craiglockhart from September 1917 to January or April 1918. *The Boston Medical Journal,* April 1918, stated that he was posted to France in April 1918. He then became Division Psychiatrist of the U.S. 2nd Division in France, where he remained until the end of the war, and received the Croix de Guerre.

206 He assumed Bryce's responsibilities: *The Hydra, the Magazine of Craiglockhart War Hospital,* New Series, no. 2, December 1917, 31.

206 Ruggles went on treating: Arthur H. Ruggles, *The Place and Scope of Psychotherapy: Viewing Fifty Years in Psychiatry* (New York: Salmon Committee on Psychiatry and Mental Hygiene, 1952), 13.

207 "I was in Scotland": Ruggles, *The Place and Scope of Psychotherapy,* 13.

207 On October 28, Brock informed Owen: Owen Collected Letters, Letter 555.

207 In the book's favor: Max Egremont, *Siegfried Sassoon: A Biography* (London: Picador, 2013), 172.

208 Sassoon's letter that night: Sassoon, *Siegfried Sassoon Diaries,* 193.

208 "Fight to a Finish": Siegfried Sassoon, *Counter-Attack and Other Poems* (New York: E. P. Dutton & Company, 1918), 29.

209 "Glory of Women": Sassoon, *Counter-Attack and Other Poems,* 32.

209 Another, "Their Frailty": Sassoon, *Counter-Attack and Other Poems,* 38.

209 "Suicide in the Trenches": Sassoon, *Counter-Attack and Other Poems,* 31.

210 Guilt at his noncombatant status: Sassoon, *Siegfried Sassoon Diaries,* 193.

210 "The Chances," in particular: Wilfred Owen, *The Poems of Wilfred Owen,* ed. Edmund Blunden (London: Chatto and Windus, 1933), 68.

211 The next evening, he delighted: Owen Collected Letters, Letter 555.

211 Although he had been under: British National Archives (BNA), War Office: Service Medal and Award Rolls Index, First World War, 133/74.

211 Owen was in no hurry: Owen Collected Letters, Letter 556.

212 After their last lesson: Owen, *The Poems of Wilfred Owen,* 134.

212 The conversation turned: Owen, *The Poems of Wilfred Owen,* 135.

Chapter Fifteen: Love Drove Me to Rebel

213 Officers with hospital blue bands: *The Hydra, the Magazine of Craiglockhart War Hospital,* New Series no. 8, June 1918, 12.

213 *The Scotsman* published a letter: Letter to the Editor, "The Castle Gun," *Scotsman,* January 14, 1918, 7.

213 **The writer's overriding concern:** Letter to the Editor, *Scotsman*, January 23, 1918, 6.

214 **"The firing of the gun":** "Edinburgh Time Gun," *Scotsman*, April 14, 1918, 4.

214 **On a more jocular note:** *The Hydra*, New Series, no. 1, November 1917, 27.

214 **One poem, "Any Private":** *The Hydra*, New Series, no. 1, 9–10. "I canna lauch the nicht" translates to "I cannot grasp [understand] the night."

215 **Thirty-year-old Berrington:** British National Archives (BNA), Ministry of Health 106/ 1887 and War Office: Service Medal and Award Rolls Index, First World War, 374/6051.

215 **inspired him to explore the countryside:** Volker M. Welter, *Revival After the Great War* (Belgium: Leuven University Press, 2020), 107–8.

215 **Another *Hydra* stalwart:** BNA, MH 106/1887.

215 **The two soldier-poets met:** Siegfried Sassoon, *Siegfried's Journey* (London: Faber and Faber, 1945), 64.

216 **The venue's usual hush:** Sassoon, *Siegfried's Journey*, 65.

216 **The present of ten pounds seemed:** Owen Collected Letters, Letter 557.

217 **Its frank intimacy was unexpected:** Owen Collected Letters, Letter 557.

218 **She took an all-night train:** Ottoline Morrell, *Ottoline at Garsington: Memoirs of Lady Ottoline Morrell*, ed. Robert Gathorne-Hardy (London: Faber and Faber, 1974), 65.

218 **She recalled that "he told":** Morrell, *Ottoline at Garsington*, 230.

219 **Ottoline cried in the train:** Morrell, *Ottoline at Garsington*, 231.

219 **Its final lines expressed better:** Morrell, *Ottoline at Garsington*, 231.

219 **On November 21, Sassoon wrote:** Siegfried Sassoon, *Siegfried Sassoon Diaries, 1915–1918*, ed. Rupert Hart-Davis (London: Faber and Faber, 1983), 195.

219 **His letter of November 21 played:** Sassoon, *Siegfried Sassoon Diaries*, 194.

219 **He wrote the same day:** Sassoon, *Siegfried Sassoon Diaries*, 196.

220 **"The Board asked if":** Sassoon, *Siegfried Sassoon Diaries*, 197.

220 **The officers on the board:** BNA, WO 339/51440.

Chapter Sixteen: Things Might Be Worse

221 **The hospital received:** British National Archives (BNA), Ministry of Health 106/1887.

221 **The Hydra published:** *The Hydra, the Magazine of Craiglockhart War Hospital*, New Series, no. 2, December 1917, 8.

222 **A full-page cartoon:** This image is reproduced on Oxford University's First World War Poetry Digital Archive at http://ww1lit.nsms.ox.ac.uk/ww1lit/collections/document/5627/5323.

222 **The boys attended King Edward's:** King Edward's School *Chronicle*, vol. 29, no. 207, October 1914, 55.

223 **Austin was wounded:** Melville Amadeus Henry Douglas Heddle de La Caillemotte de Massue de Ruvignés, *The Roll of Honour: A Biographical Record of All Members of His Majesty's Naval and Military Forces Who Have Fallen in the War*, vol. 3 (London: Standard Art Book Company, 1918), 29.

223 **In November, after a year:** BNA, War Office: Service Medal and Award Rolls Index, First World War, 339/2466.

223 **Surviving hospital records did not:** Papers of George Henry Bonner, Magdalen College Archive, Oxford, Reference Number P429.

224 **In what amounted to a manifesto:** *The Hydra*, New Series, no. 3, January 1918, 3–4.

224 **The first, "Break of Day," began:** *The Hydra*, New Series, no. 2, 6.

224 **"Base Details" harked back:** *The Hydra*, New Series, no. 2, 10.

225 **He forwarded it to another:** BNA, WO 339/51440.

225 **One, Philip Mercer-Wright, wrote:** *The Hydra*, New Series, no. 2, 12.

225 **Many patients, in addition to:** *The Hydra*, New Series, no. 3, 8.

226 **Despite his noncombat status:** Max Plowman, *Bridge into the Future: Letters of Max Plowman*, ed. Dorothy L. Plowman (London: Andrew Dakers Limited, 1944), 92.

227 **Sassoon forwarded the letter:** Imperial War Museum (IWM), Siegfried Sassoon Papers, Documents 9059.

227 **Rivers initiated a correspondence:** M. Plowman, *Bridge into the Future*, 94.

228 **On February 27, Plowman received:** M. Plowman, *Bridge into the Future*, 102.

228 **"Civil conscription for":** M. Plowman, *Bridge into the Future*, 104.

228 **"With great pleasure":** *The Hydra*, New Series, no. 4, February 1918, 29.

229 **The report of the horse's death:** *The Hydra*, New Series, no. 4, 29.

230 **"We Hear," the anonymous author:** *The Hydra*, New Series, no. 4, 28.

230 **A choral voice, in classical tradition:** *The Hydra*, New Series, no. 4, 36.

231 **He added, "Everyone interested":** *The Hydra*, New Series, no. 4, 27.

231 **The departure in late January:** Captain Hall may have been Dr. Millard W. Hall of Chicago, Illinois. The only reference to him in surviving Craiglockhart records was this brief reference in *The Hydra*. See "Craiglockhart Hospital Medical Staff," The Great War (1914– 1918) Forum, www.greatwarforum.org/topic/283613-craiglockhart-war-hospital-medical-staff/page/2.

231 **The major's posting:** Harvey Cushing, *From a Surgeon's Journal, 1915–1918* (Boston: Little, Brown and Company, 1936), 426.

231 **His heroism treating them:** "War Record of Dartmouth Men," File Name: Arthur Ruggles, 1902. Rauner Special Collections Library, Dartmouth College.

231 **He inscribed a triolet:** "Nurse Mellor's Autograph Book," National Museums of Scotland, www.nms.ac.uk/explore-our-collections/stories/scottish-history-and-archaeology/first-world -war/first-world-war/nurse-mellors-autograph-book.

231 **His preoccupation with Miss Mellor:** *The Hydra*, New Series, no. 5, March 1918, 9–10.

232 **His daughter, Betty Stein:** Wendy Holden, *Shell Shock* (London: Channel Four Books, 2001), 61.

232 **titled simply "Sonnet":** Arthur J. Bock, "The Re-Education of the Adult," *Sociological Review* A10, no. 1 (March 1918): 26–27. See also Anne-Catriona Schaupp, "The Repression and Articulation of War Experience: A Study of the Literary Culture of Craiglockhart War Hospital" (PhD thesis, University of Edinburgh, 2017), 220.

232 **A hint of shirking appeared:** *The Hydra*, New Series, no. 5, 11.

233 **The varied stanza lengths:** Schaupp, "The Repression and Articulation of War Experience," 245–48.

235 **The next editor praised him:** *The Hydra*, New Series, no. 5, 3.

235 **"I would therefore much prefer":** BNA, WO 339/2466.

235 **His commanding officer commended him:** Massue de Ruvigné, *The Roll of Honour: A Biographical Record of All Members of His Majesty's Naval and Military Forces Who Have Fallen in the War*, 29.

Chapter Seventeen: A Second Chance

236 **The first post-Bonner *Hydra*:** *The Hydra*, New Series, no. 5, March 1918, 13–14.

236 **Drama critic "LOLLIUS" described:** *The Hydra*, New Series, no. 5, 18.

237 **The onset of spring:** "Edinburgh Time Gun," *Scotsman*, April 14, 1918, 4.

237 **One patient wrote about:** *The Hydra*, no. 7, July 21, 1917, 8.

237 **Another, C. Wakelin Scott, recorded:** *The Hydra*, New Series, no. 4, February 1918, 11.

237 **The new *Hydra* editor asked Brock:** *The Hydra*, New Series, no. 6, May 1918, 4.

238 **One of the most famous psychiatrists:** Stephanie C. Linden, Edgar Jones, and Andrew J. Lees, "Shell Shock at Queen Square; Lewis Yealland 100 Years On," *Brain* 136, no. 6 (June 2013), 1976–1988, see online at 10.1093/brain/aws331. See also Lewis R. Yealland, M.D., *Hysterical Disorders of Warfare* (London: Macmillan and Co., 1918).

239 **One of those present recalled:** *The Hydra*, New Series, no. 6, 17–18.

239 **On April 5, a court-martial:** British National Archives (BNA), War Office: Service Medal and Award Rolls Index, First World War, 339/50680.

239 **That, he admitted:** Max Plowman, *Bridge into the Future: Letters of Max Plowman*, ed. Dorothy L. Plowman (London: Andrew Dakers Limited, 1944), 112.

240 **The court permitted him to read:** "Mark Plowman's Defence," *Labour Leader*, April 11, 1918, 5. See also "Max Plowman: From Army Officer to Conscientious Objector," Imperial War

Museum (IWM), www.iwm.org.uk/history/max-plowman-from-army-officer-to-conscientious -objector.

240 **It uncovered details of Plowman's:** BNA, WO 339/50680.

241 *The Tribunal*, **underground organ:** "On Active Service," *Tribunal*, April 11, 1918, 1.

241 **While no member of Parliament:** M. Plowman, *Bridge into the Future*, 114.

241 **Miss Mellor's brother:** "Gordon Highlander Killed," *Fife Free Press & Kirkcaldy Guardian*, May 11, 1918, 5.

242 **Despite living on the Craiglockhart:** Scottish Cultural Resource Access Network, "The War Poets at Craiglockhart: The Carmichael Family, Those Who Stayed at Home," https://sites .scran.ac.uk/Warp/Stay_home2.htm.

242 **Osburn, who did not know:** Arthur Osburn, *Unwilling Passenger* (London: Faber and Faber, 1932), 292.

243 **Captain E. A. E. Wilson:** *The Hydra*, New Series, no. 8, June 1918, 9.

243 **The deputy director of Medical Services:** BNA, WO 399/13071.

244 **His next posting, in November 1916:** William Brown, "The Psychologist in War-Time," *Lancet* (June 3, 1939), 1288.

245 **He detected a connection:** Dominic Hibberd, "Wilfred Owen (1893–1918): His Recovery from Shell Shock," *Notes and Queries*, New Series, vol. 23, no. 7 (July 1976): 302.

245 **"They roll about," wrote Brown:** William Brown, "Psychopathology and Dissociation," *British Medical Journal*, no. 3083 (January 31, 1920): 140.

245 **For 70 percent:** William Brown, *Psychological Methods of Hearing: An Introduction to Psychotherapy* (London: University of London Press, 1938), 12.

245 **He explained, "By the process":** William Brown, "The Treatment of Cases of Shell Shock in an Advanced Neurological Centre," *Scientific American Supplement*, no. 2240 (December 7, 1918).

Chapter Eighteen: Drastic Changes Were Necessary

246 **Their maladies, he told:** *Report of the War Office Committee of Enquiry into "Shell-Shock,"* Presented to Parliament by Command of His Majesty (London: His Majesty's Stationery Office, 1922), 56.

247 **On June 29, the Ministry:** *Report of the War Office Committee of Enquiry into "Shell-Shock,"* 120.

247 **Plowman recalled, "Of course":** *Report of the War Office Committee of Enquiry into "Shell-Shock,"* 130.

248 **His wife, Dorothy, wrote:** *Report of the War Office Committee of Enquiry into "Shell-Shock,"* 130.

248 **Henry Carmichael prepared:** *The Hydra, the Magazine of Craiglockhart War Hospital*, New Series, no. 9, July 1918, 21.

248 **Despite its idyllic grounds:** British National Archives (BNA), War Office: Service Medal and Award Rolls Index, First World War, 399/13071.

249 **Although he had left:** BNA, WO 399/5084.

249 **"Miss MacBean," he wrote:** BNA, WO 300/13071.

249 **The War Office did not respond:** BNA, WO 300/13071.

250 **Adding his voice to Wilson's:** BNA, WO 300/13071.

250 **On September 10:** BNA, WO 300/13071.

250 **Brown sent Matron MacBean:** BNA, WO 399/5084.

251 **Miss MacBean demanded:** BNA, WO 399/5084. Wilson's memo to the War Office elaborated that, while her character was not in question, "Much of the difficulty we have experienced at Craiglockhart has been due to her lack of energy and initiative (whether from age or other causes)—to her failure to co-operate with successive Commanding Officers or to inspire confidence in or get good work out of the Staff under her."

251 **Change of leadership:** "William Brown," Royal College of Physicians, https://history.rcp london.ac.uk/inspiring-physicians/william-brown.

252 Since childhood, the patient: William Brown, "The Treatment of Cases of Shell Shock in an Advanced Neurological Centre," *Scientific American Supplement*, no. 2240 (December 7, 1918): 363.

252 His left eye went foggy: William Brown, *Psychology and Psychotherapy* (London: Longmans, Green and Co., 1921), 142.

253 A twenty-four-year-old lieutenant: Brown, *Psychology and Psychotherapy*, 143.

253 Brown concluded that: Brown, *Psychology and Psychotherapy*, 147.

Chapter Nineteen: Mad Jack Returns

255 On August 17, 1918: Sassoon biographer Jean Moorcroft Wilson reported a discrepancy between the date Sassoon wrote he returned to Craiglockhart and the date he probably arrived: "SS says that his diary for this period was lost but he afterward noted that he left London on 17 Aug. and arrived at Coldstream [Lennel House] on 20 Aug. However it is unlikely that he left his Lancaster Gate Hospital on the same evening that WO [Wilfred Owen] delivered him back there." Jean Moorcroft Wilson, *Siegfried Sassoon: The Making of a War Poet; A Biography (1886–1918)* (New York: Routledge, 2014), 581, note 55.

255 Lennel House was not: Caroline Alexander, "The Shock of War," *Smithsonian*, September 2010, www.smithsonianmag.com/history/the-shock-of-war-55376701.

256 Clemmie, regarding the men: Siegfried Sassoon, *Siegfried's Journey* (London: Faber and Faber, 1945), 75.

256 Visiting psychiatrists from Craiglockhart: Alexander, "The Shock of War."

257 On January 21: Siegfried Sassoon, *Siegfried Sassoon Diaries, 1915–1918*, ed. Rupert Hart-Davis (London: Faber and Faber, 1983), 205–6.

257 His inclination was against: Frank Richards, *Old Soldiers Never Die* (Cardigan, Wales: Parthian Books, 2016), 208. Richards wrote that he handed Sassoon's telegram to Major Kearsley hoping he would act on it "as it was only once in a blue moon that we had an officer like Mr. Sassoon. But he was unable."

257 On April 4, a rumor: Sassoon, *Siegfried Sassoon Diaries*, 228.

257 On May 1, he left: Sassoon, *Siegfried Sassoon Diaries*, 241.

257 The ship docked: Sassoon, *Siegfried Sassoon Diaries*, 246.

258 A few days later, he listened: Sassoon, *Siegfried Sassoon Diaries*, 249.

258 His mood changed: Sassoon, *Siegfried Sassoon Diaries*, 259.

258 Then, in a letter: Sassoon, *Siegfried Sassoon Diaries*, 259.

258 While the 25th Battalion troops: Major C. H. Dudley Ward, DSO, MC, *Regimental Records of the Royal Welch Fusiliers (Late the 23rd Foot)*, vol. 3, *1914–1918, France and Flanders*, ed. A. D. L. Cary and Stouppe McCance (Uckfield, East Sussex, UK: Naval and Military Press Limited, 2005), 445.

260 Declining to wait: Siegfried Sassoon, *The Complete Memoirs of George Sherston* (London: Faber and Faber, 1937), 791.

260 The darkness of night: Sassoon, *The Complete Memoirs of George Sherston*, 794.

261 He returned to poetry: Siegfried Sassoon, *The War Poems* (London: William Heinemann, 1919), 35.

261 "How could I begin": Sassoon, *The Complete Memoirs of George Sherston*, 803.

262 Sassoon wrote to Graves: Robert Graves, *Goodbye to All That: An Autobiography* (London: Jonathan Cape, 1929), 346.

263 It was in the library: Sassoon, *Siegfried's Journey*, 75.

263 Sassoon, as with Owen: Sir Edward Howard Marsh Collection, Henry W. and Albert A. Berg Collection of English and American Literature, New York Public Library.

264 The thirty-three-year-old: Sassoon, *Siegfried's Journey*, 76.

264 He also met the economist: Sassoon, *Siegfried Sassoon Diaries*, 279.

264 Eddie Marsh arranged: Sassoon, *Siegfried's Journey*, 77.

265 Churchill's informality and courtesy: Sassoon, *Siegfried's Journey*, 78

266 "We met at the house": Sassoon, *Siegfried's Journey*, 71.

267 Owen wrote to Sassoon: Columbia University Archives, Rare Book and Manuscript Collections, Wilfred Owen Papers, Box 01.

267 Owen wrote again: Columbia University Archives, Rare Book and Manuscript Collections, Wilfred Owen Papers, Box 01.

Chapter Twenty: The Loathsome Ending

268 In June 1917: Owen Collected Letters, Letter 528.

268 The veteran soldier: "James Finlay Dempster," Imperial War Museum (IWM), https://livesofthefirstworldwar.iwm.org.uk/lifestory/1167184. BNA, WO 372/5/243506. The Imperial War Museum recorded that Dempster was wounded and hospitalized on June 17, 1917. That would have been two days after he met Owen in London, indicating that he was wounded at some other time.

268 Seeing Dempster in London: "James Finlay Dempster," IWM. Owen's reference to William Makepeace Thackeray related to the author's *The Book of Snobs* (London: Bradbury and Evans, 1855).

269 Among those who detected Owen's sensitivity: Wilfred Owen, *The Poems of Wilfred Owen*, ed. Edmund Blunden (London: Chatto and Windus, 1933), 30.

269 Graves went further: Robert Graves, *Goodbye to All That: An Autobiography* (London: Jonathan Cape, 1929), 327 and 464, note 8. See Dominic Hibberd, *Wilfred Owen: A New Biography* (London: Phoenix, 2002), appendix B, 470–72, for a full discussion of Owen and his self-suspected cowardice. Following Sassoon's intervention, Graves changed "accused of cowardice" to "unjustly accused of cowardice" in the second edition.

269 On September 15: "War Diary," British National Archives (BNA), War Office: Service Medal and Award Rolls Index, First World War, WO 95/2397.

270 Owen, his uniform drenched: *London Gazette*, Supplement, July 30, 1919, His Majesty's Stationery Office, 9761.

270 A poem he had been writing: Owen, *The Poems of Wilfred Owen*, 116.

271 Sassoon would call: Siegfried Sassoon, "Wilfred Owen: A Personal Appreciation," BBC Third Programme, August 22, 1948.

272 His commander, Captain Taylor: Hibberd, *Wilfred Owen*, 474.

272 "This is where I admired": Owen, *The Poems of Wilfred Owen*, 37.

273 Owen wrote to assure: Owen Collected Letters, Letter 662.

273 By October 5: Basil Liddell Hart, *History of the First World War* (Leeds: Book Club Associates, 1973), 484.

273 With British and imperial troops: Owen Collected Letters, Letter 662.

273 To avert a slackening: Hibberd, *Wilfred Owen*, 176.

273 The order infuriated Owen: Owen Collected Letters, Letter 665.

274 Owen replied on October 10: Owen Collected Letters, Letter 664.

275 There he found masses of humanity: Siegfried Sassoon, *Siegfried Sassoon Diaries, 1915–1918*, ed. Rupert Hart-Davis (London: Faber and Faber, 1983), 282.

276 When his ship anchored: Harold Owen, *Journey from Obscurity: Wilfred Owen, 1893–1918*, vol. 3 (Oxford: Oxford University Press, 1963), 198.

276 The postman delivered it: Owen, *Journey from Obscurity*, 201.

276 The suspense over Owen's fate: Siegfried Sassoon, *Siegfried's Journey* (London: Faber and Faber, 1945), 72.

277 In such good company: Owen Collected Letters, Letter 673.

278 Susan Owen, who heard the story: Hibberd, *Wilfred Owen*, 459.

279 Dr. Brock wrote: Arthur J. Brock, *Health and Conduct* (London and Edinburgh: Williams and Norgate, 1923), 171.

Epilogue

280 Over Craiglockhart's thirty months: Email from Catherine Walker, curator, Craiglockhart, Edinburgh Napier University's Craiglockhart War Poets Collection, to the author, September 23, 2019.

280 The record compared favorably: C. Stanford Read, *Military Psychiatry in Peace and War*
(London: H. K. Lewis and Company, 1920), 52.

281 His daughter, Maureen Huws: Wendy Holden, *Shell Shock* (London: Channel Four Books,
2001), 63.

282 "Hitherto, she had thought of the War": Ford Madox Ford, *Parade's End* (London: Everyman's Library, 1992), 714.

Image Credits

Index